The
Nature of the
Atonement

FOUR VIEWS

WITH CONTRIBUTIONS BY
Gregory A. Boyd, Joel B. Green,
Bruce R. Reichenbach and
Thomas R. Schreiner

EDITED BY
James Beilby and Paul R. Eddy

IVP Academic

An imprint of InterVarsity Press
Downers Grove, Illinois

InterVarsity Press
P.O. Box 1400, Downers Grove, IL 60515-1426
World Wide Web: www.ivpress.com
E-mail: email@ivpress.com

InterVarsity Press® is the book-publishing division of InterVarsity Christian Fellowship/USA®, a movement of students and faculty active on campus at hundreds of universities, colleges and schools of nursing in the United States of America, and a member movement of the International Fellowship of Evangelical Students. For information about local and regional activities, write Public Relations Dept., InterVarsity Christian Fellowship/USA, 6400 Schroeder Rd., P.O. Box 7895, Madison, WI 53707-7895, or visit the IVCF website at <www.intervarsity.org>.

Design: Cindy Kiple
Images: Jill Fromer/istockphoto.com

ISBN 978-0-8308-2570-7

Printed in the United States of America ∞

Library of Congress Cataloging-in-Publication Data

The nature of the Atonement: four views/with contributions by
*   Gregory A. Boyd . . . [et al.]; edited by James K. Beilby and Paul*
*   R. Eddy.*
*   p. cm.*
*   Includes bibliographical references and indexes.*
*   ISBN -13: 978-0-8308-2570-7 (pbk.: alk. paper)*
*   ISBN -10: 0-8308-2570-3 (pbk.: alk. paper)*
*   1. Atonement.   I. Beilby, James K.   II. Eddy, Paul R.*
BT265.3.N38 2006
232'.3—dc22

                                        2006020894

P 22 21 20 19 18 17 16 15 14 13 12 11 10 9 8 7 6 5

Y 27 26 25 24 23 22 21 20 19 18 17 16 15 14 13 12 11

To David K. Clark

Teacher, mentor, friend

Contents

The Atonement: *An Introduction*

BY PAUL R. EDDY AND JAMES BEILBY

This book is concerned with the complexities of the Christian view of the atonement—that is, the saving work of Jesus Christ. Broadly speaking, the term *atonement*—one of the few theological terms that is "wholly and indigenously English"—refers to a reconciled state of "at-one-ness" between parties that were formerly alienated in some manner.[1] According to the great eighteenth-century evangelist John Wesley, "Nothing in the Christian system is of greater consequence than the doctrine of the atonement."[2] Wesley wrote those words during the same century that gave birth to the Enlightenment. Since that time more than a few theologians have taken leave of Wesley's sentiments. Writing in the late 1980s, Colin Gunton noted that over the previous two decades, matters other than the atonement had come to capture the attention of theologians, reducing the former "flood" of works on this topic to a virtual "trickle."[3] A similar observation, no doubt, led to Colin Grant's mid-1980s announcement of "the abandonment of atonement."[4] Today however, two decades later, the waterway has begun to flow anew, and the atonement is again a matter for serious and widespread discussion at the theological roundtable.

A number of factors have served to foster renewed conversation and exploration concerning the atonement within Christian theological circles. A number of feminist and womanist critiques of traditional interpretations of the atonement have highlighted what many consider to be two troubling as-

---

[1]Robert S. Paul, *The Atonement and the Sacraments* (Nashville: Abingdon, 1960), p. 20.
[2]John Wesley, *A Compendium of Wesley's Theology*, ed. R. Burtner and R. Chiles (Nashville: Abingdon, 1954), p. 79.
[3]Colin E. Gunton, *The Actuality of the Atonement* (Grand Rapids: Eerdmans, 1989), p. xi.
[4]Colin Grant, "The Abandonment of Atonement," *King's Theological Review* 9 (1986): 1-8. Ironically, the same year that brought Grant's pessimistic announcement also brought the publication of one of twentieth-century evangelicalism's most notable reflections on the atonement—John Stott's *The Cross of Christ* (Downers Grove, Ill.: InterVarsity Press, 1986).

pects of this central Christian doctrine. Here certain traditional atonement theories (i.e., satisfaction and penal substitution) are seen as encouraging apathetic tolerance of abuse by unduly glorifying the experience of suffering. Related to this, certain models are said to foster the idea that "cosmic child abuse" (i.e., the Father's willing sacrifice of the Son) is the divinely ordained path to salvation.[5]

Another impetus behind the current renewed interest in the atonement involves the interdisciplinary reflections of literary critic René Girard and his scapegoat theory of ritual violence.[6] According to Girard, societies commonly avoid widespread internal conflict and thus preserve the social order by channeling innate human hostility toward a scapegoat. Though truly innocent, the scapegoat, typically a person or group outside of or at the margins of the society, is identified as the source of the conflict and is consequently "sacrificed," that is, punished, killed, or banished from the community. For Girard the gospel story offers what no other scapegoat scenario does: it clearly reveals that the scapegoat—Jesus—is innocent, and in doing so unmasks the ritual violence associated with the scapegoat myth for the tragic mistake that it is. In Girard's assessment, however, Christian theology through the ages has all too often slipped back into an endorsement of sacred violence by encouraging the (re)interpretation of Jesus' death in sacrificial terms and the like. While Girard's take on the atonement leaves little of the traditional understanding of Christ's saving work intact, there is no question that his theory has been an important force in the recent renaissance of atonement studies.[7]

Another factor that is highlighted in many of the current conversations

---

[5]See e.g., Joanne Carlson Brown and Rebecca Parker, "For God So Loved the World?" in *Christianity, Patriarchy, and Abuse: A Feminist Critique,* ed. Joanne Carlson Brown and Carole R. Bohn (New York: Pilgrim, 1989), pp. 1-30; and Rita Nakashima Brock, "And a Little Child Will Lead Us: Christology and Child Abuse," in *Christianity, Patriarchy, and Abuse: A Feminist Critique,* ed. Joanne Carlson Brown and Carole R. Bohn (New York: Pilgrim, 1989), pp. 42-61. For an example of an evangelical thinker who raises concerns about the penal substitution theory see Steve Chalke, *The Lost Message of Jesus* (Grand Rapids: Zondervan, 2003).

[6]See René Girard, *Violence and the Sacred* (Baltimore: Johns Hopkins University Press, 1977); *The Scapegoat* (Baltimore: Johns Hopkins University Press, 1986); *Things Hidden Since the Foundation of the World* (Stanford: Stanford University Press, 1987).

[7]For several representative interactions with Girard's thought see Ted Peters, "The Atonement and the Final Scapegoat," *Perspectives in Religious Studies* 19 (1992): 151-81; William C. Placher, "Christ Takes Our Place: Rethinking Atonement," *Interpretation* 53 (1999): 7-9; Kevin J. Vanhoozer, "The Atonement in Postmodernity: Guilt, Goats and Gifts," in *The Glory of the Atonement,* ed. Charles E. Hill and Frank A. James III (Downers Grove, Ill.: InterVarsity Press,

surrounding the work of Christ is the ongoing quest for the most suitable image or theory by which to understand the atonement. This aged quest has always been complicated by the fact that the New Testament itself offers a wide variety of images to explain the atonement. John Driver has noted no less than ten motifs around which the New Testament atonement images can be clustered: conflict/victory/liberation; vicarious suffering; archetypal (i.e., representative man, pioneer, forerunner, firstborn); martyr; sacrifice; expiation/wrath of God; redemption; reconciliation; justification; and adoption-family.[8] From the patristic period onward, Christian theologians generally can be found acknowledging the rich diversity of ways that the manifold aspects of the atonement can be expressed while at the same time seeking to identify the heart of the atonement—the primary image that most powerfully and completely expresses the crux of the saving work of Christ.[9] Particularly among evangelical theologians today, the question of how best to conceive of the atonement remains an important and contested issue, with the question of status of the penal substitution model often turning up at the core of the debate. Among the recent spate of new books on the topic, a good number represent adherents of the penal substitution theory responding to a variety of critics and in the process correcting what they perceive to be unflattering characterizations of their views.[10]

In no small part due to the landmark work of Gustaf Aulén's (1879-1978) *Christus Victor,* the variety of atonement images and theories have come to be commonly categorized under three broad paradigms: Christus Victor (or

---

2004), pp. 367-404; James G. Williams, "The Innocent Victim: Rene Girard on Violence, Sacrifice, and the Sacred," *Religious Studies Review* 14, no. 4 (1988): 320-26; James G. Williams, *The Bible, Violence and the Sacred: Liberation from the Myth of Sanctioned Violence* (San Francisco: HarperSanFrancisco, 1991). While Girard's thought has been the most notable example of a new approach to the atonement that has contributed to the recent ferment, it is certainly not the only one. Other recent works that offer novel, and not uncontroversial, interpretations of the Christ's atonement include Jon D. Levenson, *The Death and Resurrection of the Beloved Son* (New Haven, Conn.: Yale University Press, 1993); and David Seeley, *The Noble Death* (Sheffield: JSOT, 1990).

[8]John Driver, *Understanding the Atonement for the Mission of the Church* (Scottdale, Penn.: Herald Press, 1986). Others, of course, would collapse some of Driver's motifs to shorten the list. Joel Green and Mark Baker, for example, have captured the major images under five rubrics in *Recovering the Scandal of the Cross* (Downers Grove, Ill.: InterVarsity, 2000), p. 23.

[9]On the breadth of patristic understandings of the atonement see Joseph F. Mitros, "Patristic Views of Christ's Salvific Work," *Thought* 42 (1967): 415-47.

[10]For two recent collections of essays by evangelical scholars that serve to explicate and defend the penal substitution theory, see Charles E. Hill and Frank A. James III, eds., *The Glory of the Atonement* (Downers Grove, Ill.: InterVarsity Press, 2004); and David Peterson, ed., *Where Wrath and Mercy Meet* (Waynesboro, Ga.: Paternoster, 2001).

classic/dramatic), objective and subjective.[11] In essence, each of these paradigms focuses the primary emphasis of the atonement in a different direction.[12] That is, each paradigm sees the central thrust of the work of Christ as
designed to address a different fundamental problem that stands in the way
of salvation.

The Christus Victor Paradigm

The Christus Victor paradigm, known alternatively as the classic or dramatic
model, can be described as Satanward in its focus. In Aulén's words, the
central theme of this approach is "the idea of the Atonement as a Divine
conflict and victory; Christ—Christus Victor—fights against and triumphs
over the evil powers of the world, the 'tyrants' under which mankind is in
bondage and suffering."[13]

More specifically, the Christus Victor paradigm understands the work
of Christ primarily in terms of his conflict with and triumph over those
elements of the kingdom of darkness that, according to the New Testament, hold humanity in their clutches, that is, Satan and his demonic
hosts (Lk 13:10-16; Acts 10:38; 2 Tim 2:26; Heb 2:14-15), the sin power
(Jn 8:34; Acts 8:23; Rom 6; 7:14-25; 8:2), death (Rom 6:23; 1 Cor 15:56;
Heb 2:15) and even, particularly in its curse elements, the law (Rom 7:8-
13; 1 Cor 15:56; Gal 3:13). In addition, the harrowing of hell motif has
fed into the Christus Victor theme from ancient times (i.e., Eph 4:8-10;
1 Pet 3:18-20).

In one form or another, this view seems to have dominated the atonement theology of the early church for the first millennium (thus the label
"classic view"). In certain quarters this general approach crystallized into
a more defined model—the so-called ransom theory of the atonement. In
the ransom theory, this conflict-victory theme was conjoined with the re-
demption-ransom motif to produce an explanatory model in which Jesus
became the ransom by which God redeemed humanity from Satan's
power. Several elements came to characterize the theory: (1) Satan gained
mastery over humanity when the first couple chose the path of sin in the

---

[11]Gustaf Aulén, *Christus Victor: An Historical Study of the Three Main Types of the Idea of the
Atonement*, trans. A. G. Hebert (1931; reprint, New York: Macmillan, 1969).
[12]For a helpful discussion of the various meanings that have attached to the terms *objective* and
subjective vis-à-vis the atonement, see Paul S. Fiddes, *Past Event and Present Salvation* (Louisville: Westminster/John Knox, 1989), pp. 26-28.
[13]Aulén, *Christus Victor*, p. 4.

garden. Satan retains this hold on humanity through the powers of the kingdom of darkness (sin, fear, death, etc.). (2) Through death, Jesus' innocent life became the ransom price that was acceptable to Satan for the liberation/redemption of humanity. The New Testament passage often used to support this idea came from the very lips of Jesus: "The Son of Man came not to be served but to serve, and to give his life as a ransom for many" (Mt 20:28; Mk 10:45; cf. 1 Tim 2:6). (3) Finally, the ransom theory typically emphasizes that Christ's victory was achieved by outwitting the devil. The inherent injustice of taking an innocent life as a ransom is the basis on which Christ defeats Satan (a notion tied to the words of Paul in 1 Cor 2:8).

Among the more notable exponents of some version of the ransom theory are Irenaeus (at least in its embryonic form), Origen (the first to explicate the theory in any kind of detail), Gregory of Nyssa, Gregory the Great and Rufinus.[14] A good number of other writers from the early centuries of the church can be found aligning themselves with the broader Christus Victor theme to one degree or another, whether in conjunction with an explicit ransom theory or not, including Tertullian, Chrysostom, Athanasius, Augustine and John of Damascus.[15]

However, with the coming of the eleventh century and Anselm's satisfaction theory (including his critique of the more idiosyncratic elements of the ransom theory) came the demise of the predominance of the Christus Victor paradigm. Under Aulén's assessment, Martin Luther revitalized the Christus Victor approach.[16] According to Aulén, however, beginning with Melanchthon himself, Luther's reappropriation of the classic theme was quickly lost within later Protestant circles as more objective, "Latin," theories were allowed to displace it. Others question whether Aulén's reading of Luther's atonement theology as primarily rooted in the Christus Victor, as opposed to the objective, paradigm is truly reflective of his thought.[17] In recent years

---

[14]Irenaeus *Against Heresies* 2.20.3, 3.18.6, 5.1.1, 5.2.1; Origen *Commentary on Matthew* 13.9, 16.8; Gregory of Nyssa *The Great Catechism* 21-26; Rufinus *A Commentary on the Apostle's Creed* 16.

[15]Tertullian *On the Flesh of Christ* 17; John Chrysostom *Homily* 67 (John 12:25-32), 2; Athanasius *Incarnation of the Word* 25.4; Augustine *On the Trinity* 13.12-15; John of Damascus *Exposition of the Orthodox Faith* 4.4.

[16]For Aulén's reading of Luther on the atonement see *Christus Victor*, pp. 101-22. Aulén's reading of Luther has not gone unchallenged.

[17]See e.g., Ted Peters, "The Atonement in Anselm and Luther, Second Thoughts About Gustaf Aulén's *Christus Victor*," *Lutheran Quarterly* 24 (1972): 301-14.

there has been a growing consensus that the Christus Victor approach has played a central role in much Anabaptist thought on the atonement over the last several centuries.[18]

While aspects of the Christus Victor view and Aulén's presentation of it have been subjected to criticism—for example, since Anselm's famous critique, many have charged that it fosters a dangerous dualism, one that, among other things, threatens the very sovereignty of God—it nonetheless is widely acknowledged as highlighting an important element of the atonement that went largely neglected for centuries. At the very least it is clear that since the advent of Aulén's book in 1931, a number of scholars have picked up on the Christus Victor theme, and have made it an important, if not the central, theme by which to understand the atoning work of Jesus Christ.[19] Intriguingly, in recent years a number of theologians are making use of the Christus Victor paradigm and its conflict-victory motifs in order to flesh out a nonviolent liberationist (if typically demythologized) vision of the atonement.[20]

The Objective Paradigm

A central characteristic of any objective model of the atonement will be its "Godward" focus. That is, an objective theory of the atonement understands the work of Christ as primarily addressing a necessary demand of God. This trajectory of atonement theories has been denoted by such labels as "substitutionary," "Latin," "commercial" and "Anselmian." Theories that fall within this paradigm tend to emphasize such New Testament motifs as vicarious

---

[18]See e.g., Thomas N. Finger, *A Contemporary Anabaptist Theology* (Downers Grove, Ill.: Inter-Varsity Press, 2004), pp. 331-65.

[19]See e.g., S. Cave, *The Doctrine of the Work of Christ* (Nashville: Cokesbury, 1937); Thomas Finger, *Christian Theology* (Nashville: Nelson, 1985), pp. 1:303-48; Rowan A. Greer, "Christ the Victor and the Victim," *Concordia Theological Quarterly* 59 (1995): 1-30; Karl Heim, *Jesus the World's Perfector,* trans. D. H. Van Daalen (Edinburgh: Oliver & Boyd, 1959); R. Leivestad, *Christ the Conqueror* (New York: Macmillan, 1954); J. S. Whale, *Victor and Victim* (New York: Cambridge University Press, 1960). Robert Webber writes of a "new theological consensus" vis-à-vis the restoration of the Christus Victor view to a place of importance in atonement theology; see his *The Church in the World* (Grand Rapids: Zondervan, 1986), p. 267.

[20]See e.g., Simon S. Maimela, "The Atonement in the Context of Liberation Theology," *International Review of Mission* 75 (1986): 261-69; Darby Kathleen Ray, *Deceiving the Devil* (Cleveland: Pilgrim, 1998); J. Denny Weaver, *The Nonviolent Atonement* (Grand Rapids: Eerdmans, 2001).

suffering, sacrifice, justification and propitiation/expiation.[21] Those passages that reflect the sin-bearing elements of the paradigmatic Isaiah 53 are important here. Many see Paul as capturing the heart of the objective paradigm when he writes: "God made him who had no sin to be sin for us, so that in him we might become the righteousness of God" (2 Cor 5:21). And from another key Pauline text:

> Since all have sinned and fall short of the glory of God; they are now justified by his grace as a gift, through the redemption that is in Christ Jesus, whom God put forward as a sacrifice of atonement by his blood, effective through faith. He did this to show his righteousness, because in his divine forbearance he had passed over the sins previously committed; it was to prove at the present time that he himself is righteous and that he justifies the one who has faith in Jesus. (Rom 3:23-26 NRSV)

Anselm's satisfaction theory of the atonement is the classic example of this type. Although the seeds of Anselm's theory can be traced back to Tertullian (with his emphasis on penance and the satisfaction due to God from sinful humanity, a notion inspired by Roman law) and Cyprian, it was Anselm of Canterbury (1033-1109) who in his famous little book *Cur Deus Homo? (Why God Became Human)* delineated this view in a robust form.

The main outline of Anselm's theory can be summarized by the following six points: (1) The essence of sin is humanity's failure to render to God what is rightfully due him; sin dishonors God. (2) It is humanity's responsibility to restore to God what they have robbed him of, as well as to make reparation above and beyond for injuring and offending him. God's honor inherently demands such restoration and reparation. (3) Humanity can never restore such a debt. Even if humans did their best and did not sin further, they would only be rendering what God is already due; the necessary reparation

---

[21]Even among those who agree that the notion of vicarious sacrifice is central to the atonement, disagreements arise as to the nature and effect of the sacrifice with respect to God and his demands. This controversy was exemplified in the twentieth-century debate about whether the Greek word *hilaskesthai* and related terms, as used in relation to atonement within the Septuagint and the New Testament, should be translated as "propitiation" (i.e., "the appeasement/placation of an angry deity") or rather merely as "expiation" (i.e., "the removal of sin"). C. H. Dodd, arguing for the expiation view, opened up the debate with his article "*hilaskesthai*, its Cognates, Derivatives, and Synonyms in the Septuagint," *Journal of Theological Studies* 32 (1931): 352-60. Leon Morris eventually offered his well-known counterargument, first articulated in "The Use of *hilaskesthai*, Etc. in Biblical Greek," *Expository Times* 62 (1951): 227-33, and later expanded in his book *The Apostolic Preaching of the Cross,* 3rd ed. (Grand Rapids: Eerdmans, 1965), pp. 144-213.

above and beyond would always be left undone. Beyond this, humanity lives in a state of bondage to the devil. (4) God is left with two basic options: punish humanity as they deserve, or accept satisfaction made on their behalf. (5) But now the predicament: satisfaction can only be made by a human since it is humanity that owes God the debt, yet no mere human has the resources to make satisfaction for the race. (6) The sole solution is to be found in the mystery of Jesus Christ, the God-man. As God, he has the *ability* to make satisfaction; as man, his satisfaction can be made on behalf of *humanity*. Anselm grounds his discussion of both the incarnation and the atonement on terms of reason and necessity. In the final dialogical exchange between his two interlocutors, Boso says, "All things which you have said seem to me reasonable and incontrovertible . . . . For, in proving that God became man by necessity, . . . you convince both Jews and Pagans by the mere force of reason."[22]

The attractiveness of Anselm's theory in the Middle Ages is at least partly to be explained by the fact that it capitalized on a notion that was intimately tied to the church's practice of penance as well as the recently arisen feudal system—namely the idea of satisfaction. The satisfaction theory had the advantages of avoiding the eccentricities of the ransom theory while providing an explication of the work of Christ that both takes human sin seriously and offers a reasonable explanation of how Jesus' death satisfies the demands of God's honor.

With the advent of the Reformation period came not only theological innovations but societal transformations as well, changes that would prove to have a bearing on atonement theory. Within Europe the gradual fading of the feudal system and the emergence of Teutonic political theory and its notion of law paved the way for a new expression of the objective paradigm: penal substitution.[23] Here the fundamental issue is that of a legal penal transaction between God and Christ for the salvific benefit of humanity. As a righteous judge, God cannot allow his law to be broken without punishment. Christ's sacrifice satisfies God's requirements of justice. It thus propitiates God's wrath toward sinners and is the basis on which divine forgiveness can righteously be extended to them. A wide variety of biblical passages can be

---

[22]Anselm *Cur Deus Homo* 22.1, in *Saint Anselm: Basic Writings,* trans. S. N. Deane, 2nd ed. (LaSalle, Ill.: Open Court, 1962), p. 287.

[23]For two of the most influential expressions of the penal substitutionary view within twentieth-century evangelical theology, see Morris's *Apostolic Preaching of the Cross* and Stott's *Cross of Christ.*

marshaled in support of this view. Isaiah declares that the suffering Servant was "wounded for our transgressions" and "bruised for our iniquities" (Is 53:5 KJV). Paul asserts that Christ was "delivered over to death for our sins" (Rom 4:25), and that God "made him who had no sin to be sin" (2 Cor 5:21). The first epistle of John affirms a similar understanding when he states that Jesus is the "atoning sacrifice for our sins" (1 Jn 2:2).

The roots of the penal substitution view are discernable in the writings of John Calvin (1509-1564), though it was left to later expositors to systematize and emphasize it in its more robust forms. The penal substitutionary view has come to characterize the standard Reformed/Calvinist approach to the atonement. A long line of respected evangelical thinkers have embraced some version of it, including Charles Hodge, W. G. T. Shedd, Louis Berkhof, John Murray, Leon Morris and John Stott.[24]

During the Reformation period, another expression of the objective paradigm arose: the moral government theory. This theory, first championed by the erstwhile Calvinist turned Arminian Hugo Grotius (1583-1645), offers something of a third quotient over against the satisfaction theory of Anselm and the moral influence theory of Abelard—or, as the lines were drawn in Grotius's day, over against the Reformed penal substitution theory and the Socinian moral example theory. Like the penal substitutionary approach, it strives to take God's law and justice seriously. Similar to the subjective theories, however, it emphasizes that God primarily is to be viewed as loving Creator-Father rather than wrathful Judge.

The moral government theory views God as both the loving Creator and moral Governor of the universe. As loving Creator, God has no intrinsic need to punish us before forgiving us. Rather, like the father in the parable of the prodigal son, God is always waiting with open arms to forgive. On the other hand, as the just moral Governor of the universe, God cannot simply pass over human sins as if they were nothing. In Christ's death, God shows us the seriousness of violating his law, which then deters us from further sinning. While he requires that sin be dealt with, God does not necessarily require a penalty or punishment equal to the offense in every case. As

---

[24]Charles Hodge, *Systematic Theology* (New York: Scribner, 1872), 2:464-543; W. G. T. Shedd, *Dogmatic Theology,* ed. Alan W. Gomes, 3rd ed. (1894; reprint, Phillipsburg, N.J.: Presbyterian & Reformed, 2003), pp. 711-20; Louis Berkhof, *Vicarious Atonement Through Christ* (Grand Rapids: Eerdmans, 1936); John Murray, *Redemption: Accomplished and Applied* (Grand Rapids: Eerdmans, 1955); Morris, *Apostolic Preaching of the Cross;* Leon Morris, *The Cross in the New Testament* (Grand Rapids: Eerdmans, 1965); Stott, *Cross of Christ.*

long as sinners are deterred from committing future sins, God has justly upheld his governing role. Thus, rather than punish humanity, God's hatred of sin is demonstrated by the suffering of Christ. The moral government view has often been adopted by those within the Wesleyan/Arminian tradition.[25]

The Subjective Paradigm

The subjective trajectory of atonement theories—alternatively known as the moralistic, humanistic or Abelardian paradigm—are held together by the common conviction that the primary focus of the atonement is humanward, that is, the atoning work of Christ is designed first and foremost to effect a change in human beings. Subjective theories draw primarily from New Testament themes such as the reconciliation, revelatory (i.e., Jesus as revelation of God's love) and family-adoption (i.e., God as loving Father) motifs. The healing motif found throughout the Scriptures offers another important humanward dimension of the atonement (Is 53:5; Mk 2:17; 1 Pet 2:24), one that is put forward in this book by Bruce Reichenbach for consideration as the primary lens through which to understand the atoning work of Christ.[26] For many expressions of this paradigm, a banner passage is Paul's declaration in Romans: "But God demonstrates his own love for us in this: While we were still sinners, Christ died for us" (Rom 5:8). Any New Testament text that proclaims God's love for humanity and consequent desire to save sinners can be brought forth as evidence for this interpretation of the atonement (e.g., Jn 3:16; 1 Jn 4:8, 16).

It is commonly acknowledged that the most famed exponent of the subjectivist approach is Peter Abelard (1079-1142).[27] Abelard, like Anselm, had little time for the ransom theory of the early church, with its conviction that Satan possessed some sort of legitimate rights over sinful humanity. Such a dualistic view was tantamount to making the devil into a rival god. On the

---

[25]See e.g., John Miley, *The Atonement in Christ* (New York: Phillips & Hunt, 1879); J. Kenneth Grider, *A Wesleyan-Holiness Theology* (Kansas City: Beacon Hill, 1994), pp. 330-35. For a concise articulation of the moral government theory—alongside similar presentations of the penal substitutionary and Christus Victor theories—see Gregory A. Boyd and Paul R. Eddy, "The Atonement Debate," in *Across the Spectrum* (Grand Rapids: Baker, 2002), pp. 113-31.

[26]Margaret Barker has argued that the Hebrew word for atonement *(kpr)* is best understood as to "restore, recreate or heal" ("Atonement: The Rite of Healing," *Scottish Journal of Theology* 49 [1996]: 14).

[27]Some, however, have questioned to what extent this is a fair reading of Abelard. See Alister McGrath, "The Moral Theory of the Atonement: An Historic and Theological Critique," *Scottish Journal of Theology* 38 (1985): 205-20.

other hand, Abelard was also repulsed by certain features of the Anselmic satisfaction theory, which (at least in its easily caricatured forms) one could construe as turning God into a wrathful devil. Abelard's primary answer to the atonement question came in the form of a third broad paradigm: The work of Christ chiefly consists of demonstrating to the world the amazing depth of God's love for sinful humanity. The atonement was directed primarily at humanity, not God. There is nothing inherent in God that must be appeased before he is willing to forgive sinful humanity. The problem rather lies in the sinful, hardened human heart, with its fear and ignorance of God. Humanity refuses to turn to God and be reconciled. Through the incarnation and death of Jesus Christ, the love of God shines like a beacon, beckoning humanity to come and fellowship. Abelard's view, which has come to be known as the moral influence theory, was joined with a fairly strong doctrine of election (something missing from most of the contemporary Abelardian reconstructions). Abelard was eventually challenged in his views by Bernard of Clairvaux, condemned by the Council of Sens (1140), and finally excommunicated. His general approach to the atonement, however, has lived on in various forms throughout the last millennium.[28]

During the Reformation era another form of the subjective view was proposed by Faustus Socinus (1539-1604). It is rooted in a basic rejection of vicarious satisfaction as having anything to do with the work of Christ. Socinus's view, which has come to be known as the moral example theory, emphasizes that the true value of Jesus' death is to be found in the fact that it offers us a perfect example of self-sacrificial dedication to God. Thus, according to Socinus, "Jesus Christ is our savior because he announced to us the way of eternal salvation, confirmed, and in his own person, both by the example of his life and by rising from the dead, clearly showed it, and will give that eternal life to us who have faith in him."[29] Socinus has, of course, been charged with any number of heretical teachings, including an antitrinitarian theology proper, a mistaken Christology, and a Pelagian view of humanity and sin. To these castigations, critics of the subjective paradigm would also add an anemic, overly human-centered theory of the work of Christ.

The rise of modern liberal theology brought a new appreciation for the

---

[28]For a contemporary articulation see Philip Quinn, "Abelard on Atonement: 'Nothing Unintelligible, Arbitrary, Illogical, or Immoral About It,' " in *Reasoned Faith,* ed. Eleonore Stump (Ithaca, N.Y.: Cornell University Press, 1993), pp. 281-300.

[29]Faustus Socinus, cited in Robert Culpepper, *Interpreting the Atonement* (Grand Rapids: Eerdmans, 1966), pp. 104.

Abelardian approach to the atonement. In North America, Horace Bushnell became a well-known exponent, and his counterpart in Britain was Hastings Rashdall.[30] Others whose thought evinces sympathies with the subjective paradigm include Fredrick Schleiermacher, Albrecht Ritschl and R. S. Franks.[31]

Four Views on the Atonement: An Evangelical Dialogue

The purpose of this book is to foster dialogue between four different interpretations of the atonement. Each contributor offers an essay explicating and defending their particular view of the atonement. Each of the four major essays is followed by responses from the other three contributors. The four views offered are (1) the Christus Victor view, presented by Gregory Boyd;[32] (2) the penal substitution view, presented by Thomas Schreiner;[33] (3) the healing view, presented by Bruce Reichenbach;[34] and (4) a kaleidoscopic view, presented by Joel Green.[35] The first two views, of course, fall squarely

---

[30]Horace Bushnell, *The Vicarious Sacrifice, Grounded in Principles of Universal Obligation* (New York: Scribner, 1866); Hastings Rashdall, *The Idea of the Atonement in Christian Theology* (London: Macmillan, 1920).

[31]Frederick Schleiermacher, *The Christian Faith,* ed. and trans. H. R. Mackintosh and J. S. Stewart, 2nd ed. (1830; reprint, Edinburgh: Clark, 1928), pp. 458; Albrecht Ritschl, *The Christian Doctrine of Justification and Reconciliation,* ed. and trans. H. R. Mackintosh and A. B. Macaulay (Edinburgh: Clark, 1900); R. S. Franks, *The Atonement* (London: Oxford University Press, 1934).

[32]Boyd has presented his Christus Victor theory in Gregory A. Boyd, "*Christus Victor:* The Warfare Significance of Christ's Death," in *God at War* (Downers Grove, Ill.: InterVarsity Press, 1997), pp. 238-68. Boyd is currently working out a comprehensive vision of Christian spiritual warfare in a four-volume series titled Satan and Evil. Volume one *(God at War)* and volume two (*Satan and the Problem of Evil* [Downers Grove, Ill.: InterVarsity Press, 2001]) have been published. Volume three, *The Myth of the Blueprint,* is currently underway. A fourth volume focusing on practical implications for the Christian life will eventually round out the series.

[33]Schreiner's approach to the atonement clearly has been shaped by his prior work on Pauline theology. See Thomas R. Schreiner, *The Law and Its Fulfillment* (Grand Rapids: Baker, 1993); *Romans* (Grand Rapids: Baker, 1998); and *Paul, Apostle of God's Glory in Christ* (Downers Grove, Ill.: InterVarsity Press, 2001). Along with Ardel Caneday, Schreiner has also explored the implications of the atonement for the security of the believer in *The Race Set Before Us* (Downers Grove, Ill.: InterVarsity Press, 2001).

[34]Reichenbach has presented his ideas on the atonement as healing in Bruce R. Reichenbach, "By His Stripes We Are Healed," *Journal of the Evangelical Theological Society* 41 (1998): 551-60; and "Inclusivism and the Atonement," *Faith and Philosophy* 16 (1999) 43-54.

[35]Green has presented his kaleidoscopic perspective in Green and Baker, *Recovering the Scandal of the Cross.* He has also explored matters related to the atonement in other publications including Joel B. Green, *The Death of Jesus* (Tübingen: Mohr-Siebeck, 1988); *Salvation* (St. Louis: Chalice, 2003); and John T. Carroll and Joel B. Green, eds., *The Death of Jesus in Early Christianity* (Peabody, Mass.: Hendrickson, 1995).

within one of the standard paradigms—the Christus Victor and the objective, respectively. The third view, atonement as healing, while not reducible to a merely subjective approach, does emphasize the subjective dimension of the atonement in a way that other common evangelical models do not. Finally, the kaleidoscopic view suggests that the wide variety of New Testament atonement images should lead us to conclude that, while each of the paradigms play an important role in explicating the work of Christ, none of them has a claim to priority. It is important to note that all of the contributors represented in this book acknowledge that the New Testament provides a plethora of images by which to understand Christ's work, and that each of them provides a valuable window into the workings of the atonement. However, each of the first three views (Christus Victor, penal substitution, and healing) will contend that their particular theory has a justifiable claim to priority over the others, while the kaleidoscopic view argues that none of the views has a priority status and that to emphasize only one is to misunderstand the atonement.

We would like to thank each of our contributors—Greg Boyd, Joel Green, Bruce Reichenbach and Tom Schreiner—for their valuable role in this project and for their collegiality throughout the process. Our thanks also goes to our IVP editor Dan Reid, who encouraged and nurtured this project from start to finish. We also offer a word of grateful remembrance for Philip Quinn. Professor Quinn began this project as one of our contributors but passed away before the project was brought to completion. He will be remembered for many things, among them being the way that he brought his acute philosophical sensibilities to a variety of theological considerations, including the atoning work of Christ.[36] As always, we are forever grateful for the loving encouragement of our families, especially our wives, Michelle Beilby and Kelly Eddy. Finally, we want to express our gratitude to our teacher, our mentor and our friend David K. Clark. It is to him that we dedicate this book.

---

[36]Philip L. Quinn, "Christian Atonement and Kantian Justification," *Faith and Philosophy* 3 (1986): 440-62; "Aquinas on Atonement," in *Trinity, Incarnation, and Atonement,* eds. Ronald Feenstra and Cornelius Plantinga (Notre Dame, Ind.: University of Notre Dame Press, 1989), pp. 153-77; "Abelard on Atonement: 'Nothing Unintelligible, Arbitrary, Illogical, or Immoral about It," in *Reasoned Faith,* ed. Eleonore Stump (Ithaca, N.Y.: Cornell University Press, 1993), pp. 281-300; "Swinburne on Guilt, Atonement and Christian Redemption," in *Reason and the Christian Religion,* ed. Alan G. Padgett (Oxford: Clarendon Press, 1994), pp. 277-300.

ONE

Christus Victor View

GREGORY A. BOYD

*"The Son of God was revealed for this purpose,
to destroy the works of the devil."*

1 JOHN 3:8

One mark of great intelligence is that a person can solve a number of problems with a single stroke. I believe this is why Paul speaks of the "rich variety" of God's secret and hidden wisdom in having his Son become incarnate and die on Calvary (Eph 3:10; cf. 1 Cor 1:30; 2:7). Through the incarnation, life, death and resurrection of Jesus Christ the infinitely wise God solved a number of problems. Among other things, through Christ God defeated the devil and his cohorts (Heb 2:14; 1 Jn 3:8); revealed the definitive truth about himself (Rom 5:8, cf. Jn 14:7-10); reconciled all things, including humans, to himself (2 Cor 5:18-19; Col 1:20-22); forgave us our sins (Acts 13:38; Eph 1:7); healed us from our sin-diseased nature (1 Pet 2:24); poured his Spirit on us and empowered us to live in relation to himself (Rom 8:2-16); and gave us an example to follow (Eph 5:1-2; 1 Pet 2:21). God's wisdom is displayed in a "rich variety" indeed!

Given the multifaceted design of Christ's life, death and resurrection, it is not at all surprising that over time the church created a diversity of conceptual models of the atonement. Hence we have various Christus Victor models, substitutionary models, healing models, exemplary models, apotheosis models, recapitulation models and moral government models of the atonement. Each model legitimately expresses a facet of what the incarnation, life, death and resurrection of Christ accomplished.

Some in our postmodern context argue that we should simply leave it at that. While various cultural and personal contexts may call for one model to be at times emphasized over others, these people argue that we should not attempt to defend any one view as more fundamental than others or attempt to fashion the various models into a single coherent framework. I'm deeply sympathetic to the sentiment. Yet it seems to me perfectly natural and, if carried out with an irenic spirit, potentially beneficial to strive for an encompassing conceptual model that might reveal an "inner logic" to all aspects of Christ's work. Consider that every advance we have ever made in human understanding has been the result of sticking to the conviction that *reality is unified* while striving to comprehend it as such. We strive to integrate apparently disparate facts into a unified framework. If we believe in the *reality* of the atonement, therefore, I do not see why we should avoid trying to integrate the various facets of the "rich variety" of God's wisdom into a coherent whole.

This is not a merely theoretical interest. As has been the case with every advance in science, matters of practical consequence may be at stake. How we understand the "rich variety" of God's wisdom behind the atonement may affect how we apply the atonement to areas of our life (a point I will return to at the end of this chapter).

I obviously cannot try to accomplish this unifying task in the limited space of this present essay. Yet I want to at least propose a framework within which such a project might be carried out. More specifically, I'm suggesting that a unifying framework may be found in the view of Christ's work that dominated the thinking of the church for the first thousand years of its history: namely the Christus Victor model. This model centers on the truth that through the incarnation, life, death and resurrection of Christ, God defeated the devil. In this essay I will argue that this aspect of Christ's work can plausibly be construed as more fundamental than other aspects of Christ's work and that other aspects of the "rich variety" of the wisdom behind Christ's work can be best understood within this context.[1]

---

[1]While the Christus Victor model has for the most part taken the back seat to Anselm's "satisfaction theory" (and later to the Reformers' "penal substitution theory") for the last nine centuries, the Christus Victor model has in the last century been experiencing something of a Renaissance, especially since the publication of Gustaf Aulén's now classic work, *Christus Victor: An Historical Study of the Three Main Types of the Idea of the Atonement,* trans. A. G. Hebert (Eugene, Ore.: Wipf & Stock, [1931]). For a sampling of other recent advocates see references in Gregory A. Boyd, *God at War: The Bible and Spiritual Conflict* (Downers Grove, Ill.: InterVarsity Press, 1997), pp. 238-68, as well as Thomas Finger, *Christian Theology: An Eschatological Approach,* vol. 1 (Scottdale, Penn.: Herald Press, 1985). Interestingly, a growing number

I start by providing the scriptural background for the Christus Victor model. I follow this with a brief examination of those New Testament passages that are most central to this understanding of Christ's life and work. I then discuss five clues we find in the New Testament that suggest something about *how* Christ defeated the devil while also revealing that the atonement concerns every aspect of Christ's life and teaching, not just his death and resurrection. This is followed by a brief sketch of how other facets of Christ's work might be understood in the context of the Christus Victor model. I conclude by summarizing eight points that I believe support my thesis that the Christus Victor model of the atonement is more fundamental and more encompassing than other atonement models.

Background: The Warfare Motif in Scripture

The Christus Victor view of the atonement cannot be appropriately understood without an appreciation for the broader spiritual warfare motif that runs throughout Scripture. Though the motif of spiritual warfare is rarely given its full due, the biblical narrative could in fact be accurately described as a story of God's ongoing conflict with and ultimate victory over cosmic and human agents who oppose him and who threaten his creation.[2]

Hostile waters, monsters and gods. In the Old Testament this warfare is most commonly depicted in terms of God's battle with hostile waters and vicious sea monsters that were believed to surround and threaten the earth. Whereas non-Israelites looked to various deities (e.g., Marduk and Baal) to resist these sinister cosmic forces, the Hebrews declared that it was Yahweh alone who warred against, rebuked, guarded and trampled on the malevolent waters, and who vanquished the cosmic monsters (e.g., Ps 29:3-4, 10; 74:10-14; 77:16, 19; 89:9-10; 104:2-9; Prov 8:27-29; Job 7:12; 9:8, 17; 26:12-13; 38:6-11; 40:15-34; Ezek 29:3; 32:2; Jer 51:34; Hab 3:8-15; Nahum 1:4).

We also read a great deal about rebel gods in the Old Testament, created

of nonevangelical theologians have embraced various more-or-less "demythologized" versions of the Christus Victor motif, often with helpful insights. See e.g., Walter Wink, *Engaging the Powers: Discernment and Resistance in a World of Domination* (Minneapolis: Fortress, 1992); J. Denny Weaver, *The Nonviolent Atonement* (Grand Rapids: Eerdmans, 2001); Darby Kathleen Ray, *Deceiving the Devil: Atonement, Abuse and Ransom* (Cleveland, Ohio: Pilgrims Press, 1998); John Macquarrie, *Principles of Christian Theology,* 2nd ed. (New York: Charles Scribners, 1977), pp. 318-21; cf. also John Macquarrie, "Demonology and the Classic Idea of Atonement," *Expository Times* 68 (1956): 3-6, 60-63.

[2]For a full exposition of the spiritual warfare motif throughout Scripture, see Boyd, *God at War.*

spirit beings with whom God and his heavenly host do battle. As is the case with the hostile waters and cosmic monsters, ancient Israelites never separated battles that took place on earth from battles that took place among the gods (e.g., 2 Sam 5:23-24; 1 Chron 12:22; Judg 11:21-24).[3] What went on in (what we today would call) the "spiritual realm" affects what transpires in history, and vice versa. So in the ancient Israelite worldview, part of the explanation for why a prayer is not answered quickly, why people suffer injustice and are in poverty and why "natural" disasters fall on someone may have something to do with the contingent activity of these rebel gods (e.g., Dan 10; Ps 82; Job 1—2).[4]

These depictions of evil in terms of hostile waters, cosmic monsters and rebel gods are in varying degrees clearly influenced by standard ancient Near Eastern mythological imagery. Yet they nevertheless powerfully communicate the understanding that the earth and its inhabitants exist in a *cosmic war zone*. Order in the cosmos and the preservation of Israel depend on God's continually fighting against these evil cosmic forces. In contrast to their pagan neighbors, Old Testament authors of course express unprecedented confidence that Yahweh is capable of keeping these cosmic forces of chaos at bay and ultimately overthrowing them. At the same time, however, it's clear they understand Yahweh's victory over these forces to be praiseworthy precisely because they believe these opposing cosmic forces are *formidable* and that the battles in the spiritual realm are *real*.[5]

Satan in the New Testament. Owing to a number of historical factors, the understanding that the earth is a war zone between good and evil cosmic forces intensified significantly among Jews in the two centuries leading

---

[3]For discussions, see Neil Forsyth, *The Old Enemy: Satan and the Combat Myth* (Princeton, N.J.: Princeton University Press, 1987); Jon D. Levenson, *Creation and the Persistence of Evil: The Jewish Drama of Divine Omnipotence* (San Francisco: Harper & Row, 1988); Carola Kloos, *YHWH's Combat with the Sea: A Canaanite Tradition in the Religion of Ancient Israel* (Leiden: E. J. Brill, 1986); Mary K. Wakeman, *God's Battle with the Monster: A Study in Biblical Imagery* (Leiden: E. J. Brill, 1973); John Day, *God's Conflict with the Dragon and the Sea: Echoes of a Canaanite Myth in the Old Testament* (Cambridge: Cambridge University Press, 1985); Patrick D. Miller, *The Divine Warrior in Early Israel* (Cambridge, Mass.: Harvard University Press, 1973); E. Theodor Mullen Jr., *The Assembly of the Gods* (Chico, Calif.: Scholars Press, 1980). See other references in Boyd, *God at War,* pp. 73-142.

[4]I have argued elsewhere that the activity of rebel gods is one of several missing aspects of traditional theodicy. See Gregory A. Boyd, *Is God to Blame?* (Downers Grove, Ill.: InterVarsity Press, 2003).

[5]See Levenson, *Creation and the Persistence of Evil,* pp. 14-27.

up to Christ, commonly referred to as the apocalyptic period.[6] While there is significant theological diversity among apocalyptic writers, all attribute far more influence to gods, angels and demons than Old Testament canonical writings do.[7] What is more, all share an acute awareness that the earth is held hostage by evil forces to such a degree that it can only be freed by a radical in-breaking of God, something they believed was going to happen in the very near future.

It was into this world that Jesus came, and all indications are that he and his earliest followers shared and in some respects intensified still further this apocalyptic worldview. For example, the role given to Satan by Jesus and his followers is without precedent in previous apocalyptic writings. According to John, Jesus believed that Satan was "the ruler of this world" (Jn 12:31; 14:30; 16:11).[8] The word translated "ruler" *(archōn)* customarily referred to "the highest official in a city or a region in the Greco-Roman world."[9] While Jesus and his followers of course believed that God was the *ultimate* Lord over all creation, they clearly viewed Satan as the *functional* lord of earth at the present time.

Along the same lines, Satan is depicted as possessing "all the kingdoms of the world"—to the point where *he* gives authority to rule these kingdoms to anyone he pleases (Lk 4:5-6). In fact, the various kingdoms of the world can be described as *a single kingdom* under Satan's rule (Rev 11:15, cf. Rev 13). John goes so far as to claim that the *entire world* is "under the power of the evil one" (1 Jn 5:19), and Paul does not shy away from labeling Satan "the god of this world" (2 Cor 4:4) and "the ruler of the power of the air" (Eph 2:2). Because of this pervasive and oppressive diabolic influence, Paul, in typical apocalyptic fashion, depicts this present world system as fundamentally evil (Gal 1:4).

Everything Jesus was about was centered on vanquishing this empire, taking back the world that Satan had seized and restoring its rightful viceroys—humans—to their position of guardians of the earth (Gen 1:26-28; cf. 2 Tim 2:12; Rev 5:10). Each one of Jesus' many healings and deliverances diminished Satan's hold on the world and liberated people, to whatever de-

---

[6]See Boyd, *God at War,* pp. 172-76.

[7]With the possible exception of Daniel, though most scholars argue this is because Daniel was composed in the second century B.C., during the apocalyptic period.

[8]Unless otherwise indicated, Scripture quotations are from the New Revised Standard Version.

[9]Clinton E. Arnold, *Powers of Darkness: Principalities and Powers in Paul's Letters* (Downers Grove, Ill.: InterVarsity Press, 1992), p. 81.

gree, from his stronghold.[10] Peter succinctly summarized Jesus' ministry to Cornelius when he said that Jesus "went about doing good and healing *all who were oppressed by the devil.*" (Acts 10:38, emphasis added). Gustaf Wingren captures this central motif well:

> When Jesus heals the sick and drives out evil spirits, Satan's dominion is departing and God's kingdom is coming (Mt 12:22-29). All Christ's activity is therefore a conflict with the Devil (Acts 10:38). God's Son took flesh and became man that he might overthrow the power of the Devil, and bring his works to nought (Heb 2.14f.; I John 3.8).[11]

The battle against the powers. Intensifying the apocalyptic view of the time, Jesus and the New Testament authors saw demonic influences not only in demonized and diseased people but directly or indirectly in everything that was not consistent with God's reign. For example, swearing oaths, temptation, lying, legalism, false teachings, anger, spiritual blindness and persecution were all seen as being satanically inspired.[12] This ought not surprise us since, again, Jesus and his followers all believed the devil had significant control of the entire world (1 Jn 5:19). The kingdom of the roaring lion (1 Pet 5:8) was an ever-present reality to Jesus and his earliest disciples. For this reason Paul taught that whatever earthly struggles disciples found themselves involved in, they must understand that their *real* struggle was against "the rulers, against the authorities, against the cosmic powers of this present darkness, against the spiritual forces of evil in the heavenly places" (Eph 6:12; cf. 2 Cor 10:3-5).

This last Pauline passage brings up a final and very important aspect of the New Testament's apocalyptic worldview. Beyond the frequent references to Satan and demons throughout the New Testament, we find Paul (and others, e.g., 1 Pet 3:21-22) making reference to other spiritual powers, most of which have their counterpart in the apocalyptic literature of the time. Thus we read about "rulers," "principalities," "powers" and "authorities" (Rom 8:38; 13:1; 1 Cor 2:6, 8; 15:24; Eph 1:21; 2:2; 3:10; 6:12; Col 1:16;

---

[10]On the centrality of healings and exorcisms in Jesus' ministry, see Boyd, *God at War,* pp. 171-214.

[11]Gustaf Wingren, *The Living Word,* trans. T. V. Pague (Philadelphia: Muhlenberg, 1960), p. 53. I have elsewhere argued that even Jesus' "nature miracles" (e.g., calming the raging sea, cursing the barren tree) are manifestations of the kingdom of God over and against the kingdom of Satan (see *God at War,* pp. 205-14).

[12]See e.g., Mt 5:37; 6:13; 13:19, 38; Acts 5:3; 1 Cor 7:5; 10:20; 2 Cor 2:7, 10-11; 4:4; 11:3, 13; Gal 1:8; 4:8-10; Eph 4:26-27; Col 2:8; 1 Thess 3:5; 1 Tim 4:1-5; 1 Jn 4:1-4; 2 Jn 7.

2:10, 15), along with "dominions" (Eph 1:21; Col 1:16), "cosmic powers" (Eph 6:12), "thrones" (Col 1:16), "spiritual forces" (Eph 6:12), "elemental spirits" (Col 2:8, 20; Gal 4:3, 8-9) and other spiritual entities.[13] For the sake of brevity I will follow the precedent set by Walter Wink and simply refer to this vast array of cosmic powers as "the powers."

There has been a good deal of discussion surrounding what precisely Paul and others were referring to with these various titles, and while certain matters continue to be debated, there is widespread consensus that these powers are at the very least closely related to (and, some argue, identical with) the destructive spiritual force of various social structures and people groups—nations, governments, religions, classes, races, tribes and other social groups, for example.[14]

It is arguably for this reason that Paul does not see "sin" first and foremost as a matter of *individual* behavior, as most modern Westerners do. He rather conceives of "sin" (and related concepts such as the "law" and the "flesh") as a quasi-autonomous power that holds people groups as well as individuals in bondage (e.g., Rom 3:9; 6:6-12; 7:7-20, 23, 25). This is why people can never hope to break the power of sin and fulfill the law by their own effort. As in much apocalyptic thought, Paul believed what was needed was nothing less than God breaking into human history to destroy the power of sin and rescuing us from the cosmic powers that keep us in bondage to sin. This is precisely what Paul and all early Christians believed happened with the advent of Jesus Christ. And this is the essence of the Christus Victor view of the atonement.

Christ's Victory over the Powers

For Luther and other Reformers the central theological issue that needed addressing was how individual sinners could be made righteous before an all-holy God who cannot leave sin unpunished. But as numerous scholars in the last several decades have confirmed, this was not the main problem

---

[13]For example, it's likely Paul is referring to demonic entities in Rom 8:39. See James D. G. Dunn, *Romans 1-8,* Word Biblical Commentary 38A (Waco, Tex.: Word, 1988), p. 513.

[14]For an overview of the discussion, see Peter O'Brien, "Principalities and Powers: Opponents of the Church," *Evangelical Review of Theology* 16 (1992): 353-84. No one has explored and developed this thesis more thoroughly and insightfully than Walter Wink in his acclaimed "Powers" trilogy. See especially Walter Wink, *Naming the Powers: The Language of Power in the New Testament* (Philadelphia: Fortress, 1984). Unfortunately, in my estimation, Wink denies the "powers" are personal, transcendent agents. See my critique of his view in Boyd, *God at War,* pp. 273-76.

most first century Jews struggled with.[15] As was the case with Paul, the central concern of most first-century Jews was over how people could get free from the oppressive and destructive force of the cosmic powers that had seized the world. Most fundamentally it was in *these categories* that the followers of Jesus came to understand the significance of his life, death and resurrection.

Christ's victory over enemies. According to the New Testament, the central thing Jesus did was drive out the "ruler of this world" (Jn 12:31). He came to "destroy the works of the devil" (1 Jn 3:8). He came to "destroy the one who has the power of death, that is, the devil" in order to "free those who all their lives were held in slavery by the fear of death" (Heb 2:14-15). Jesus lived, died and rose again to establish a new reign that would ultimately "put all his enemies under his feet" (1 Cor 15:25). Though "the strong man" was "fully armed," one who was "stronger than he" had finally arrived who could attack and overpower him (Lk 11:21-22). While the cosmic "thief comes only to steal and kill and destroy," Jesus came into the world to vanquish the thief so that all "may have life, and have it abundantly" (Jn 10:10). Jesus "disarmed the rulers and authorities and made a public example of them, triumphing over them" (Col 2:15). In a word, Jesus came to end the cosmic war that had been raging from time immemorial and to set Satan's captives free (Lk 4:18; Eph 4:8).

The first messianic prophecy given in Scripture—indeed the first prophecy *period*—announced just this: a descendent of Eve would crush the head of the serpent who originally deceived humanity into joining in his rebellion (Gen 3:15).[16] It is therefore not surprising that the original disciples expressed what the Messiah accomplished in terms of *a victory over the ancient serpent*.

The very first Christian sermon, according to Luke, centered on Christ's

---

[15]The now classic work on this theme is E. P. Sanders's *Paul and Palestinian Judaism: A Comparison of Patterns of Religion* (Philadelphia: Fortress, 1977). We do not have to embrace all of the particulars of Sanders's proposal in order to appreciate this and other aspects of his "new view" of Paul. From my perspective, a balanced approach to Paul in our post-Sanders world is represented in the work of N. T. Wright. See e.g., Wright's *The Climax of the Covenant: Christ and the Law in Pauline Theology* (Minneapolis: Fortress, 1992); and "A Fresh Perspective on Paul?" *Bulletin of the John Rylands University Library of Manchester* 83 (2001): 21-39.

[16]On the messianic interpretation of Gen 3:15, see Ralph A. Martin, "The Earliest Messianic Interpretation of Genesis 3:15," *Journal of Biblical Literature*, 84 (1965): 425-27. This reading seems to lie behind several New Testament texts (e.g., Rom 16:19-20; 2 Cor 11:3; Rev 12).

cosmic victory. After the Holy Spirit was poured out on the day of Pentecost, Peter stood up and preached:

This Jesus God raised up, and of that all of us are witnesses. Being therefore exalted at the right hand of God, and having received from the Father the promise of the Holy Spirit, he has poured out this that you both see and hear. For David did not ascend into the heavens, but he himself says,

"The Lord said to my Lord,
'Sit at my right hand,
until I make your enemies your footstool.'"

Therefore let the entire house of Israel know with certainty that God has made him both Lord and Messiah, this Jesus whom you crucified. (Acts 2:32-36).

The central thing Jesus did, according to Peter, was *fulfill* Psalms 110:1. Jesus had been raised to a position of divine power (the Lord's "right hand") over his defeated and humiliated enemies (who are now his "footstool"). In an apocalyptic Jewish context, to say the kingdom of God has come was to say the *kingdom of Satan has been defeated*.

This theme of victory over cosmic foes pervades the entire New Testament. Indeed Psalm 110 is the most frequently cited passage in the New Testament, and it always, in a variety of ways, is used to express the truth that Christ is Lord *because he has defeated God's enemies*.[17] The significance of this is difficult to overstate. In the words of Oscar Cullman:

Nothing shows more clearly how the concept of the present Lordship of Christ and also of his consequent victory over the angel powers stands at the very center of early Christian thought than the frequent citation of Ps. 110:1, not only in isolated books, but in the entire NT.[18]

Through his incarnation, life, teachings, death and resurrection, Jesus manifested the power of God over Satan, demons and the entire spectrum of rebellious principalities and powers. The one who created "thrones . . . dominions . . . rulers . . . [and] powers" (Col 1:16) became incarnate, died and was resurrected in order for God "to reconcile to himself all things, whether on earth or in heaven, by making peace through the blood of his

---

[17]See, e.g., Mt 22:41-45; Mk 12:35-37; Lk 20:41-44; 1 Cor 15:22-25; Heb 1:13; 5:6, 10; 6:20; 7:11, 15, 17, 21; 10:12-13, cf. Mt 26:64; Mk 14:62; Lk 22:69; Acts 5:31; 7:55-56; Rom 8:34; 1 Cor 15:25; Eph 1:20; Col 3:1; Heb 1:3; 8:1; 10:12-13; 1 Pet 3:22; Rev 3:21.

[18]Oscar Cullman, *Christ and Time*, trans. F. V. Wilson, rev. ed. (London: SCM, 1962), p.193. For a thorough exposition of the importance of Psalms 110 in the New Testament, see David M. Hay, *Glory at the Right Hand: Psalm 110 in Early Christianity* (Nashville: Abingdon, 1973).

cross" (Col 1:20). *This* is what Christ accomplished. In the words of Karl
Heim, the cross is "God's final settlement of the Satanic opposing power
which has arisen against God."[19]

Salvation as deliverance from the devil. Because the main thing
Christ accomplished was that he defeated the devil, we are not surprised to
find that salvation in the New Testament is frequently depicted as freedom
from the devil's oppression. For example, the message Paul received when
he first encountered Christ was that he was being sent to the Gentiles "to
open their eyes so that they may turn from darkness to light and from the
power of Satan to God, so that they may receive forgiveness of sins and a
place among those who are sanctified by faith in [Christ]" (Acts 26:17-18).

Through Paul, God was going to free Gentiles from "the god of this
world" who had "blinded the minds of the unbelievers" (2 Cor 4:4) and
thereby set them free from the power of Satan and bring them into the
power of God. Because of this—and *note closely the logical order*—they
would be in a position to "receive forgiveness of sins" as well as a place
among the community that is set apart ("sanctified") by God. Salvation
clearly involves forgiveness of sins, but this forgiveness is itself rooted in a
person getting freed from Satan's grip, and therefore freed from the control-
ling power of sin.

A multitude of other passages captures the same dynamic. Salvation is
most fundamentally about escaping "from the snare of the devil, having been
held captive by him to do his will" (2 Tim 2:26). It's about being "set free
from the present evil age" (Gal 1:4) and liberated from our "enslave[ment] to
the elemental spirits of the world" (Gal 4:3; cf. Rom 6:18; 8:2; Gal 5:1; Heb
2:14-15). It's about being "enabled . . . to share in the inheritance of the saints
in the light" by being "rescued . . . from the power of darkness and transferred . . . into the kingdom of his beloved Son" (Col 1:12-13). This inheritance involves receiving "redemption, the forgiveness of sins" (Col 1:14), but
we have this inheritance only because we've been "transferred" out of Satan's
dominion and brought under the reign of God through his Son.

Similarly, Peter notes that baptism saves believers "through the resurrection of Jesus Christ, who has gone into heaven and is at the right hand of
God, with angels, authorities, and powers made subject to him" (1 Pet 3:21-
22). The ordinance of baptism has meaning, Peter says, not because it is a

---

[19]Karl Heim, *Jesus the World's Perfecter*, trans. D. H. Van Daalen (Edinburgh: Oliver & Boyd,
1959), p. 70.

literal washing (v. 21) but because it connects the believer with the death and resurrection of Christ. And the foremost thing that the death and resurrection of Christ accomplished, we see once again, was the subjugation of all cosmic powers under him. In baptism, therefore, believers express and participate in Christ's cosmic victory. Indeed, Peter seems to suggest (however cryptically and controversially) that because of the cosmic significance of what Christ has accomplished, even some who "in former times did not obey" can now be set free (1 Pet 3:19-20).

So too Paul writes that our trust in Christ means that we die to the "elemental spirits" in Christ (Col 2:20) and grow into the fullness of Christ who now is "the head of every ruler and authority" (Col 2:10). Through the cross and resurrection, Christ disarmed and defeated these powers, to the point of making them a "public example" (a term used when military leaders would parade defeated soldiers through their city). Consequently, all who trust in Christ are incorporated into him and therefore share in this cosmic victory. This is the essential meaning of "salvation" in the New Testament. Everything Satan and the diabolic powers had on us—all the sin that put us under their oppression—has lost its power and we have therefore been set free from all condemnation (Col 2:14-15).

The cosmic and soteriological significance of the cross. I might summarize what I have been saying by noting that in the Christus Victor view of the atonement—in sharp contrast to all other views—the *cosmic* significance of Christ's work is ontologically more fundamental than its *soteriological* significance. Of course, the soteriological significance of the cross is the meaning that is perhaps most important *to us,* and we should never minimize it. But we only accurately understand and appreciate this significance if we understand it in the context of the cosmic significance of Christ's victory.

It is for this reason that Paul discusses the cosmic significance of Christ's work—how he has in principle brought an end to the war with the principalities and powers (Col 1:15-20)— and only then concludes:

> And *you* who [like the rebel powers] were once estranged and hostile [to God] in mind, doing evil deeds, he has now reconciled in his fleshly body through death, so as to present you holy and blameless and irreproachable before him. (Col 1:21-22, emphasis added).

We are reconciled because the cosmos has been reconciled. Because the rebel powers have been put in their place, we can be presented "holy and blameless" before God.

Similarly, in Ephesians 1—2, Paul first glories in Christ's cosmic significance, whereby all God's enemies were placed "under his feet" (Eph 1:20-
22) before he celebrates the fact that we who once followed "the course of
this world" and "the ruler of the power of the air" have been "made . . . alive
together with Christ" (Eph 2:2, 5). This freedom involves forgiveness for the
trespasses that placed us under the rulers' authority and thus made us spiritually dead (Eph 2:1). But this soteriological significance is simply an aspect
of the broader cosmic significance of Christ's work. Because the "strong
man" has been disarmed and tied up—and only because the strong man has
been disarmed and tied up—his "property" (the earth) gets "plundered," and
the captives get set free (Lk 11:21-22)!

The move from cosmic to soteriological significance is manifested in a
number of ways in the New Testament, especially when it speaks of the disciple's life in Christ. For example, it's only because the devil has been defeated, together with sin and the law, which sin used against us, that we can
be assured that the accuser can no longer condemn us of sin (Rom 8:1, 31,
33; Col 2:13-15; cf. Rev 12:10). And it's only because the one who once ruled
the world has in principle been driven out (Jn 12:31), disarmed (Col 2:15)
and destroyed (1 Jn 3:8) that disciples can be assured that no cosmic power
can separate us from the love of God (Rom 8:35-39).

Similarly, it's only because we who are disciples know that the same
power that positioned Christ "far above all rule and authority and power and
dominion" is now at work in us that we can have unwavering confidence
that we too shall overcome (Eph 1:18-21). Only because Christ conquered
Satan and sin can we be confident that through Christ we can "overcome the
evil one" (1 Jn 2:13-14) and overcome the power of sin (1 Jn 5:18). Only because the one who held the keys of death has been destroyed can we who
trust in Christ live free from the fear of death (Heb 2:14-15). Only because
the cross defeated the devil can we who trust in Christ overcome "that ancient serpent, who is called the Devil and Satan," for we war against him "by
the blood of the lamb and by the world of [our] testimony" (Rev 12:9, 11).

In other words, *our* personal and social victories participate in *Christ's*
cosmic victory. Everything the New Testament says about the soteriological
significance of Christ's work is predicated on the cosmic significance of his
work. Yet only the Christus Victor view captures the centrality of this cosmic,
warfare significance and thus properly expresses the soteriological significance of Christ's work.

Salvation as a cosmic and anthropological reality. As alluded to earlier, the New Testament concept of salvation is centered on our participation in Christ's cosmic victory over the powers. It does not first and foremost mean "salvation from God's wrath" or "salvation from hell," as many Western Christians mistakenly assume—often with negative consequences for their mental picture of God or with antinomian consequences for their life. Rather, as James Kallas says:

> Since the cosmos itself is in bondage, depressed under evil forces, the essential content of the word "salvation" is that the world itself will be rescued, or renewed, or set free. Salvation is a cosmic event affecting the whole of creation. . . . Salvation is not simply the overcoming of my rebellion and the forgiveness of my guilt, but salvation is the liberation of the whole world process of which I am only a small part.[20]

Christ has in principle freed the cosmos from its demonic oppression and thus freed all inhabitants of the cosmos who will simply submit to this new loving reign. The cosmos that had been "groaning in labor pains" because it was subjected to "the bondage [of] decay" has now been and is yet being set free (Rom 8:19-22). And we who were the originally intended viceroys of the earth (Gen 1:26-28) have also been and are yet being released from bondage and reestablished to our rightful position as co-rulers of the earth with Christ (2 Tim 2:12; Rev 5:10).[21] We are saved from the power of God's archenemy, saved from the destruction that would have been the inevitable consequences of our sin, saved from our fallen inability to live in right relatedness with God, saved from the idolatrous, futile striving to find "life" from the things of the world, saved from our meaninglessness and saved to forever participate in the fullness of life, joy, power and peace that is the reign of the triune God.

This is what the New Testament means by "salvation." It is a cosmic reality before it is an anthropological reality, and it is the latter because it is the former. So far as I can see, only the Christus View adequately expresses this truth.

---

[20]James Kallas, *The Satanward View: A Study in Pauline Theology* (Philadelphia: Westminster, 1966), p. 74.

[21]Christ has defeated the devil "in principle." Yet we obviously do not see this victory fully manifested. This is the well-known already–not yet tension in the New Testament's eschatology. It's significant to note that Satan is yet identified as the "god of this world," the "principality and power of the air" and in "control of the entire world" *after* the resurrection (2 Cor 4:4; Eph 2:2)!

Overcoming Evil with Good

The ancient Christus Victor theories. That Christ came to defeat the devil and his works is as clear as could be in the New Testament. But how exactly Christ's life, death and resurrection accomplished this feat is not so clear. Early church theologians offered an assortment of speculations about this.

One popular train of thought was that God offered Jesus to Satan in exchange for the humanity Satan held captive, but then God retracted the offer, as it were, when he raised Jesus from the dead. Another even more popular line of thought was that by sending Jesus into Satan's domain as a vulnerable human, God was using Jesus as "bait." God knew Satan and his cohorts would not be able to resist seizing Christ, and yet God also knew that since Jesus was divine and sinless, Satan could not "stomach" him, as it were. Jesus was therefore spewed out on the third day, but when he left hell he took imprisoned humanity with him. For the first millennium of church history, when Christians thought about what Christ accomplished they usually thought along these lines.

If taken too literally and pressed for details, both theories are obviously problematic—which is, in part, why they largely fell out of favor after Anselm proposed his alternative perspective. And yet I wonder if perhaps the church has not tended to throw the biblical baby out with the speculative bathwater. I suggest that there is some profound truth in these ancient ways of thinking about Christ. In the process of fleshing this out, I hope to show how the Christus Victor motif cannot be limited to Christ's death but rather permeates Christ's life and teaching as well.

The "secret" wisdom of God. Five pieces of biblical data may provide clues (though not detailed explanations) as to how Christ defeated the devil. First, it may be significant that throughout Christ's ministry, demons seem to know who Jesus is but have no idea why he's come into their domain (Mk 1:23-24; 3:11; 5:7; Lk 8:28). Second, the rich variety of God's wisdom that led to the crucifixion was for some reason kept "secret and hidden" until after the crucifixion (Rom 16:25; 1 Cor 2:7; Eph 3:9-10; Col 1:26). Third, it's pretty clear that Satan and his minions were instrumental in bringing about Christ's crucifixion. It was, after all, Satan who entered into Judas and inspired him to betray Jesus (Jn 13:27). Fourth, Paul tells us that had the "rulers of this age" understood the secret wisdom of God, "they would not have crucified the Lord of glory" (1 Cor

2:8, cf. vv. 6-7).[22] And fifth, it was by means of the cross that the rulers were defeated and humanity, along with the whole of creation, was reconciled to God. Whatever the spirit rulers in their twisted minds thought they were accomplishing by crucifying Jesus, it backfired.

We need not embrace any of the speculative and mythic features of the ancient Christus Victor theories to sketch a plausible story line that makes sense of these five facts. The principalities and powers that presently rule the world recognized who Jesus was but could not fathom why the Son of God had entered their domain, for they could not discern the wisdom of God, as Paul says. The wisdom of God centered on Jesus dying out of love for the race that Satan and the powers had held captive for ages, and these powers, being evil, apparently lack the capacity to imagine action that is motivated by this kind of self-sacrificial love. The only thing the powers could understand was that, for whatever reasons, Jesus had in fact entered their domain, *and this made him fair game*. Working with cooperative human agents, therefore, the powers orchestrated Jesus' crucifixion, only to learn that by doing so they had played into God's secret plan all along (Acts 2:22-23; 4:28). No wonder Paul says Christ not only disarmed the powers; he reduced them to a laughingstock (Col 2:14-15).

As I see it, the truth embodied in the most ancient ways of thinking about the atonement was that God did, in a sense, deceive Satan and the powers, and that Jesus was, in a sense, "bait." But there was nothing duplicitous or unjust in God's behavior. To the contrary, God was simply acting in an outrageously loving way, knowing all the while that his actions could not be understood by the powers whose evil blinds them to love. Like an infinitely wise military strategist, God knew how to get his enemies to use their self-inflicted blindness against themselves and thus use their self-chosen evil to his advantage. He wisely let evil implode in on itself, as it were, and thereby freed creation and humanity from evil's oppression.[23]

Paul tells us that one of the jobs of the church is to continually proclaim

---

[22]On issues surrounding the meaning of "rulers" in 1 Cor 2:7, see Boyd, *God at War*, pp. 256-59.

[23]Obviously, this account leaves unanswered a number of questions we might like answered. E.g., precisely how did Calvary and the resurrection defeat the powers? In my estimation, the ancient Christus Victor models of the atonement, like some other models, became incredulous precisely because they too vigorously pressed for details. I believe we have enough revealed to understand the broad outlines of the multifaceted wisdom of God in sending Christ to die and defeat the devil. But at the end of the day we must humbly acknowledge that our understanding is severely limited.

God's victorious, loving wisdom to the powers. As Paul writes, he was commissioned

> to make everyone see what is the plan of the mystery hidden for ages in God who created all things; so that through the church the wisdom of God in its rich variety might now be made known to the rulers and authorities in the heavenly places. This was in accordance with the eternal purpose that he has carried out in Christ Jesus our Lord. (Eph 3:9-11)

Recall that the powers are, among other things, the demonic force of destruction behind fallen social structures. Paul is thus telling all who have pledged their life to Christ that we are to individually and collectively live in such a way that the powers are continually reminded of the victorious wisdom of God's self-sacrificial love—the love that conquered them on Calvary and that will ultimately transform the world. With our lives and our words, in other words, we are to manifest the wisdom of Calvary-like love in response to all forms of evil.

The divine wisdom of self-sacrificial love is of course foolishness to the world, as Paul freely acknowledges (1 Cor 1:18). The way of the world—for it is the way of the powers that dominate the world—is the way of the sword, not the cross. Indeed, nothing seems more absurd in our present age than following Christ's example—loving your enemies, refusing to retaliate when another does you wrong or serving those who persecute you. This perhaps explains why Calvary-like attitudes and behaviors are rarely seen, even among those who profess faith in Christ. Yet, according to Paul, a central part of the church's mission is to proclaim that it is the way of self-sacrificial love, not the way of violent force, that in principle defeated the powers and that will ultimately win the day. As disciples of Jesus mimic Jesus' Calvary-like life (Eph 5:1-2), we remind the powers of their defeat on Calvary and manifest once again the foolish-looking secret wisdom of God that is in the process of freeing the world from the death grip of the violent powers.

Love overcomes all. This brings us to a final aspect of the Christus Victor motif, one that was largely absent in the early church's thinking about Christ's conquest over evil, but that has been justifiably receiving a good deal of attention in recent years by advocates of the Christus Victor view.[24]

---

[24]For the following I am significantly indebted to Walter Wink, *Engaging the Powers;* J. Denny Weaver, *The Nonviolent Atonement;* and John Howard Yoder, *The Politics of Jesus* (Grand Rapids: Eerdmans, 2002).

When we understand that the powers are destructive systemic forces, and when we view Jesus' life in the light of Calvary, it becomes apparent that every aspect of his life was an act of warfare, for every aspect of his life reflects Calvary-like love.

When Jesus broke religious taboos by fellowshiping with tax collectors, prostitutes and other sinners (e.g., Mt 11:19; Mk 2:15; Lk 5:29-30; 15:1; cf. Lk 7:31-37), and when he forsook religious traditions to lovingly heal and feed people on the sabbath (Mt 12:1, 10; Lk 13:10-18; 14:1-5; Jn 5:9-10), in the light of Calvary we can understand him to be waging war against the powers and exposing the systemic evil that fuels religious legalism and oppression. He was conquering evil with love while giving his followers an example to follow. This is what the reign of God looks like, and therefore this is what confronting the destructive powers looks like.

When Jesus boldly crossed racial lines, fellowshipping and speaking highly of Samaritans and Gentiles (e.g., Mt 8:5-10; 15:22-28; Lk 10:30-37; 17:11-16; Jn 4), and when he crossed other social barriers—fellowshiping with and touching lepers, for example (Mt 8:1-3)—he was exposing and resisting the evil of the powers that fuel racism and social marginalization. He was conquering evil with love while giving his followers the example they are to follow. This is what the reign of God looks like, and therefore this is what resisting the reign of the destructive powers looks like.

So too when in the midst of an extremely patriarchal culture Jesus treated women with remarkable dignity and respect (Mt 26:6-10; Lk 7:37-50; 8:1-32; 10:38-40; 13:11-18; Jn 4:7-29; 8:3-10; 11:5; 12:1-7), in the light of Calvary we must understand him to be battling and exposing the powers that fuel sexism. He was conquering evil with love and giving his followers the model they are to follow. This is what the reign of God looks like, and therefore this is what confronting the reign of the destructive powers looks like.

And when Jesus expressed mercy to people who knew they deserved judgment and whom the culture stipulated should be judged (Mk 2:15; Lk 5:29-30; 7:47-48; 19:1-10; Jn 8:3-10), he was resisting and exposing the powers that fuel social and religious cruelty and judgmentalism. This is what the reign of God looks like, and therefore this is what defying the destructive powers looks like.

This ongoing resistance to and exposure of the powers, and those who do their bidding, evoked the wrath of the powers and ultimately led to Jesus' crucifixion. So it is that Jesus' life, death and resurrection cannot be separated from each other, not even theoretically. Whereas other models of the atonement tend to isolate the meaning of Jesus' death from other aspects of his life, the Christus Victor model (at least as I'm presently fleshing it out) sees every aspect of Christ life—from his incarnation to his resurrection—as being most fundamentally *about one thing:* victoriously manifesting the loving kingdom of God over and against the destructive, oppressive kingdom of Satan.

Every aspect of Christ's life is best understood along these lines. For example, though he by nature enjoyed every divine prerogative, Jesus' love for lost humanity led him to set these prerogatives aside and enter into solidarity with us (Phil 2:6-11). Jesus rightfully owned the entire cosmos, but in loving service to others he put himself in a position where he had no place to lay his head (Mt 8:20). Though he had all power in heaven and earth, John reminds us, he used it to wash the dirty, smelly feet of his disciples—the very ones who would betray, deny and abandon him in a couple of hours (Jn 13:3-5). So too when Peter cut off a guard's ear in self-defense, Jesus lovingly healed the attacker's ear and rebuked Peter (Lk 22:50-51). And when he could have called legions of angels to fight for him, out of love Jesus instead let himself be crucified (Mt 26:53). Everything Jesus was about manifested Calvary-like love and should therefore be seen as acts of war against the destructive powers that seek to keep people from living in God's love.

The central call of every disciple is to imitate *this* life, manifest *this* kingdom, and thereby engage in *this* warfare. We are to purge our lives of every thought, attitude and behavior that is inconsistent with God's character and reign, as defined by Calvary, and we are therefore to manifest, in defiance of the powers, the loving character and reign of God in all we think, feel and do. We are to put off all that is "old" in order to manifest all that is "new." We are to imitate God by living in Calvary-like love (see, e.g., Eph 4:22—5:2). In this way we participate in and further expand the victory Christ accomplished. We become bearers of the kingdom of God and proclaim to the powers the victorious wisdom of the cross.

The Calvary teachings of Jesus. Jesus' incarnation, his countercultural lifestyle as well as his healing and deliverance ministry were about the same thing his death and resurrection were about. So was his teaching ministry. All of it directly or indirectly concerned manifesting the reign of God and vanquishing the reign of the destructive powers.

For example, few things in this demonically oppressed world are as "natural" to humans as resorting to violence to defend or advance our personal, political, religious or national interests. Indeed, this "natural" sentiment is the cornerstone of how things operate in "this present evil age" (Gal 1:4) and the primary reason why human history is largely a history of mindless, diabolical, cyclical carnage. So instinctive is our tendency to resort to violence when we deem it "justified" that most consider it foolish *not* to do so. Yet expressing that "secret wisdom of God" that alone defeats the demonic, violent powers, Jesus expressly forbids his followers to give into this "natural" instinct. Jesus says:

> You have heard that it was said, "An eye for an eye and a tooth for a tooth." But I say to you, Do not resist an evildoer. But if anyone strikes you on the right cheek, turn the other also. . . . You have heard that it was said, "You shall love your neighbor and hate your enemy." But I say to you, Love your enemies and pray for those who persecute you, so that you may be children of your Father in heaven; for he makes his sun rise on the evil and on the good, and sends rain on the righteous and on the unrighteous. (Mt 5:38-39, 43-45).

We are to love indiscriminately—as the sun shines and the rain falls—without any consideration of the merit of the person we love. This is to be a distinguishing mark of the "children of [the] Father." And it centrally includes expressing Calvary-like love *to our worst enemies.*[25]

As Wink and others have noted, the word translated "resist" *(anthistēmi)* in Matthew 5:39 does not imply passivity in the face of evil. It rather connotes using a forceful action in response to a similar forceful action.[26] Jesus is thus forbidding responding to violent action with similar violent action. Instead followers of Jesus are to respond to their "enemies" in ways that are consistent with loving them and blessing them (cf. Lk 6:28). Feeding our enemy when they're hungry and giving them something to drink when they're thirsty rather than retaliating against them is the only way we can keep from being "overcome by evil" and the only way we can "overcome evil with

---

[25]Jesus' harsh words to the Pharisees (e.g., Mt 23) reveal that expressing love is not always flowery, at least not when you're a first-century Jewish prophet trying to protect people from wayward Jewish leaders. Still, Jesus befriended and dined with Pharisees when they permitted (e.g., Lk 7:36), and of course he eventually gave his life for them. I discuss Jesus' loving-yet-confrontational treatment of the Pharisees further in Gregory A. Boyd, *The Myth of a Christian Nation* (Grand Rapids: Zondervan, 2006).

[26]Wink notes, "Jesus . . . abhors both passivity and violence" (Walter Wink, *The Powers That Be* [New York: Doubleday, 1998], p. 111, see also pp. 99-100).

good"—both in ourselves and in our "enemies" (Rom 12:17-21). As Mohandas Gandhi and Dr. Martin Luther King Jr. so wonderfully demonstrated, our Calvary-like response to our enemies exposes the evil of what they are doing, breaks the tit-for-tat cycle of violence that keeps the demonically oppressed world spinning, and lovingly opens up the possibility that our enemy will repent of their ways (cf. 1 Pet 2:23; 3:13-18).[27]

The point here is that Jesus' countercultural teachings, as much as his countercultural lifestyle and his healing and deliverance ministry, are part and parcel of his work on the cross and his resurrection. Jesus confronted destructive, violent powers with Calvary-like love at every turn. Whereas other models of the atonement tend to isolate the work of the cross from other aspects of Jesus' life, the Christus Victor model highlights a missional unity that interweaves them all. They cannot be separated, even theoretically. Everything Jesus was about centered on manifesting the outrageously loving reign of God over and against the destructive reign of the powers.

What is more, the Christus Victor model weaves together our understanding of what Christ did *for* us with the reality of what Christ is doing *in* us and *through* us. To have faith in Christ inseparably involves living faithful to the kingdom he embodied and manifested in every aspect of his life. It is to trust that the Calvary way of life alone has the power to ultimately conquer the destructive powers that oppress humanity.

The Christus Victor Motif and Other Facets of the Atonement

Though I cannot demonstrate this now, it is my contention that not only can every aspect of Christ's life be understood in the context of the Christus Victor motif, but every aspect of what the New Testament says about Christ's work and about salvation can be best understood in this context as well. Hence I argue that the Christus Victor model is able to encompass the es-

---

[27]It is worth noting that the centrality of Christ's teaching on and example of self-sacrificial love, especially toward one's enemies, was largely abandoned, at least at an institutional level, with the advent of "Constantinian Christianity." Once the church acquired worldly power, it revisioned its task as *conquering* the world in Jesus' name rather than sacrificially serving the world in Jesus' name. I have elsewhere argued that nothing has done—and is yet doing—more harm to the advancement of the kingdom of God than the Constantinian model of Christianity (see Boyd, *The Myth of a Christian Nation*). For an insightful discussion of how Constantinian Christianity has undermined the essence of Christian discipleship, see L. Camp, *Mere Discipleship: Radical Christianity in a Rebellious World* (Grand Rapids: Brazos, 2003). Some have argued that the Constantinian transformation factored into the eventual demise of the Christus Victor motif. See Weaver, *Nonviolent Atonement,* pp. 81-92, and J. Denny Weaver, "Atonement for the Non-Constantian Church," *Modern Theology* 6, no. 4 (1990): 309-11.

sential truth of other atonement models. Indeed it is able to do so while avoiding some of their potential difficulties when they are considered alone.

For example, the Christus Victor model can strongly affirm the essential truth of substitutionary models of the atonement. Jesus indeed died as our substitute, bore our sin and guilt, was sacrificed for our forgiveness, and was punished by the Father in our place (see e.g., Is 53:4-5, 10; Rom 3:23-25; 2 Cor 5:21; Heb 2:17; 9:26; 1 Jn 2:2). From a Christus Victor perspective it was the outrageous act of love in entering into complete solidarity with fallen, cursed, oppressed humanity that broke the back of the cosmic evil that held us in slavery. But because it construes Christ's substitutionary role in organic, warfare terms rather than primarily in legal terms, the Christus Victor model can potentially affirm Christ's substitutionary work without embracing some of the more problematic aspects of the penal substitutionary theory. For example, the Christus Victor model need not hold that our individual sins, guilt and deserved punishment were somehow legally transferred onto Jesus, that Jesus literally experienced the Father's wrath or that the Father *needed* to punish his Son in order to be able to forgive us. The cross reconciles the world to God, not God to the world (2 Cor 5:19).

In the Christus Victor view, we might rather hold that Jesus died as our substitute and bore our sin and guilt by voluntarily experiencing the full force of the rebel kingdom we have allowed to reign on the earth. As the new Adam—our new representative, the originator of a new humanity (Eph 2:14-15)—Jesus stood in our place, bearing the full consequences of our sin. This very act of self-sacrificial love, anticipated in everything Jesus was about, exposed and disempowered the evil of the destructive powers, erased the condemnation of the law that stood against us, and freed us to receive the life-giving Holy Spirit who now draws us into the triune fellowship and empowers us to walk in right relatedness with God and one another.

What is more, in the Christus Victor view, we might hold that Jesus was afflicted by the Father not in the sense that the Father's rage burned directly toward his Son—as though the eternal love between the Father and the Son could be suspended—but in the sense that for a greater good God surrendered his Son over to evil agents to have their way with him (Rom 8:32). This is how God's wrath was usually expressed toward Israel in the Old Testament (e.g., Judg 2:11-19; Is 10:5-6). It's just that with Jesus the greater good was not to teach Jesus obedience, as it usually was with Israel in the Old

Testament. Instead, God the Son bore the Father's wrath, expressed through the destructive powers, for the greater good of demonstrating God's righteousness against the powers and sin (Rom 3:25) while defeating the powers and setting humans free from their oppression. [28]

So too the Christus Victor model can wholeheartedly affirm that Jesus gave his life as a ransom for many, but without supposing that Jesus literally had to in some sense buy off either God or the devil (Mt 20:28; Mk 10:45; cf. 1 Tim. 2:6; Heb 9:15). The word *ransom* simply means "the price of release" and was most commonly used when purchasing slaves from the slave market.[29] Hence the Christus Victor model can simply take this to mean that Christ did whatever it took to release us from slavery to the powers, and this he did by becoming incarnate, living an outrageously loving life in defiance of the powers, freeing people from the oppression of the devil through healings and exorcisms, teaching the way of self-sacrificial love, and most definitively by his sacrificial death and victorious resurrection. He "paid the price" needed to bring us and the whole of creation into God's salvation.

Something similar could be said about other facets of Christ's work and thus of other theories about the atonement. For example, the Christus Victor model can completely affirm various versions of the recapitulation model of the atonement. It simply adds that it was as a decisive act of war against the powers and for the sake of the enslaved creation and humanity that Jesus became the new Adam and reversed what the old Adam had done when he succumbed to the devil's temptation. The loving obedience of the new Adam gives humanity a fresh start; by his obedience the violent powers have been vanquished, the Spirit has been released and we are given a new nature.

So too the Christus Victor model can affirm the healing model of the atonement. In manifesting the reign of God and therefore in vanquishing the devil, Jesus heals us of the disease that is our sin and frees us from all its destructive consequences. In love Jesus absorbs within himself all that is part of the "old" creation, and it is this very love that makes all things new (2 Cor 5:17). Moreover, in the process of defeating the devil through his life

---

[28]For an insightful discussion of this understanding of how Jesus bore the Father's wrath, see Finger, *Christian Theology,* pp. 327-30.

[29]John Stott, *The Cross of Christ* (Downers Grove, Ill.: InterVarsity Press, 1986), p. 176; and Leon Morris, *The Atonement* (Downers Grove, Ill.: InterVarsity Press, 1983), pp. 106-31.

and on Calvary, Jesus removed the blinders on our spiritual eyes that had kept us from seeing the true nature of God. Jesus is the "truth" precisely because he unveils the true, loving nature of the Father in contrast to all the ugly, untrustworthy and demonically polluted ideas about God's nature we're inclined to have in our state of bondage. This too is part of how God reconciles us to himself and further heals us from our sin bondage. As we behold the beautiful revelation of God in Christ—dying on Calvary for those who crucified him—we are healed from our deception-induced sickness and increasingly transformed into the likeness of Christ (2 Cor 3:12—4:6).

Along the same lines, by having his Son absorb within himself the violent terror of the powers for the sake of our sin, God demonstrates his righteous stance against all sin (Rom 3:25), as the moral government model of the atonement stresses. At the same time, in overcoming evil with good on Calvary, Jesus gives us a beautiful (and difficult) example to follow, and in freeing us from the powers that cut us off from God's life, he empowers us to actually follow this example and participate in the divine nature (2 Pet 1:4). The Christus Victor model can thus embrace fundamental aspects of exemplar and apotheosis models of the atonement.

Sketchy as this overview has necessarily been, I hope it is enough to at least demonstrate the possibility that the distinctive truth of each model of the atonement can be encompassed in a single, coherent framework. And remember, this framework is the one that dominated the church for the first millennium of its existence. If I am correct, just as all facets of Christ's life are ultimately about one thing, so all models of the atonement can be understood as distinctive aspects of one thing: overcoming evil with good. Christ came to overthrow the powers that hold us in bondage by revealing and establishing in the earth the perfect love of the triune God. In short, he came to manifest and establish the reign of God and therefore to vanquish the reign of the violent, destructive, rebellious powers.

Yes, Jesus died in our place, brought about our forgiveness, heals us, shows us the just consequences of sin, recapitulates our humanity and undoes what Adam did, opens the way for us to become participants in the divine nature, provides an example for us to follow and motivates us to follow it by revealing God's love. But, I submit, all these marvelous aspects of Christ's work can be understood, and are best understood, as distinctive aspects of the "rich variety" of God's "secret and hidden" wisdom by which he overcame evil with good and calls us to do the same.

Conclusion

I conclude this chapter by summarizing eight reasons why I believe the Christus Victor model of the atonement should be considered more foundational to our thinking about Jesus than other atonement models.

1. The Christus Victor model is the only model that does full justice to the centrality of the motif of Christ's victory over Satan in the New Testament.

2. The Christus Victor model was, in various forms, the dominant model for the first millennium of church history.

3. Whereas other models make little or no connection between Christ's life, death and resurrection on the one hand, and the warfare motif that runs throughout Scripture on the other, the Christus Victor model expresses this connection and puts it on center stage.

4. Whereas other models tend to isolate the meaning of Christ's death from his lifestyle, his healing and deliverance ministry, his teachings and even (in some cases) his resurrection, the Christus Victor model reveals the profound interconnectedness of everything Christ was about. All these things are ultimately *about one thing:* establishing the reign of God by vanquishing the reign of Satan and the powers through the power of self-sacrificial love.

5. Only the Christus Victor model does full justice to the apocalyptic context of Jesus' life and the kingdom revolution he started, a consideration that should, in my estimation, carry a good bit of exegetical weight.

6. Other models of the atonement say little or nothing about the cosmic significance of Christ's work—as though the only problem in creation was that humans sin! The Christus Victor model captures the interconnectedness of humans and the broader creation and shows how the cosmic and soteriological aspects of Christ's work are really two aspects of one reality. For this reason the Christus Victor motif best elucidates how Christ's work restores humans to our originally intended place of dominion on the earth, a point that is central to the story line of the Bible (Gen 1:26-28; 2 Tim 2:12; Rev 5:10).

   Along these same lines, while I cannot make the case presently, I should at least mention that the cosmic focus of the Christus Victor model arguably leads to advantages in working out a plausible theodicy. Because of their more anthropocentric focus, no other model of the atonement as adequately expresses the truth that the problem of evil God confronted on the cross involved the whole of creation (Rom 8:18-23). Hence no other model as effectively articulates how Christ's work on the cross (let alone how every facet of Christ's life) rectified this cosmic problem of evil.[30]

7. The Christus Victor model is arguably able to encompass within a single coherent framework the elements of truth expressed in other models of the atonement, but so far as I can see, the converse is not true. Not only this but the Christus Victor model is arguably able to embrace these truths while avoiding some of the difficulties that are found in the other models when considered alone.

8. One final consideration deserves more extensive comment. Namely, I believe there are a number of practical advantages to viewing the whole of Christ's life as manifesting the Christus Victor motif, especially for those of us who are considering this model from within the current situation of the church in Western culture.

For example, in the Christus Victor model what Christ does *for* us cannot be separated, even theoretically, from what Christ does *in* us and *through* us. There is, therefore, no temptation to think about Christ's work on the cross as a "legal fiction." Related to this, there is no temptation to even theoretically divorce justification from sanctification.[31] Rather, in the Christus Victor model we either participate in Christ's cosmic victory over the powers or we don't. Which is to say, we either participate in the ever-expanding reign of God, confronting at every turn the reign of the destructive powers, or we don't. Stated otherwise, what it means to experience "salvation" is that we participate in the cosmic liberation Christ won through his incarnation, life, ministry, death and resurrection. Hence, to have faith in what Christ *did* is to walk faithful to what Christ *is doing*.

Of course, we do so imperfectly. As the kingdom takes hold in our lives, we are gradually being transformed from one degree of glory to another (2 Cor 3:17-18). But with the Christus Victor model there's no temptation for people to mistakenly suppose they are participating in the kingdom when there's no evidence of the kingdom in their life. There is no "legal fiction" version of freedom from the powers and Calvary-like love.

---

[30]See Boyd, *God at War,* chap. 8.

[31]On the inseparability of justification and sanctification in the Christus Victor model of the atonement, see William M. Greathouse, "Sanctification and the Christus Victor Motif in Wesleyan Theology," *Wesleyan Theological Journal* (Spring 1972): 47-58.

Given the multitude of people, especially in Western culture, who seem to buy into some version of the "legal fiction" view of Christ's work and who therefore profess faith in Christ without any significant effect on their life, this advantage of the Christus Victor model strikes me as carrying significant weight.

A related practical advantage of the Christus Victor model for the Western Church is that, in sharp contrast to the hyperindividualistic outlook of most Westerners, the Christus Victor model puts on center stage the easily overlooked demonic dimension of all fallen social structures. By calling on disciples to join Christ's rebellion against and victory over the ever-present powers, the Christus Victor perspective inspires disciples to live countercultural lives that aggressively resist the demonically seductive pull of nationalism, patriotism, culturally endorsed violence, greed, racism and a host of other structural evils that are part of the spiritually polluted air we all breathe.[32]

More specifically, the Christus Victor model motivates believers to take seriously the revelation that the devil, though in principle defeated on Calvary, is yet the "god of this world" (2 Cor 4:4) and still has power over the whole world (1 Jn 5:19), including all the nations of the world (Lk 4:5-6). It thereby helps disciples guard against all forms of nationalistic idolatry while motivating them toward radical, nonviolent, Jesus-like social action. Given the tragic extent to which Western Christianity today accepts and often even Christianizes demonic aspects of Western culture, the advantage of a model of the atonement that centralizes the call for disciples to identify and defy the powers is of considerable importance. Most significantly, given the extent to which American Christianity in particular tends to accept and even Christianize nationalistic interests and the use of violence to advance or protect these interests, and given how dangerous this mindset is in our present world situation, and how damaging this nationalistic association is to global Christian missions, the advantage of a model of the atonement that centralizes our call to be ambassadors

---

[32]For an excellent exposition, see L. Camp, *Mere Discipleship*. Because of this emphasis on the Christus Victor model, a number of black, liberation and feminist theologians have been making explicit or implicit use of Christus Victor themes (though often in a demythologized form). See e.g., James H. Cone, *The God of the Oppressed*, rev. ed. (Maryknoll, N.Y.: Orbis, 1997); Ray, *Deceiving the Devil*; and Thelma Megill-Cobbler, "A Feminist Rethinking of Punishment Imagery in Atonement," *Dialog* 35, no. 1 (1996): 14-20. For a helpful overview and constructive proposal, see Weaver, *Nonviolent Atonement*.

of a kingdom *that is not of this world* (Jn 18:36) and that centralizes our call to resist the powers by imitating Christ's way of nonviolence and self-sacrificial love can hardly be overestimated.[33]

As Christ established the kingdom of God by the way his life, ministry, teachings and death contrasted with the power-dominated, violence-oriented kingdom of the world, so his followers are called to advance the kingdom by living lives that sharply contrast with the kingdom of the world. Just as it was with Christ, our witness is centered on this contrast—this persistent defiance of the powers, this refusal to conform to "the pattern of this world" (Rom 12:2 NIV), this obstinate commitment to walk in Calvary-like love, regardless of the practical consequences. Instead of trusting the power of worldly force, followers of Jesus are called to trust the "foolish" power of the cross and thereby proclaim its wisdom to the gods of this age (Eph 3:10). Following the example of our Captain, we are to always overcome evil with good, trusting that, however ineffective it looks in a Good Friday world, when Easter morning for the cosmos comes, it will be goodness that will have won the day—and the entire cosmos.

The Christus Victor motif is the one model of the atonement that makes the call to resist the powers and imitate Christ in these ways the centerpiece of what it means to follow Christ. And given how little the Western church looks like Jesus, and, conversely, given how much the Western church looks like little more than a religious version of Western culture itself, embracing this model of the atonement is perhaps not only advantageous; in the West, at least, it is arguably a kingdom necessity.

---

[33]For a fuller discussion of the harm of nationalistic and patriotic idolatry and the centrality of the kingdom call to confront them, see Boyd, *Myth of a Christian Nation*.

Penal Substitution Response

THOMAS A. SCHREINER

Greg Boyd rightly underlines the importance of the Christus Victor theme in the Scriptures, for the significance of Christ's death and resurrection on our behalf is not exhausted by a single model of the atonement. The defeat and dismantling of the principalities and powers has too often been ignored by Western evangelicals. Boyd highlights the story line in the Scriptures and the importance of the coming of God's kingdom in Jesus of Nazareth. We must see, as Boyd emphasizes, the cosmic dimensions of Christ's victory over demonic powers. We have too often succumbed to individualism, failing to see that God is working out all things in all places for the honor of his name. Boyd also reminds us that the atonement should lead to a transformed life, a life of self-giving love and radical discipleship.[1]

Boyd is mistaken, however, in claiming that the Christus Victor theme is fundamental and the main thing that God accomplished in Christ's death. Boyd says very little about human sin and the need for forgiveness of sins, but in the story line of the Scriptures the need for forgiveness is more pervasive than victory over the powers. The centrality of forgiveness of sins is evident in the ministry of John the Baptist (Mk 1:4-5), and also in Jesus' ministry in which he embodied and preached forgiveness and in his death where he poured out his life for the forgiveness of sins (Mt 26:28). The proclamation of the Baptist and Jesus has antecedents in Old Testament sacrifices that were given to provide forgiveness of sins. The primacy of forgiveness is fleshed out in the early apostolic preaching where people are summoned to repentance (e.g., Acts 2:38; 3:19; 5:31; 10:43; 13:38). Furthermore, it is quite clear in Paul (cf. Rom 1:18—3:26; Gal 3:10-13; 2 Cor 5:21), the author

---

[1]We may disagree on some points as to what a life patterned after Jesus involves. Boyd hints that he supports pacifism, with which I would disagree. But perhaps I misread him here, and that is a discussion for another book!

of Hebrews (Heb 7:11—10:25), John (1 Jn 1:7—2:2; 2:12; 4:10), and Peter (1 Pet 2:21-24; 3:18; 2 Pet 1:9) that forgiveness of sins is fundamental, and hence cannot be dismissed merely as Western individualism. Boyd correctly argues that the theme of forgiveness must be placed into a larger apocalyptic and salvation historical canvas, which also involves the defeat of demonic powers, but I believe that he wrongly elevates the theme of the defeat of demonic powers.

Boyd also claims that the Scriptures depict sin as a power that enslaves and does not focus on individual behavior. He is correct in saying that sin is a power that overwhelms us, but he downplays, perhaps inadvertently, the notion of individual responsibility. Even though sin is a power that holds us in bondage, such a reality does not lessen individual responsibility. Paul believes we are sinners in Adam and under bondage to sin, but Paul also maintains that we are fully responsible for the sins we commit. In making his case regarding the significance of evil powers, Boyd reduces the importance of individual accountability and guilt, and thus does not guard his view sufficiently from the notion that human beings are merely victims of sin. He stresses that sin is "satanically inspired" and that the "*real* struggle" is against spiritual powers (p. 28). Boyd departs from the biblical balance by overemphasizing the influence of Satan and demons. He is correct in saying that sin is a power that enslaves human beings as sons and daughters of Adam, but we are also fully responsible for allowing sin to reign over us, and we choose to follow the desires of the flesh (cf. Eph 2:1-3), and hence are personally guilty for the sins we commit (Rom 3:19-20).

Nor is Boyd convincing in saying that E. P. Sanders has demonstrated conclusively that the problem in the first century was not self-righteousness (p. 30 n. 15). The view promoted by Sanders has been subjected to significant criticism in the work of Friedrich Avemarie, *Tora und Leben;* Mark A. Elliott, *The Survivors of Israel;* Simon J. Gathercole, *Where is Boasting?* Stephen Westerholm, *Old and New Perspectives on Paul;* and the work edited by D. A. Carson, Peter T. O'Brien, and Mark A. Seifrid, *Justification and Variegated Nomism,* vol. 2. Boyd shows no awareness of the scholarship that takes issue with the paradigm advanced by Sanders.

Greg Boyd's one-sided reading of the biblical evidence manifests itself in the claim that first people are saved from spiritual and satanic powers, and *then* they receive forgiveness of sins. Boyd claims the cosmological has logical priority and then the soteriological follows, and hence the former is more fundamental than the latter. Space is limited here, but I found Boyd's logic and exegesis to be unconvincing. The New Testament regularly argues that forgiveness and justification were accomplished when Christ died and was raised, and it does not clearly subordinate forgiveness to victory over demons and Satan. It is certainly the case that forgiveness of sins does not occur in isolation from victory over Satan, but Boyd does not clearly show from the biblical text that the latter is the causal ground for the former. For example, contrary to Boyd, it is unclear in Colossians 1:15-23 that we will be holy on the last day *because* demonic powers are defeated (in the sense that the latter precedes the former). In the same way, it does not follow logically, nor is it demonstrated exegetically that Christ's exaltation over all his enemies (Eph 1:20-22) takes priority over his soteriological work on behalf of his people (Eph 2:1-5).

Boyd also lacks clarity in explaining *how* Christ's death led to triumph over demonic powers. He claims repeatedly that Jesus defeated demons and Satan on the cross, but I could not clearly see how or why the death of Jesus was necessary to procure such victory on Boyd's terms. He says that the Father did not need to punish the Son to forgive us, that there is no basis for seeing a legal transaction, and that the wrath of God was not inflicted on the Son, whereas I argue that forgiveness could not come apart from the Son bearing our sins on the cross and thereby satisfying God's wrath. But I wonder why the Son had to, according to Boyd, stand "in our place, bearing the full consequences of our sin." How is that he "erased the condemnation of the law that stood against us" (p. 43)? Boyd says he believes in a kind of organic warfare view of substitution rather than a legal model. So how did Christ's death dismantle the principalities and powers? Boyd says Christ's solidarity with us in his radical love defeated the power of evil. This contention is not worked out with any exegesis. It is asserted rather than demonstrated. Boyd suggests in a footnote that the Scriptures do not explain how this is so, and so we must take it on faith (p. 37 n. 23). But since he does not back up his case with exegesis, I see no reason to accept his position.

I would argue (all too briefly!) that the reason demonic powers reign over us is because of human sin. The apocalyptic and anthropological are woven together in the New Testament. Jesus came "to destroy the works of the devil" (1 Jn 3:8) by coming to "take away sins" (1 Jn 3:5). And Jesus, according to 1 John 4:9-10, was sent "to be the propitiation for our sins" (cf. 1 Jn 1:7, 9; 2:2). The devil and demons rule over us because we are sinners, not because we are in some mysterious way at the mercy of outside powers. Jesus destroyed the works of the devil by suffering in our place as the propitiation for our sins, so that we now stand forgiven before God. Jesus did not conquer the devil merely by showing us how much he loved us. The Scriptures are more specific than this. The devil's hold over us was broken when our sins were forgiven on the cross by virtue of Christ taking our place and suffering our punishment.

The letter to the Hebrews points in the same direction. In Jesus' death he destroyed the power of the devil (Heb 2:14-15) so that we are freed from the fear of death. We need to read all of Hebrews to discern how this liberation was accomplished. Hebrews explicates Christ's death in light of the Old Testament sacrificial system. His death cleansed believers from the guilt that was theirs because of sin (Heb 1:3; 9:14). The judgment of death comes because of sin (Heb 9:27), and Christ freed believers from this judgment by procuring forgiveness of sins. His death has accomplished propitiation, that is, satisfaction for sins (Heb 2:17). Believers can now boldly enter God's presence because of the blood of Jesus (Heb 10:19). When we put the whole of Hebrews together, we see that Satan is deprived of the power of death when Christ accomplishes forgiveness and cleansing of sin for his people by his sacrifice. Since the guilt of sin has been atoned for, Satan no longer has any power over those who put their trust in Christ. Revelation 12:11 points in the same direction. We conquer the devil as our accuser "by the blood of the lamb"—the death of Jesus that delivers us from sin (cf. Rev 7:13-14). Victory over Satan is rooted in Christ's work on the cross in which he pardons sinners.

Greg Boyd rightly reminds us that victory over demonic powers and Satan is a glorious part of what Christ accomplished for us, but Christ's victory over Satan is anchored in his sacrifice for sinners where he bore the wrath of God and took the punishment we deserved.

Healing Response

BRUCE R. REICHENBACH

Frankly, if Greg Boyd's thesis is true, a Christian should have some significant worries. It is not that Boyd's warfare model lacks biblical support or is illogical. Rather, making divine warfare the centerpiece of creation and redemption and giving enormous powers to Satan and his minions has serious implications for Christian faith.

Before developing this, let me first acknowledge areas of agreement between us. I agree that if God is to have agents who participate in his triune love in ways that allow them to return God's love to God, they must be free. But if they are free to say yes to God, they likewise are free to say no. Further, granting this freedom implies risk on the part of God, a risk that exists whether or not God has foreknowledge of future contingent events.[1] Neither ignorance of the future nor simple foreknowledge increases God's control over events, for even if God foreknows future events, they will occur and no one can change what he knows will occur. Likewise, Boyd is correct that risk creates moral responsibility.[2]

So what are the serious questions? According to Boyd's account, the satanic hosts, though originally created by God, not only rebelled against him but managed to gather substantial power and seize control over both human beings and nature, both terrestrial and cosmic. Creation now belongs to Satan, not to God. Over the billions of years the enemy in one way or another denuded the cosmos, leaving it empty and desolate *(tohu wabohu)*. Thus God had to refashion it to make it hospitable for humans.[3] Hence, when Boyd treats creation, he restricts the original creation to the first verse of

---

[1]Gregory A. Boyd, *Satan and the Problem of Evil* (Downers Grove, Ill.: InterVarsity Press, 2001), p. 86.
[2]Ibid., p. 165.
[3]Ibid., pp. 313-14.

Genesis 1. He suggests that a great gap lies between the first two verses of Genesis 1, so that whereas Genesis 1:1 "describes the original creation," Genesis 1:2 describes the restoration required to correct the cosmic destruction wrought either by the demonic forces or by the battle to repel them.[4] I have serious qualms about Boyd's reading of Genesis 1. As I have argued elsewhere, there is no reason to see chaos and destruction between verses 1 and 2.[5] Rather, the verses are continuous; whereas verse 1 describes the creating per se, the subsequent verses describe the filling of that creation, so that in the end God is justified in laying claim to everything on the grounds that everything comes from him.

Further, I see no grounds for thinking that God has given powers of "twisting the laws of nature governing the cosmos" to personal beings, so that they can "infiltrate the evolutionary process."[6] Even if demonic powers are connected with nations (Dan 10),[7] and even if Satan is the "god of this age" (2 Cor 4:4), that is a far cry from giving him almost unlimited destructive powers over the universe.

Moreover, according to Boyd's restoration reading of Genesis, God has been about the business of destroying Satan for billions of years—without any apparent success. The first battle required recreating the universe, an act that gave at best temporary respite.[8] Though the restoration removed the carnivorous animals[9] (though paleontological evidence of such a dramatic fauna change is absent), it is clear that they soon returned with a vengeance. The second battle required a devastating flood to wash clean the Earth (Gen 6—9). The first divine counteroffensive left the demonic powers in charge of nature; the second proved likewise unsuccessful, for humans immediately returned to emulate the deeds of their master. We are told that God will take another shot at recreation at the end of this age (Rev 21:1, 5). In the meantime, we have the atonement, by which God defeated the devil, destroyed his works and established the church to continue the war.

Two critical issues arise. First, why is it not more apparent who is winning? After all, neither moral evils nor natural evils, both ascribed to the

---

[4]Franz Delitzsch, *A System of Biblical Psychology* (Grand Rapids: Baker, 1996), pp. 74-76.
[5]Bruce R. Reichenbach, "Genesis 1 as a Theological-Political Narrative of Kingdom Establishment," *Bulletin for Biblical Research* 13, no. 1 (2003): 56-59.
[6]Boyd, *Satan and the Problem of Evil*, p. 314.
[7]Gregory A. Boyd, *God at War* (Downers Grove, Ill.: InterVarsity Press, 1997), pp. 137-38.
[8]Boyd, *Satan and the Problem of Evil*, p. 314.
[9]Ibid., p. 315.

causal powers of Satan, have significantly declined. Rather, the former have increased (more people were killed by wars in the twentieth century than in all the previous centuries combined), and the destructiveness of natural disasters has not abated, either in intensity or in deadliness. If Satan and his hosts were conquered at the cross, one would expect to find more empirical evidence of this victory. The failure of the church, Boyd notes, results because "the church has always been a very human and a very fallen institution, exhibiting all the carnality, pettiness, narrowness, self-centeredness and abusive power tendencies that characterize all other fallen human institutions. On the surface we hardly look like trophies God would want to showcase." However, Boyd continues, "this does not disqualify us from this divine service" for God "has always chosen to use the foolish and weak things of the world to overthrow the 'wise' and 'strong' in the world who resist him (I Cor 1:18-30)."[10] But the weakness of the church is not what is in view here, but its sinfulness. And sin is the work of Satan. Hence, if Satan has that much control over the church, it is very hard to see that this "trophy" can play a successful part in God's campaign against Satan. The point here is not that Boyd's view runs counter to New Testament assertions that Satan remains active.[11] It is rather that this claim is difficult to reconcile with the claim that Christ's victory over Satan in the battle for the cosmos is the *dominant* atonement motif.

Second, Greg Boyd continually assures us that God will triumph in the end. On this he, I and the Scriptures agree. Boyd portrays God conducting not a skirmish or a battle, but an all-out war with (at least for now) apparently equal enemies. But with this scenario in place, why should one think that God ultimately will succeed in wresting control from the satanic powers? Boyd's history of God's battles with Satan over billions of years does not inspire much confidence about the final outcome. Given the perspective of an open view of God, it seems that God keeps trying various tactics to defeat this formidable enemy, perhaps even becoming desperate enough to send his own Son to die to achieve the victory.

Boyd responds to this by introducing two important principles: the freedom God gives is irrevocable, and that freedom is finite. By the first principle, Boyd means that unless the power to influence is irrevocable, God has not granted genuine freedom. Genuine freedom means that free agents pos-

---

[10]Boyd, *God at War,* pp. 252-53.
[11]See relevant passages in ibid., pp. 276-77.

sess the power to "exercise this influence over time." God cannot "immediately" revoke this freedom upon the agents' misuse of it.[12]

Although this principle of irrevocability is true, Boyd's application of it is mistaken. It is true that if one grants free agency to another, one cannot constantly intervene to make sure that the agent acts according to the grantee's will. The grantor of the freedom has to let go; immediate intervention at the first misstep destroys any meaningful sense of freedom. However, this principle does not entail that no restrictions may be placed on the agent's freedom, that God must allow Satan to seize control not only of humans but also of the cosmos. God is justified in revoking the freedom when the power is continuously and with increasing seriousness misused. Surely, if the Allies were justified in curtailing Hitler's evil intentions or, less dramatically, if the civil authorities are justified in restricting criminals' freedom by incarcerating them, so too God would be justified in revoking or limiting the freedom of those who seriously and persistently violate his commands. Granting freedom does not entail unlimited toleration of what those agents do; the very structures of law and morality must be factored into the freedom equation. Thus, since the demonic powers breach both divine law and morality, we are back to the question why God does not intervene more often and more forcefully in human affairs. Boyd's answer that we cannot understand because of our finitude and the complexity of the situation[13] puts him squarely in the camp of those theodicists he critiques.

Boyd proposes that although freedom is irrevocable, it is finite. This principle allows him to be certain that God ultimately will be victorious.[14] "While the gift of life God gives to those who choose him is eternal, the gift of freedom to choose against him is apparently not."[15] But if God, consistent with his delegation of freedom, can limit delegated power, why has God tolerated both the duration and extent of the activities of the demonic powers for so long? Enough is enough, one might say; decisive intervention, not temporary

---

[12]Boyd, *Satan and the Problem of Evil*, p. 181. "Apparently out of integrity for the gift of freedom he has given, God endures for a time the wrath of these destructive rebels. To do otherwise would undoubtedly render the gift of freedom disingenuous" (Boyd, *God at War*, p. 287).

[13]See appendix one of Boyd's *Satan and the Problem of Evil*.

[14]Ibid., pp. 185-86.

[15]Boyd, *God at War*, p. 287. The contrast, not between freedoms but between eternal life and limited freedom, is puzzling. That is, apparently the freedom of those who choose for God is extended as long as they love him, but not that of those who oppose him. Is the freedom of the former continued conditionally on their continuing to love God?

battles, and limitation of freedom are long overdue.

Boyd replies that Satan's power "to become evil and to harm others had to be proportionate to his potential to become loving and to bless others."[16] But there is good reason to doubt that the amount of power delegated to Satan to either bless or destroy accords with divine justice. John Rawls advances what he terms the "maximin principle," according to which to achieve a just outcome between various alternatives, one ought to set up structures that maximize the minimum good that can be achieved, even at the cost of lowering attainability of some higher goods.[17] In determining those structures, we should deliberate as if we are behind a veil of ignorance, not knowing where we would fall in that social structure. We might be among the most privileged, but equally we might be among the least privileged. Hence, in establishing just structures, the rational thing to do, even out of self-interest, is to construct a structure whose worst possible outcome is better than the worst possible outcome presented by the other alternatives. On Boyd's open view of God, God lies behind a veil of ignorance, for he cannot know what the future holds. Thus, justice would indicate that God ought to create a cosmic structure where the proportionate freedom granted to do either good or evil is consistent with the best overall outcome for the least privileged. That is, it would be unjust and unwise for God to grant a freedom to do either good or evil that creates the possibilities of horrifically catastrophic situations, even at the price of less bliss. Since God has alternative courses of action where people might be less blessed by the heavenly powers but also less damaged, and since this situation presents a significantly better possible world consistent with liberty, justice indicates that this route be followed. God's justice, as represented by Boyd's proportionality principle, dictates a severe curbing of the power God grants to the heavenly forces, both to do good and to do evil and render havoc. In effect, Boyd's view magnifies freedom at the cost of God's justice.

This brings us finally to the issue of the atonement. Two questions must be asked. First, with the above problems looming, can one rightly claim that the Christus Victor view of the atonement is as dominant a motif as Greg Boyd suggests? We are not contending that the motif is absent from Scripture. Boyd presents the key New Testament passages that clearly establish the importance of this model. Rather, we question whether it can rationally

---

[16]Boyd, *Satan and the Problem of Evil,* p. 205.
[17]John Rawls, *A Theory of Justice,* rev. ed. (Cambridge, Mass.: Harvard University Press, 1999).

and adequately function as the *central* motif, the motif that organizes all other atonement metaphors. Boyd writes that the "central thing Jesus did was drive out the 'ruler of this world,' " the "main thing Christ accomplished was that he defeated the devil," and "salvation is most fundamentally about escaping 'from the snare of the devil'" (pp. 30, 32). But none of the passages cited (Jn 12:31; Acts 26:17-18; 2 Tim 2:26) speak of Christ's act in terms that suggest that the conquest of Satan is the *fundamental* or main way to interpret the atonement. One might wonder whether Boyd's centrality thesis is continually brought *to* the text, not derived from it. In part, his thesis depends on his argument that the soteriological depends on the cosmic, which he defends as arising out of Colossians 1:15-22 and Ephesians 1:22—2:8. Whether these texts support or demand his interpretation is at issue.

We might note a similar situation with the way he treats Peter's preaching in Acts 10:38. The statement that Jesus healed "all who were oppressed by the devil" should not be misread to say that "all those whom Jesus healed were oppressed by the devil."[18] This assumption that all illness is demonic lies behind Boyd's contention that "all these things are ultimately *about one thing:* establishing the reign of God by vanquishing the reign of Satan" (p. 46).

Second, how has this victory been accomplished? In Boyd's discussion of the Old Testament's God-at-war motif, power provides the means of victory.[19] The battles with Leviathan and Rahab are power plays: God "crushed the heads of Leviathan" (Ps 74:13-14) and "cut Rahab to pieces" (Job 26:12-13). Likewise with "crushing the head of the serpent" in Genesis 3:15 (p. 30). Yet when Boyd discusses Christ's victory, love is the means to victory. The centrality of love is scripturally correct but provocative and questionable within a Christus Victor context. Indeed, the final successful battle is not one of love but of all-out horrific war (Rev 19—20).[20]

But how does love bring about the conquest of Satan and our atonement? Boyd notes that "at the end of the day we must humbly acknowledge that our understanding is severely limited" (p. 37 n. 23). This admission is proper, but it does seem puzzling that we have little idea of how the atonement works on the Christus Victor view, especially if this view is the essen-

---

[18]For Boyd's tendency in that direction, see *God at War,* p. 250.

[19]Boyd, *Satan and the Problem of Evil,* pp. 31-32.

[20]On an open view of God, how can we know what the outcome will be or that it will be as described or symbolized in Revelation?

tial and central understanding of the atonement. Indeed, describing how the atonement is accomplished has been a major stumbling block for accepting the Christus Victor model. Explanations of the how are certainly more forthcoming in the healing, sacrificial and satisfaction models.

In sum, Greg Boyd's Christus Victor model provides a powerful understanding of the atonement. He has constructed a strong case for the importance of understanding atonement in terms of Christ's victory over Satan. But is the Christus Victor the dominant motif of salvation? The success of that part of the project remains in doubt.

Kaleidoscopic Response

JOEL B. GREEN

Greg Boyd's presentation of the Christus Victor view of the atonement is admirable in many ways. First, it demonstrates how pervasively this model fills the pages of the Scriptures. Those of us who are concerned to articulate a *biblical* model of the atonement are in Boyd's debt for showing both how this model resides in many of our biblical texts and its basis within the canonical drama of salvation history itself. Second, it is worth noting how well his position accounts for the historical realities of Jesus' death on a Roman cross. Faithful models of the atonement cannot be abstracted from the narrative of Jesus' life, a life that resulted in his death as an enemy of the state, and the Christus Victor model takes that history with seriousness. Third, Boyd rightly observes that this model has cosmic repercussions; this is surely a needed emphasis today. Fourth, he justifiably observes how well-grounded in the tradition of Christian interpretation of the crucifixion his position is; clumps of our theological roots intermingle in this venerable model, and our theological work ought to proceed accordingly. Fifth, in Boyd's hands, this model helpfully accounts for the objective nature of the atonement. Finally, he shows how seriously the Christus Victor model takes the presence of evil, and to what lengths God must go to deliver his people.

I have real appreciation for Boyd's presentation, then, and the questions I need to raise ought to be understood underneath the broader umbrella of our agreement on a range of key issues. I have two basic concerns. The first, which I hope he will welcome, focuses on areas where his presentation of the Christus Victor model might be strengthened. Second, I want to show why we cannot accept Boyd's claim that Christus Victor provides "an encompassing conceptual model that might reveal an 'inner logic' to all aspects of Christ's work" (p. 24).

I have four suggestions how Greg Boyd's presentation of Christus Victor might be fortified.

First, Boyd might make even more of the historic liberation of God's people from Egypt as the prototype for salvation as this is developed in Scripture, where exodus serves as the pattern for new exodus. In countless ways the Scriptures weave the story of Israel's life with strands of yarn spun out of exodus,[1] and, especially in Isaiah, the exodus story is transformed for its role in the service of new exodus hope. The actualization of the promise of new exodus—including images of battle, liberation and sojourn—is a common thread in New Testament theology.[2] Tracing the biblical narrative in these terms would only strengthen Boyd's presentation.

Second, is it really true that, according to the New Testament, "the central thing Jesus did was drive out the 'ruler of this world'" (p. 30)? Though speaking of a minion of Satan, Luke 11:24-26 is nonetheless apropos; it is never enough to drive out an evil spirit—lest it return, find its former home "swept and in order," then go and bring "seven other spirits more evil than itself, and they enter and live there; and the last state of that person is worse than the first." One might better find the "center" of Jesus' mission in his proclamation of the kingdom of God in word and deed. Boyd might rightly argue that this would *include* driving out the ruler of this world, but he would also need to sketch the alternative "rule" Jesus announced and embodied, together with the human response engendered by the inbreaking kingdom of God.

Third, Boyd's discussion of "the powers" arrayed against God in the New Testament are surprisingly spiritual (contrast the social and political opponents in the Old Testament). For good reason, he faults Walter Wink for clothing "the powers" in the letters of Paul so fully in the garb of social institutions, but I fear that Boyd has lost his balance in the other direction. In Mary's Song (Lk 1:46-55), for example, salvation is depicted in unavoidably this-worldly terms:

> He has brought down the powerful from their thrones,
>   and lifted up the lowly;
> he has filled the hungry with good things,
>   and sent the rich away empty. (Lk 1:52-53)

---

[1]Cf. Göran Larsson, *Bound for Freedom* (Peabody, Mass.: Hendrickson, 1999); Rikki E. Watts, "Exodus," in *New Dictionary of Biblical Theology*, ed. T. D. Alexander and Brian S. Rosner (Downers Grove, Ill.: InterVarsity Press, 2000), pp. 478-87.

[2]E.g., Rikki E. Watts, *Isaiah's New Exodus and Mark*, Wissenschaftliche Untersuchungen zum Neuen Testament 2:88 (Tübingen: Mohr/Siebeck, 1997); David W. Pao, *Acts and the Isaianic New Exodus*, Wissenschaftliche Untersuchungen zum Neuen Testament 2:130 (Tübingen: Mohr/Siebeck, 2000).

My own view is that only rarely, if ever, can one attribute to Paul (or other New Testament writers) a concern with spiritual forces of evil devoid of their expression in human institutions; and neither can one attribute to Paul (or other New Testament writers) a theology of human institutions aligned against God that does not account for the diabolic animation of those institutions. In his presentation of "the powers," then, I worry that Boyd has stripped the Christus Victor model of one of its most impressive assets—namely, its capacity to show that the death of Jesus addresses profoundly the sociopolitical realities that continue to array themselves against the saving purpose of God.

Fourth, given the self-evident reality that opposition toward God and God's people continues in our contemporary world, what is the role of God's people in warfare? The God of Israel is portrayed in Exodus as sovereign over the world's powerful structures aligned against his purpose, seeking and shaping new structures within which his aims and character are incarnate; accordingly, God's people participate with God in the battle. What is the role of God's people on the battleground of new exodus? The book of Revelation helps to orient us. In a book that is seemingly overrun with images of violence, Revelation 12:11 is thematic: "They have conquered him by the blood of the Lamb and by the word of their testimony, for they did not cling to life even in the face of death." God's people are called to overcome the enemy with the weapons of patient endurance and faithfulness (Rev 2:3, 7, 10, 11, 25, 26; 3:5, 12; 13:10; 14:12; 15:2), and the blood of the Lamb and the testimony of the word (Rev 12:11; 19:10). What more might be said about the role of Christians in the battle?

Well-grounded as it is in both Scripture and the theological tradition, the Christus Victor model of the atonement has a secure place within contemporary articulations of the saving significance of Jesus' death. For a number of reasons, however, we can regard as only hyperbole Greg Boyd's claim that Christus Victor is "more fundamental" as a way to construe the work of Christ on the cross (p. 33).

First, Boyd presumes erroneously that the nature of reality is such that there *ought* to be a single, encompassing model of the atonement. Beginning with the conviction that "*reality is unified*," he urges that "the reality of the atonement" has as its corollary a single, unified framework for all atonement models (p. 24). Tempting though this logic might be, we need to recognize that Boyd is apparently using the word *reality* in two different ways.

When folks appeal to the unity of reality, they usually refer to something like "things as they actually exist," but in his reference to the "reality of the atonement," Boyd takes us further, locating "reality" within a particular interpretive network. Hence, although we might all agree on the reality that Jesus was crucified under Pontius Pilate, this is not the same thing as admitting the reality of a particular interpretation of that event. Interestingly, when the theologian Colin Gunton argued for "the actuality of the atonement" (a phrase that seems a close relative of Boyd's "the reality of the atonement"), he articulated this "actuality" as "a victory," "an act of justice" and "a sacrifice"—using not a single, unified metaphor but a triad of them.[3]

The effect of my criticism is not to sound a retreat into postmodern perspectivalism, as though the atonement were not "real" or as though nothing certain might be said of it. It is rather to admit that the only way to speak of "the reality of the atonement" in the way Boyd desires is to speak from God's perspective about "the way the atonement actually is." But why should we imagine that a God who so obviously delights in diversity (consider, e.g., the world he has created, or the mix of peoples gathered for end-time worship [Rev 7]) would establish a single, unifying framework for interpreting the saving work of his Son? Among Christians, how we articulate the nature of the solution provided by the cross of Christ is very much dependent on how we understand the nature of the problem requiring resolution, and Scripture develops this in a dizzying array of possibilities. Missiological and pedagogical concerns press our models in different directions as well.[4] This does not make the cross of Jesus any less "real," but it does demonstrate that we construe the same "reality" ("something that actually exists") according to different "realities" (different worldviews or lifeworlds). In any case, what we know of God's perspective is only what God has disclosed, and God's revelation in Scripture points to the cross of Christ as the focal point of the drama of salvation without thereby identifying a single interpretation of the cross.

Second, as important as Christus Victor might be, the interpretive canopy it provides simply cannot cover all of the ground occupied by the atonement theologies championed within Scripture and among theologians today. Boyd himself seems to be aware that penal substitution lies outside the circle

---

[3]Colin E. Gunton, *The Actuality of the Atonement* (Grand Rapids: Eerdmans, 1989).
[4]This is the burden of Joel B. Green and Mark D. Baker, *Recovering the Scandal of the Cross* (Downers Grove, Ill.: InterVarsity Press, 2000).

drawn by Christus Victor; thus, immediately on affirming that the Christus Victor model undergirds penal substitution, he reinterprets this substitutionary model in warfare rather than legal terms (p. 43). Whether Boyd has space for penal substitution in the pantheon of atonement theologies, it should not escape our notice that to evacuate "substitution" of its "legal" concerns is to deny the "penal" in "penal substitution."

Other models are more easily set alongside Christus Victor than subsumed beneath it. How should we understand "sacrifice" in warfare terms? Against whom is God engaged in battle in models emphasizing forgiveness? In Romans 5:8-10, Paul has it that while we were sinners, enemies, God did not declare war on us but proved his love through Christ's offering himself for us. Christus Victor handles the objective side of the atonement well, but falters when it comes to drawing out the subjective side of the atonement. It may be that, on the cross, God engages in battle *for us* and wins our salvation, but this is not the same thing as describing the work of the atonement *in us*. Even if we allow that Christus Victor could lead us to transformation, as Boyd urges, it remains unclear how, in this model, we are in fact made holy.

In a book entitled *Salvation,* I argued that the biblical portraits of Yahweh as warrior and as healer were overlapping, complementary images, each irreducible in terms of the other.[5] In the same way that the Lord God can be understood only through multiple portraits, so the human condition requires development along multiple lines. Atonement theology sits at the crossroads of our doctrines of God and of humanity, so atonement theology cannot help but reflect those multiple portraits. Consequently, Scripture itself, together with the theological tradition, incorporates, authenticates and invites the coexistence of multiple, irreducible models of the atonement.

---

[5]Joel B. Green, *Salvation,* Understanding Biblical Themes (St. Louis, Missouri: Chalice, 2003).

Penal Substitution View

THOMAS R. SCHREINER

The theory of penal substitution is the heart and soul of an evangelical view of the atonement.[1] I am not claiming that it is the *only* truth about the atonement taught in the Scriptures. Nor am I claiming that penal substitution is emphasized in every piece of literature or that every author articulates clearly penal substitution.[2] I am claiming that penal substitution functions as the anchor and foundation for all other dimensions of the atonement when the Scriptures are considered as a canonical whole.[3] I define penal substitution as follows: The Father, because of his love for human beings, sent his Son (who offered himself willingly and gladly) to satisfy God's justice, so that Christ took the place of sinners. The punishment and penalty we deserved was laid on Jesus Christ instead of us, so that in the cross both God's holiness and love are manifested.

The riches of what God has accomplished in Christ for his people are not exhausted by penal substitution. The multifaceted character of the atonement must be recognized to do justice to the canonical witness. God's people are impoverished if Christ's triumph over evil powers at the cross is slighted, or Christ's exemplary love is shoved to the side, or the healing bestowed on believers by Christ's cross and resurrection is downplayed. While not denying the wide-ranging character of Christ's atonement, I am arguing that penal substitution is foundational and the heart of the atonement.

---

[1] I want to thank Jim Hamilton, Bruce Ware and Justin Taylor for reading this essay carefully and providing some helpful suggestions on how to improve it. Unless noted otherwise all scripture references in this essay are from the ESV.

[2] For a recent, brief defense of penal substitution, see Simon Gathercole, "The Cross and Substitutionary Atonement," *Scottish Bulletin of Evangelical Theology* 21 (2003): 152-65; Henri Blocher, "The Sacrifice of Jesus Christ: The Current Theological Situation," *European Journal of Theology* 8 (1999): 23-36.

[3] For a robust and convincing defense of this claim, see John R. W. Stott, *The Cross of Christ* (Downers Grove, Ill.: InterVarsity Press, 1986), pp. 133-63.

The fundamental nature of penal substitution is evident if we consider some of the other theories of the atonement. For example, the Christus Victor motif recognizes rightly that Christ has conquered demonic powers and has liberated us from the dominion of evil in our lives.[4] But if the Christus Victor motif is not tethered to penal substitution, we might conclude that human beings are merely victims of sin, held in thrall by evil powers. Penal substitution reminds us that sinners are enslaved to demonic powers because of our own moral failure and guilt.[5] Our fundamental problem as human beings is not that outside powers victimize us. The root problem is that we ourselves are radically evil and that we are wrongly related to God himself. Evil powers reign over us because of the evil within us. We are victims of sin because we have failed to glorify and thank God the way we should (Rom 1:21).

A therapeutic view of the atonement prizes the healing that we experience because of Christ's death for us.[6] We praise God that his grace repairs those whom he saves, that the deforming effect of sin is removed (progressively, not instantaneously) by the work of Christ. Identifying the therapeutic view as central, however, is mistaken. The focus shifts from the glory of God to the good accomplished for human beings. We diminish the objective work of Christ and exalt the subjective experience of people. Sin may be so redefined that it becomes a disease that disfigures us instead of being a radical egocentricity, pride and rebellion that corrupts and condemns us.

The governmental theory of the atonement emphasizes that God desires to show how seriously he takes the law without requiring a full payment for every infraction. According to this view, God's law needs to be honored in order for sinners to be forgiven. Still, the governmental view is flawed because it sunders God's law from his person and hence undercuts the biblical teaching of God's awful and beautiful holiness. The governmental view suggests that God desires to demonstrate the importance of the law and his moral standards. The governmental view does not succeed, however, be-

---

[4]The Christus Victor motif was brought to the forefront of modern discussion by the work of Gustaf Aulén, *Christus Victor: A Historical Study of the Three Main Types of the Idea of Atonement*, trans. A. G. Herbert (London: SPCK, 1931).

[5]So also Blocher, "Sacrifice of Jesus Christ," p. 31.

[6]Stanley P. Rosenberg points out that Augustine's preaching on the atonement emphasized the reformation and restoration of human beings deformed by sin ("Interpreting Atonement in Augustine's Preaching," in *The Glory of the Atonement,* ed. Charles E. Hill and Frank A. James III [Downers Grove, Ill.: InterVarsity Press, 2004], pp. 235-38).

cause it does not uphold the truth that God's justice must be satisfied *entirely,* not merely approximately.

Some might claim that reconciliation speaks to our contemporaries better than justification, for the former addresses relationships and the latter focuses on legality.[7] It is sometimes said that people today cannot relate to the legal categories that inhabit penal substitution whereas the warm and personal dimensions of reconciliation speak to their hearts. No one should diminish the importance of reconciliation, but neither should we make the mistake of exalting reconciliation and minimizing justification.[8] The reason human beings need to be reconciled to God is because of their sin and guilt. Sin is an objective reality that separates sinners from a holy God. Reconciliation between God and humans does not become a reality merely on the basis of human repentance and a desire for forgiveness. If human beings could be reconciled to God by repentance alone, then the sacrifice of Christ on the cross would be completely unnecessary. All people would need to do to receive forgiveness would be to feel sorry for their sins, and we could dispense entirely with the work of Christ. Reconciliation is a precious reality, but it is anchored in the sin-bearing work of Christ on the cross by which the wrath of God was appeased.[9]

The example theory of the atonement rightly sees that Jesus functions paradigmatically for Christians. Some might think that a focus on penal substitution displaces the call to imitate Jesus. On the contrary, the love of Jesus Christ, demonstrated supremely in the cross, becomes the paradigm of love for believers (e.g., Mt 20:25-28; Jn 13:1-17; Rom 15:1-4; 2 Cor 8:8-9; Eph 5:2; Phil 2:5-11; 1 Pet 2:21-25; 1 Jn 3:16-18; 4:10-11). Jesus' self-giving on the cross functions as the model of love for believers; those who belong to Christ are to imitate him and to walk in his steps. As important as it is to imitate Jesus, we would be badly mistaken if we conceived of his example as the primary truth with respect to the atonement. Such a view undercuts the radical pervasiveness of sin in human beings and suggests that we pri-

---

[7]So Ralph P. Martin, "Reconciliation: Romans 5:1-11," in *Romans and the People of God,* ed. Sven K. Soderlund and N. T. Wright (Grand Rapid: Eerdmans, 1999), p. 47.

[8]Leon Morris rightly argues that justification, reconciliation and redemption are all rooted in substitution (*The Cross in the New Testament* [Grand Rapids: Eerdmans, 1965], pp. 404-19).

[9]Martin Hengel comments, "In other words, men no longer need to assuage the wrath of God through their actions. God as subject of the saving event, reconciled to himself his unfaithful creatures, who had become his enemies" (*The Atonement: The Origins of the Doctrine in the New Testament,* trans. John Bowden [Philadelphia: Fortress, 1981], p. 32). Note also his comments to this effect on p. 74.

marily need a model and paradigm of love. Jesus functions, according to this scheme, as a model to imitate rather than a Savior who rescues us from ourselves. The depth of human evil is glossed over in the example view, and an optimistic view of human nature comes to the forefront. The penal substitution view rightly heralds that human beings stand in debt before God and that they desperately need more than anything else in the world his forgiveness. Such forgiveness is secured through the cross and resurrection of Jesus Christ.

The wisdom of God displayed in the cross is rejected by the wise of this age. Penal substitution is an object of indignation and regularly pilloried by many of the educated class.[10] For instance, many radical feminists claim that penal substitution sanctions domestic abuse of women and children.[11] In a recent book Denny Weaver emphatically rejects penal substitution and advocates nonviolent atonement.[12] Scholars regularly complain that penal substitution is abstract, legal and impersonal. They lament that it pits the Father against the Son, puts the law above God and places the emphasis on a wrathful God.[13] Even in the evangelical camp there is the claim that penal substitution is "cosmic child abuse" and contrary to the love of God.[14]

Criticisms of penal substitution also hail from the evangelical commu-

---

[10]See the brief survey of objections in Blocher, "Sacrifice of Jesus Christ," pp. 24-27.

[11]For an introduction to this thesis, see Joanne Carlson Brown and Rebecca Parker, "For God So Loved the World?" in *Christianity, Patriarchy and Abuse: A Feminist Critique,* ed. Joanne Carlson Brown and Carole R. Bohn (New York: Pilgrim, 1989), pp. 1-30; Darby Kathleen Ray, *Deceiving the Devil: Atonement, Abuse, and Ransom* (Cleveland: Pilgrim, 1998), pp. 1-18. It is not my purpose to counteract such charges in detail here. Laying the charge of abuse at the door of penal substitution is unpersuasive since the Scriptures never defend the moral legitimacy of those who crucified Christ and subjected him to an agonizing death. Hence, no basis exists in the Scripture for justifying those who inflict abuse on others. Those who maintain that the Father abused the Son overemphasize the distinctions between the persons of the Trinity, failing to see that the Father experienced grief (not malevolent pleasure) at the death of his Son, and they also reduce the death of Jesus to a human perspective, identifying it completely with the decision of a human father to send his son to death.

[12]J. Denny Weaver, *The Nonviolent Atonement* (Grand Rapids: Eerdmans, 2001). See also Anthony W. Bartlett, *Cross Purposes: The Violent Grammar of Christian Atonement* (Harrisburg, Penn.: Trinity Press International, 2001); C. D. Marshall, *Beyond Retribution: A New Testament Vision for Justice, Crime and Punishment* (Grand Rapids: Eerdmans, 2001).

[13]Cf. John Goldingay, ed., *Atonement Today: A Symposium at St. John's College Nottingham* (London: SPCK, 1995). Many of the authors who contributed to this work reject penal substitution for reasons stated above.

[14]Steve Chalke, *The Lost Message of Jesus* (Grand Rapids: Zondervan, 2003), pp. 182-83. D. A. Carson shows the astonishing weaknesses in Chalke's claim, so that what he says about penal substitution does not qualify as serious scholarship (*Becoming Conversant with the Emergent Church* [Grand Rapids: Zondervan, 2005], pp. 185-87).

nity. Joel Green and Mark Baker have recently written a book titled *Recovering the Scandal of the Cross.*[15] They claim that penal substitution is one metaphor among many for understanding the cross of Christ, and they are certainly right in saying that penal substitution does not exhaust what Scripture teaches about the atonement.[16] And yet their claim to accept penal substitution seems to be contradicted by the content of the book, for they criticize penal substitution frequently. Often in the book their criticisms of penal substitution are directed against popular views and misunderstandings. Still, they do not clearly commend a version of penal substitution shorn of distortions, nor do they present a positive perspective of penal substitution stripped of popular misrepresentations. Indeed, many of the same criticisms in the book raised against popular views are also raised against Charles Hodge. They criticize Hodge's defense of the theory, saying that it (1) only has the "appearance of being biblical" and "is foreign to the Bible";[17] (2) divides the Father from the Son; (3) supports an abstract view of justice that doesn't speak to people today and departs from the relational and covenantal views found in the Scriptures; (4) wrongly understands "God's wrath as retributive punishment";[18] (5) restricts God's love by this "abstract concept of justice";[19] (6) omits the necessity of the resurrection; (7) distorts what the Bible says; (8) removes the need for ethics.

Green and Baker level many of the same criticisms against popular views of penal substitution and against Hodge, who is surely a sophisticated proponent of penal substitution. It seems, therefore, that many of the objections raised against popular views also apply to sophisticated proponents of penal substitution. Since Green and Baker speak against both popular and sophisticated explanations of penal substitution and do not present a positive version of it, we can see why they say that even when it is defended "by its

---

[15]Joel B. Green and Mark D. Baker, *Recovering the Scandal of the Cross: Atonement in New Testament & Contemporary Contexts* (Downers Grove, Ill.: InterVarsity Press, 2000).

[16]Though I differ from them in maintaining that it is the most important metaphor. In addition, Henri Blocher rightly argues that the use of metaphorical language does not cancel out the centrality and clarity of penal substitution in the Scriptures ("Biblical Metaphors and the Doctrine of the Atonement," *The Journal of the Evangelical Theological Society* 47 [2004]: 629-45).

[17]Green and Baker, *Scandal of the Cross,* pp. 146-47. They say Hodge "distorts biblical words and phrases to the point that they are no longer recognizable in their biblical contexts" (p. 147).

[18]Ibid, p. 147.

[19]Ibid.

most careful and sophisticated advocates" it "remains susceptible to misunderstanding and bizarre caricature."[20]

Even though Green and Baker claim that penal substitution is one motif for the atonement, nowhere do they commend it in the book. In effect, then, penal substitution is rejected in their theology of the cross. Indeed, Green and Baker also seem to endorse a view of God's wrath quite similar to that proposed by C. H. Dodd, who limited God's wrath to the negative consequences that flow from our sins and rejected the idea that God's anger needs to be appeased.[21]

I conclude that the penal substitution view needs defending today because it is scandalous to some scholars. We know that it is scandalous to radical feminists who see it as a form of divine child abuse, or to scholars like Denny Weaver who promote nonviolent atonement. Indeed, among all the views of the atonement, penal substitution provokes the most negative response.

Such a response, of course, does not prove that penal substitution is biblically grounded.[22] We must demonstrate from the Scriptures themselves that penal substitution is the heart and soul of God's work in Christ. I will defend penal substitution by appealing to three theological themes: (1) the sinfulness and guilt of humanity, (2) the holiness of God, and (3) the sacrifice of Christ. There is some overlap among these three categories, and they are not neatly segregated from one another in this essay.[23] But before defending penal substitution from the Scriptures, I should clarify what is meant by penal substitution. The penalty for sin is death (Rom 6:23). Sinners deserve eternal punishment in hell from God himself because of their sin and guilt. God's holy anger is directed (Rom 1:18) against all those who have sinned and fall short of the glory of God (Rom 3:23). And yet because of God's great love, he sent Christ to bear the punishment of our sins. Christ died in our place,

---

[20]Ibid., p. 30.

[21]Ibid., pp. 51-56. They say, "The Scriptures as a whole provide no ground for a portrait of an angry God needing to be appeased in atoning sacrifice" (p. 51). One might say that they differ from Dodd since God's wrath is defined as "the active presence of God's judgment," and they speak of God handing people over to their sin (p. 54). The authors, however, reject retributive justice and appear to define this active presence of God in terms of God allowing people to "receive the fruits of their own misplaced hopes and commitments" (p. 54). The wrath of God is explained as follows: "letting us go on our own way" (p. 55). The difference from Dodd's view is a matter of degree rather than kind in my judgment.

[22]For recent defenses, see David Peterson, ed., *Where Wrath and Mercy Meet* (Carlisle, U.K.: Paternoster, 2001); Hill and James, eds., *Glory of the Atonement*.

[23]For example, I will focus on sin in the second section in order to articulate God's holiness.

took to himself our sin (2 Cor 5:21) and guilt (Gal 3:10), and bore our penalty so that we might receive forgiveness of sins.[24] The forgiveness of our sins by virtue of the death of Christ is the wellspring of ethics; we love God because he first loved us (1 Jn 4:19), and such love is the wellspring of a life of obedience. It should be noted that such forgiveness would not be ours apart from the death *and resurrection* of Christ (Rom 4:25). Too often evangelicals refer to the substitutionary atonement but fail to say anything about the resurrection.[25]

The Sinfulness of Humanity

Human beings need a penal substitute since "all have sinned and fall short of the glory of God" (Rom 3:23).[26] Adam and Eve were evicted from the garden and subjected to judgment for one sin. The standard in the garden was not that Adam and Eve should trust God the majority of the time or even 99 percent of the time. God condemns them to death after they violated his requirements once. That God demands perfection fits with James 2:10, where James says, "For whoever keeps the whole law but fails in one point has become accountable for all of it."[27] One transgression constitutes a person as a lawbreaker. James 2:11 illustrates the point. If a person faces trial for murder, he or she will hardly help the case by protesting during the trial, "I should not be condemned, for I have never committed adultery!" Such a defense would be completely irrelevant because the issue before the court is whether he or she murdered someone. So too James teaches us that we can-

---

[24]Some scholars prefer the word *representation* instead of *substitution*. J. I. Packer demonstrates that the term *representation* either includes the concept of substitution or is less than faithful to the biblical witness ("What Did the Cross Achieve?" in *Celebrating the Saving Work of God* [Carlisle, U.K.: Paternoster, 1998], 1:102-5, 112-13). Leon Morris also criticizes the imprecision of language of some who opt for *representation* rather than *substitution* (*Cross in the New Testament,* pp. 407-9). Cf. also Colin Gunton who argues that the term *representation* cannot be used to exclude *substitution* (*The Actuality of the Atonement* [Grand Rapids: Eerdmans, 1989], pp. 160-67), though he does not concur with the view of penal substitution argued for in this essay.

[25]See Richard Gaffin, "Atonement in the Pauline Corpus: 'The Scandal of the Cross,'" in *The Glory of the Atonement,* ed. Charles E. Hill and Frank A. James III (Downers Grove, Ill.: InterVarsity Press, 2004), pp. 142-44, 160. It follows then that the cross and resurrection together secure salvation; the cross without the resurrection would not be a saving event. Hence, when I speak of the cross in the remainder of this essay, the resurrection is also implied, so that both are essential to God's saving work in Christ.

[26]See also the insightful discussion on sin in Gaffin in which he takes aim at some defective views current in scholarship, "Atonement in the Pauline Corpus," pp. 145-50.

[27]See Roger T. Beckwith, "Sacrifice in the World of the New Testament," in *Sacrifice in the Bible,* ed. Roger T. Beckwith and Martin J. Selman (Grand Rapids: Baker, 1995), p. 109.

not defend ourselves before God by claiming that we usually keep the law. One failure to keep the law brands us as a law-breaker and hence guilty before God.

Sometimes scholars say that the Old Testament does not demand perfect obedience to the law. We must address this matter carefully because there is a sense in which the Old Testament requires perfect obedience and a sense in which it doesn't. Let me explain. God saves his people, Israel, by grace. He enters into covenant with them and delivers them at the exodus. He does not demand that they obey the law perfectly to remain in covenant with him. But Yahweh threatens exile if his people become enslaved to evil. They will be judged by God if they harden their hearts, forsake the Lord and turn away from him. They will be blessed as his people if they keep the Torah. Such blessing is not conditioned on perfect obedience. Israel will show its faith in Yahweh by obeying him significantly and substantially, but not perfectly.

We might conclude from the above that God does not demand perfect obedience. But the sacrificial system instituted by God reveals that perfect obedience was required to maintain a relationship with him. The sacrifices atoned for sins committed. The sacrifices on the Day of Atonement (Lev 16) were required for Israel to maintain its relationship with God. The Old Testament nowhere teaches that sacrifices are only required of notorious sinners. Any individual who sinned, whether once or many times, was required to offer sacrifice. Indeed, in a number of places the Old Testament recognizes that no one is exempt from sin. Ecclesiastes says, "Surely there is not a righteous man on earth who does good and never sins" (Eccles 7:20). A temple where sacrifices are offered is necessary because of human sin. Solomon remarks, "If they sin against you— for there is no one who does not sin . . ." (1 Kings 8:46; cf. 2 Chron 6:36). Proverbs recognizes that all deviate from the right way. "Who can say, 'I have made my heart pure; I am clean from my sin' "? (Prov 20:9; cf. Job 15:14; 25:4). David recognized that he was sinful from conception (Ps 51:5). If God merely required substantial and significant obedience, sacrifice would not be demanded from those who trusted God most of the time. Sacrifices were still needed to atone for sins, however, because God demands perfect obedience.

The need for perfect obedience is also found in the New Testament. We have already seen such a requirement in James. Peter acknowledges that both Jews and Gentiles need the grace of Jesus Christ to be saved because they are unable to keep the stipulations of the law. "Now, therefore, why are you putting God to the test by placing a yoke on the neck of the disciples that neither our fathers nor we have been able to bear? But we believe that we will be saved through the grace of the Lord Jesus, just as they will" (Acts 15:10-11).[28] Jews were unable to bear the yoke of the law because of their failure to keep it. Peter concludes that circumcision cannot be imposed on the Gentiles for salvation. The only way to be saved is through the grace of Christ.

Galatians 3:10 also teaches that God's standard is perfection. The Pauline argument here is particularly crucial because virtually everyone acknowledges that Galatians 3:10-14 is one of the most important texts in the Galatian letter. Galatians 3:10 says, "For all who rely on works of the law are under a curse; for it is written, 'Cursed be everyone who does not abide by all things written in the Book of the Law, and do them.' "[29] The argument of this verse can be explained as a syllogism.

> One must obey the law perfectly to be saved.[30]
> No one keeps the law perfectly.
> Therefore, those who rely on the works of the law to be saved stand under
> God's curse.

It is sometimes objected that the verse does not contain the second proposition. But Paul could easily omit the second proposition, for it is assumed in his argument and was a well-known fact from both the Old Testament Scriptures and human experience. Paul particularly emphasizes that one must do "all" that is written in the law. Partial or even significant obedience

---

[28]In support of the interpretation of Acts 15:10-11 offered here, see John Nolland, "A Fresh Look at Acts 15.10," *New Testament Studies* 27 (1980): 105-15.

[29]This verse is the subject of much controversy today. See further Thomas R. Schreiner, *The Law and Its Fulfillment: A Pauline Theology of Law* (Grand Rapids: Baker, 1993), pp. 44-59.

[30]Stephen H. Travis mistakenly excludes individuals from the text, failing to see that erecting a separation between individuals and groups is a false dichotomy ("Christ as Bearer of Divine Judgment in Paul's Thought About the Atonement," in *Jesus of Nazareth: Lord and Christ*, ed. Joel B. Green and Max Turner [Grand Rapids: Eerdmans, 1994], p. 334). Travis, contrary to the position argued here, maintains that the notion of Christ bearing retributive punishment cannot be sustained from the Scriptures. See pp. 332-45 in his essay and his *Christ and the Judgment of God: Divine Retribution in the New Testament* (Basingstoke, U.K.: Marshall, Morgan and Scott, 1986). Against the view propounded by Travis, see Blocher, "Sacrifice of Jesus Christ," p. 32, and his "Justification of the Ungodly *(Sola Fide)*: Theological Reflections," in *Justification and Variegated Nomism*, vol. 2: *The Paradoxes of Paul*, ed. D. A. Carson, P. T. O'Brien and M. A. Seifrid (Grand Rapids: Baker, 2004), pp. 473-78.

is insufficient. Only perfect obedience qualifies. So how can the curse be removed? We are not surprised to see three verses later that the curse can only be removed by the cross of Jesus Christ (Gal 3:13).

The locus classicus for Paul's doctrine of sin is Romans 1:18—3:20. He argues in this text that God's wrath is revealed against all people, both Jews and Gentiles, because of human sin. The fundamental sin is the failure to glorify and thank God for his goodness (Rom 1:21). Even those who know about God only through the created order (and not his written law) suppress and reject what they know about God (Rom 1:18-20). And the Jews, who were blessed with the possession of God's law, failed to keep it. The Jews are not condemned merely because they passed judgment on the Gentiles. They are condemned because they also failed to keep the Torah (Rom 2:1-5). Possessing the law and observing circumcision constitute no advantage if the Jews do not observe the prescriptions of the law (Rom 2:17-29). Paul summarizes the argument of Romans 1:18—3:20 in Romans 3:9-20. He concludes that not even one person is righteous. All without exception have sinned and are guilty in God's sight. No one seeks God on his or her own. All human beings have sinned in word and deed. Hence, the law does not pronounce anyone righteous (Rom 3:19-20). Those who stand before God the judge have no word of defense. The works of the law have not led to justification because the sin of human beings reveals that they do not stand in the right before God. Human beings need atonement, then, because they are sinners, because they have failed to measure up to God's law. God demands perfect obedience, and no one has met the standard.[31]

It's not only the case that human beings have sinned, but they are guilty for the sin they have committed (cf. Rom 2:1). All those who have sinned in Adam stand condemned before God (Rom 5:16, 18). The payment and wages for sin is death (Rom 6:23). God's wrath rests on those who refuse to obey the Son (Jn 3:36; cf. Jn 3:18). Those who have hard and resistant hearts will face God's righteous judgment on the last day (Rom 2:5, 16). God's righteous judgment means that those who have disobeyed the gospel will face eternal destruction when Jesus comes again (2 Thess 1:5-10). Judgment is according to works (Rom 2:6-11), and all those who have practiced evil will be judged before the great white throne (Rev 20:11-15).

---

[31]Stott rightly argues that many people do not accept substitutionary atonement because of a light view of sin (*Cross of Christ*, pp. 87-110). We recall Anselm's famous remark, "Have you considered how great is the weight of sin?" (*Cur Deus Homo* 1.21).

The Holiness of God

The theme of God's holiness is closely related to human failure to obey God's law. I will endeavor to establish three points in this section: (1) law-breaking is not impersonal, (2) God judges sin retributively, and (3) God is personally angry at sin. We begin, then, by considering sin; God's holiness cannot be grasped without comprehending the nature of sin. I am not merely recapitulating what I have already said about sin, for here the nature of sin is considered from a different angle. Some scholars complain that the requirement to keep the law is abstract and impersonal, exalting law-keeping over a personal relationship. Such an objection ultimately fails because God's law describes his moral character.[32] The moral norms of the law are not externally imposed on God. *The norms of the law express God's character, the beauty and holiness of his person.*[33] Sin certainly involves the violation of God's law (1 Jn 3:4), but violation of the law is so heinous because it constitutes rebellion against God's lordship. Those who transgress the law reject God's authority over their lives. In Romans 7 Paul explains that human beings are drawn toward transgression of the law. The very presence of commands prompts a desire among sinful and rebellious humans to contravene them.

Failure to keep the law stems from rebellion, a fierce desire for independence and a refusal to submit to God's lordship. We recall from Romans 1:21 that the heart of sin is a refusal to glorify God and to give him thanks. It makes sense, then, that "whatever does not proceed from faith is sin" (Rom 14:23), because when we trust God we glorify him (Rom 4:20). Faith finds satisfaction in Jesus, and we worship whatever we delight in the most.[34] Sin, in other words, is finding delight in the praise of people instead of seeking the glory of God (Jn 5:44), exchanging the truth for the lie by worshiping the creature rather than the Creator (Rom 1:25). Another way of putting it is that sin is spiritual adultery. The Old Testament prophets often teach that transgression of the law stems from a spirit of harlotry.[35] Hence, the charge

---

[32]See also Morris, *Cross in the New Testament*, pp. 382-89.

[33]See especially Garry Williams, "The Cross and the Punishment of Sin," in *Where Wrath and Mercy Meet,* ed. David Peterson (Carlisle, U.K.: Paternoster, 2001), pp. 81-97. Cf. also Derek Tidball, *The Message of the Cross* (Downers Grove, Ill.: InterVarsity Press, 2001), p. 73.

[34]See John Piper, *Desiring God: Meditations of a Christian Hedonist,* 3rd. ed. (Sisters, Ore.: Multnomah, 2003).

[35]Raymond C. Ortlund Jr., *God's Unfaithful Wife: A Biblical Theology of Spiritual Adultery* (Downers Grove, Ill.: InterVarsity Press, 2002).

that law-breaking is impersonal is as unconvincing as saying that adultery against one's spouse is impersonal. The prohibition against adultery constitutes a moral norm, but we all know that breaking one's marital vow is a deeply personal act.[36]

We have seen that sin is personal rebellion against God, and that brings us to the second truth in this section: *Those who sin face the retributive judgment of God.* The Scriptures emphasize repeatedly that God is holy (e.g., Lev 19:2; Ps 71:22; Is 6:3). Indeed, the cleanliness regulations and the elaborate ritual required for sacrifices and entrance into God's temple indicate that sinful human beings are unworthy to enter into God's awesome presence. Access into the holy of holies, the inner sanctum of the temple, was available only once a year on the day of atonement (Lev 16; Heb 9:6-8). When God's holiness is defiled, judgment follows as a retribution. This is evident from the earliest pages of the Bible: Adam and Eve were expelled from the garden because of their sin; the world was engulfed by a flood because of the wickedness of human beings (cf. Gen 6:5); those who erected the tower of Babel were dispersed because of their arrogance (Gen 11:1-9). The theme of judgment permeates the Old Testament: the Canaanites were driven from their land because of their sin; God afflicted Israel during the time of the judges because the people had forsaken him; both the northern and southern kingdoms of Israel were conquered and sent into exile because of their sin. The prophets declared that the Day of the Lord would be one of judgment because God's people were guilty of spiritual prostitution.

The New Testament presents the same theme. The Baptist warned Israel of a coming judgment from God unless they repented (Mt 3:1-12). Jesus proclaimed the same message of judgment, and he did so in the most uncompromising terms when addressing the religious leaders (Mt 23:1-36). The apostolic speeches in Acts (e.g., Acts 2:14-39; 3:12-26; 4:8-12) called on all to repent and believe or face judgment because of their sin. Paul spoke often of God's eschatological judgment or the punishment of sinners on the last day (cf. Rom 2:5, 16; 6:23; 9:22; 1 Cor 1:18; 5:5; 2 Cor 2:16; Gal 1:8-9; 6:8; Phil 3:18-19; 1 Thess 1:10; 2:14-16;

---

[36]In fact, as Williams demonstrates, those who reject penal substitution are actually guilty of subscribing to an impersonal and mechanistic view of the atonement ("Cross and the Punishment of Sin," pp. 94-97). The consequences of sin are conceived of as a natural process or the inevitable effects of sin and are thereby separated from God's person.

5:9).[37] Further, it is clear that the judgment God inflicts is retributive (2 Thess 1:5-9). Those who do not know God or obey the gospel will be recompensed for their obstinacy. The penalty will be "eternal destruction" (2 Thess 1:9), and this retribution will be meted out on the day of the Lord's return. Paul emphasizes in verse 6 that retributive and eternal punishment for sin is "just" *(dikaios)*. God's retribution is not considered to be a primitive kind of justice, nor is it swallowed up by God's love. God's punishment of the wicked manifests his justice and holiness.

Warnings about judgment also pervade the letters of Hebrews, 2 Peter and Jude. Finally, the book of Revelation closes the canon with the promise of eschatological reward for the righteous but wrath and judgment for the disobedient. The theme of judgment permeates Revelation and cannot be demoted to a subsidiary motif. The author of Revelation emphasizes that God's punishment of the wicked is retributive. In judging the ungodly God gives them what they deserve as repayment for their deeds (Rev 16:5-7; 18:4-7; 19:2-4; 20:12-15; 22:12, 18-19). Indeed, those who think that the New Testament mutes the Old Testament emphasis on judgment have failed to read the New Testament carefully, for the New Testament regularly declares that a final judgment awaits those who forsake God and live disobedient lives. Modern-day Marcionism has by no means disappeared, but its kinder and gentler view of judgment can only be sustained by a more radical surgery than even Marcion attempted!

God as the holy One judges sin, and that leads us to the third truth in this section: *God's judgment of sin represents his personal anger against sin.* The Lord judges sin because of his holiness—the beauty of his goodness that separates him so radically from human beings. God's judgment is not imposed abstractly, as if judgment is merely the inevitable and impersonal consequence of sin. Sin does lead to judgment, but in the biblical worldview judgment represents the personal response of the holy Lord to human sin. Indeed, Scripture regularly teaches that God is personally angry at sinners. Protestant liberalism rejects the notion that God's wrath is directed against sinners. C. H. Dodd argued that judgment is merely the natural consequence

---

[37]D. A. Carson observes that Rom 2:5-9 clearly teaches that God's justice is retributive over against the view of Stephen Travis ("Atonement in Romans 3:21-26: 'God Presented Him as a Propitiation,' " in *The Glory of the Atonement,* ed. Charles E. Hill and Frank A. James III [Downers Grove, Ill.: InterVarsity Press, 2004], p. 131). On God's wrath and retribution, see the incisive comments of Gaffin, "Atonement in the Pauline Corpus," pp. 150-52.

of sin.[38] It is like the law of gravity. If a person jumps off a high building, he or she will die. It is rather surprising, then, that those who identify themselves with the evangelical camp endorse a view quite similar to Dodd's.[39] Such a view of God's wrath strays severely from the biblical witness and succumbs to a deistic view of God instead of embracing the personal God of the Scriptures. In the Scriptures God's wrath is his personal response to sin and cannot be restricted to the law of cause and effect, as if such laws operate outside the parameters of God's person.[40] God's wrath and judgment are personally directed against sinners who have failed to praise, honor and thank him. Sin is not merely the violation of God's law but spiritual adultery. We sin in forsaking and abandoning God who is the fountain of living waters (Jer 2:13).

God is angry, then, because of human rejection of his lordship. Now I must immediately note that God's wrath is not like most human anger, which is often ill-founded. God's anger is not capricious or whimsical or arbitrary. We are prone to anger if someone accidentally steps on our foot. God's anger is remarkably different from the Greco-Roman gods who are little more than glorified human beings and become enraged for trivial reasons. The wrath of the true God flows from his holiness—from the perfection of his character and the beauty of his goodness. God does not become angry because he loses control of himself. His anger flows from his goodness, his matchless character. God's anger does not call into question his goodness but is a manifestation of it: God's goodness necessarily approves what accords with his character and repulses what stands contrary to it. So goodness necessarily loves what is right and hates what is evil. God's wrath, then, is holy, righteous and unstained by any evil motive.[41]

God's just anger at sin colors all of the biblical witness. The flood is not merely the consequence of human sin but is God's personal response of judgment to the massive incursion of human evil (cf. Gen 6:5). God is ever

---

[38]C. H. Dodd, *The Epistle of Paul to the Romans,* Moffatt New Testament Commentary (London: Hodder & Stoughton, 1932), pp. 21-24.

[39]E.g., Green and Baker, *Scandal of the Cross,* pp. 53-55.

[40]See especially Leon Morris, *The Apostolic Preaching of the Cross,* 3rd ed. (Grand Rapids: Eerdmans, 1965), pp. 144-213; Roger R. Nicole, "C. H. Dodd and the Doctrine of Propitiation," *Westminster Theological Journal* 17 (1954-1955): 117-57. Contra Paul S. Fiddes, *Past Event and Present Salvation: The Christian Idea of Atonement* (Louisville: Westminster John Knox, 1989), p. 93.

[41]For further development of this theme, see John M. Frame, *The Doctrine of God* (Phillipsburg, N.J.: Presbyterian & Reformed, 2003), pp. 463-68.

and always the holy One.[42] Nadab and Abihu may have considered the offering of different fire to be a legitimate instance of human creativity and choice, but the Lord consumes them with fire and the stunning words of Leviticus 10:3 provide an explanation: "This is what the LORD has said, 'Among those who are near me I will be sanctified, and before all the people I will be glorified.' " In other words, God's wrath burned against Nadab and Abihu because they failed to honor God as the One who is wholly other, and they thought they could enter into God's presence casually instead of following prescribed instructions. If someone were to object that the God of the New Testament is different, we recall the Lord striking down Ananias and Sapphira in Acts 5:1-11. Achan doubtless viewed taking the banned material from Jericho as his right, but God's anger burned against Israel (Josh 7:1), and he and his family were destroyed. We rightly tremble before the flaming fire of our awesome holy God.

God displayed his wrath against Korah, Dathan, Abiram and their cohorts when the earth opened up and swallowed them (Num 16:1-35). When Israel sinned in the wilderness we read of God's anger burning and consuming some of the people (Num 11:1). Even David faced God's anger when he murdered Uriah and committed adultery with Bathsheba (2 Sam 11—20). When Judah was sent into exile, we are told that God's anger burned against them (2 Kings 17:25; cf. Jer 7:20; 32:29; Lam 2:3; Zeph 2:3). The New Testament speaks with the same voice. Jesus was full of compassion and love, and yet with righteous invective he upbraided the Pharisees (Mt 23:1-36). John declares that the "wrath of God remains" on those who refuse to obey the Son (Jn 3:36). Paul begins his indictment of human sin with the words, "For the wrath of God is revealed from heaven against all ungodliness and unrighteousness of men, who by their unrighteousness suppress the truth" (Rom 1:18). The subsequent verses explain that God's anger stems from the refusal of human beings to honor and glorify him as God (Rom 1:21). God is righteously angry when people do not put him first in their affections, when they worship and serve other gods. Those with hard and stubborn hearts are "storing up wrath" for themselves "on the day of wrath when God's righteous judgment will be revealed" (Rom 2:5). Indeed, all people everywhere are by nature "children of wrath" (Eph 2:3).

Is gentle Jesus also full of wrath? Revelation 6 announces that the final

---

[42]Cf. David Peterson, "Atonement in the Old Testament," in *Where Wrath and Mercy Meet,* ed. David Peterson (Carlisle, U.K.: Paternoster, 2001), pp. 7-9.

day of judgment will be one in which people will beg to be spared "from the wrath of the Lamb" (Rev 6:16; cf. Rev 19:11-21). The final judgment is described as the expression of God's wrath (Rev 11:18). The eternal torment of hell is graphically described in Rev 14:9-11, and those who experience it "drink the wine of God's wrath" (Rev 14:10). What is remarkable is how pervasively Scripture refers to God's wrath in judgment. Indeed, many other references could have been mentioned. Let's admit that the intensity and frequency of the references to God's wrath constitute a countercultural word. For us sin becomes routine and it doesn't seem to deserve such awful punishment. We are tempted to domesticate the God of the Bible whose holiness reaches heights that we can only partially grasp. When we read in text after text about God's personal anger against sin, we recognize that those who define God's anger solely in cause-and-effect terms deviate from revelation and have substituted a conception of God that fits their own sensibilities. The sacrifice of Christ is so precious because the judgment we deserve is so horrendous.

The Sacrifice of Christ

Since all human beings have sinned, and God as the holy One judges retributively and does not merely overlook sin, sin must be atoned for by sacrifice. There must be a penal substitute. We begin by thinking of Old Testament sacrifices.[43] It should be said at the outset that Old Testament sacrifices have a diversity of purposes, for not all of them were offered to atone for sin (cf. Lev 1—7).[44] Nevertheless, the fundamental reason for the sacrifices is atonement, so that sinners could be forgiven by the holy One.[45] The laying

---

[43]The substitutionary character of sacrifices is hinted at by Genesis 22. A ram is provided by God in place of the sacrifice of Isaac. Indeed, one of the themes of that chapter is that the Lord himself will provide.

[44]Deuteronomy 21:1-9 also suggests substitutionary atonement. In support of this see the forthcoming essay by Frank Thielman, "Substitutionary Atonement," in a work tentatively titled *Basic Biblical Theology*, ed. Scott Hafemann and Paul House (Leicester, U.K.: Inter-Varsity Press). I am grateful to Thielman for sharing with me a prepublication version of his essay.

[45]Gordon J. Wenham remarks, "They all presuppose that the animal victim is a substitute for the worshipper, makes atonement for him, and thereby restores him to favour with God" ("The Theology of Old Testament Sacrifice," in *Sacrifice in the Bible*, p. 84). Cf. also the discussion of Angel Manuel Rodriguez on burned offerings and peace offerings ("Substitution in the Hebrew Cultus and in Cultic-Related Texts," [Ph.D. diss., Andrews University Seventh-day Adventist Theological Seminary, 1979], pp. 225-32). Though neither of these sacrifices focuses on expiation of sin, he concludes that expiation is included since laying on of hands, slaughtering and a tossing ritual is included (cf. Ezek 45:17).

of hands on animals most likely means that the animal functions as a substitute for a person.[46] The sins of human beings are transferred, so to speak, to the animal.[47] For many of us the sacrifice of animals remains abstract. But reflect on the violence of the activity: the blood, the entrails and the goriness of it all. The death of the animals shows that the penalty for sin is death. When we are told that the sacrifices are a soothing aroma, this image indicates that they satisfy God's wrath, that they appease his anger.[48] I concur with Hebrews that ultimately the blood of animals cannot atone for sin (Heb 10:4). Still, the requirement of sacrifice points ahead to the death of Christ and reminds us of the utter seriousness of sin.[49]

If the laying on of hands symbolizes the transfer of sin from the person to the animal, then it seems to follow that the death of the animal is substitutionary.[50] Wenham comments, "What he [the worshiper] does to the ani-

---

[46]Fiddes thinks propitiation cannot be in view because sin cannot be transferred to a pure animal because then the latter would no longer be pure (*Past Event and Present Salvation*, p. 73). Rodriguez, however, argues from Lev 10:16-18 that the animal was still considered to be holy and at the same time bore the sin of the people ("Substitution in the Hebrew Cultus," pp. 217-19). Such a conclusion is borne out by the New Testament. In 2 Cor 5:21 we see that God made the sinless one, Jesus, to be sin so that our sins could be forgiven. Jesus bore our sin, and yet in another sense he remained sinless.

[47]Against Jacob Milgrom, who says laying on of a single hand designates ownership instead of transference (*Leviticus 1-16*, Anchor Bible [New York: Doubleday, 1991], pp. 151-52). Emile Nicole is more persuasive in suggesting that substitution is in view ("Atonement in the Pentateuch: 'It is the Blood That Makes Atonement for One's Life,' " in *The Glory of the Atonement*, ed. Charles E. Hill and Frank A. James III [Downers Grove, Ill.: InterVarsity Press, 2004], pp. 44-45). Rodriguez maintains that two hands were applied in sacrifices and argues that the notions of transference and sacrificial substitution are involved ("Substitution in the Hebrew Cultus," pp. 193-224). The objection that substitution cannot be in view because some of the sacrifices were meal offerings is not compelling (Fiddes, *Past Event and Present Salvation*, p. 73). Rodriguez observes that even though expiation is not the central purpose of meal offerings, the notion of expiation can't be excluded (Lev 5:11-13; 1 Sam 3:14) ("Substitution in the Hebrew Cultus," pp. 146-47). Even if it were established that some of the offerings in the Old Testament were not expiatory, Hebrews makes it plain that forgiveness of sins doesn't occur without the spilling of blood (Heb 9:22), and clarifies that animal sacrifices function as a type of Christ's sacrifice. On this last point, compare the comments of Emile Nicole, who wisely notes that the grain offering was "an exception among exceptions" and hence cannot become the lodestar by which sacrifices are interpreted ("Atonement in the Pentateuch," p. 45).

[48]The notion that sacrifices soothe God's anger indicate that they placate his anger. So John E. Hartley, *Leviticus*, Word Biblical Commentary (Dallas: Word, 1992), p. lxviii; Wenham, "Theology of Old Testament Sacrifice," p. 84.

[49]The burned offering "propitiates God's wrath against sin" (so Gordon J. Wenham, *The Book of Leviticus*, New International Commentary on the Old Testament [Grand Rapids: Eerdmans, 1979], p. 57); Nicole, "Atonement in the Pentateuch," p. 43. The idea that God's wrath is appeased is found in a number of texts (Num 15:24; 2 Sam 24:25; Job 1:5; 2 Chron 29:7-8).

[50]In defense of substitution in the Old Testament, see also Garry Williams, "The Cross and the Punishment of Sin," in *Where Wrath and Mercy Meet*, pp. 68-81.

mal, he does symbolically to himself. The death of the animal portrays the death of himself."[51] We think of the elaborate ritual and prescriptions of the various Old Testament sacrifices. Human beings were required to approach God in the way specified. If they deviated from what he commanded, they would experience his wrath. Most remarkably, access to the inner sanctum, the holy of holies where God's presence was specially manifested, was permitted only once a year on the day of atonement (Lev 16). On this day sacrifices were offered in order to obtain forgiveness of sins for all Israel. The high priest could not enter God's presence without offering the prescribed sacrifices and following the approved ritual. The sacrifices, it appears, were given in place of the worshipers, so that the punishment due to Israel was averted.

We should note the wording in Leviticus 16:21-22: "[Aaron] shall lay both hands on the head of the live goat and confess over it all the wickedness and rebellion of the Israelites—all their sins—and put them on the goat's head. He shall send the goat away into the desert in the care of a man appointed for the task. The goat will carry on itself all their sins to a solitary place; and the man shall release it in the desert" (NIV). These verses demonstrate clearly that laying on of hands signifies substitution. When Aaron lays his hands on the goat, he confesses the sins of Israel, and the sins are conveyed to the head of the goat, the very place where Aaron lays both his hands.[52] Verse 22 confirms that substitution is in view, for the goat bears the sins of the Israelites into the desert.[53] The live goat functions as the substitute that bears the penalty (eviction to the desert) for Israel's sins. It may also be the case that the goat was sent into the wilderness to die.[54] In any case, Geerhardus Vos rightly argues that both of the goats must be taken together to grasp the truth being conveyed, for there was

> in reality one sacrificial object; the distribution of suffering death and of dismissal into a remote place simply serving the purpose of clearer expression,

---

[51]Wenham, "Theology of Old Testament Sacrifice," p. 77. He proceeds to say, "The animal is a substitute of the worshipper. Its death makes atonement for the worshipper. Its immolation on the altar quietens God's anger at human sin" (ibid., p. 82).

[52]So ibid., p. 79.

[53]Milgrom objects that Azazel was not sacrificed or punished for others (*Leviticus 1-16*, p. 1021). It is true that the Azazel rite is not an example of *sacrificial* substitution, but Rodriguez rightly argues that the role of laying on of hands in the rite signals that when a sacrifice is offered, substitution is in view ("Substitution in the Hebrew Cultus," pp. 219-20).

[54]In support of the view that Azazel was sent away to die, see Peterson, "Atonement in the Old Testament," p. 15; Williams, "The Cross and the Punishment of Sin," p. 79.

in visible form, of removal of sin after expiation had been made, something which the ordinary sacrificial animal could not well express, since it died in the process of expiation.[55]

It seems that there is a reference to substitution in Leviticus 17:11 as well. "For the life of the flesh is in the blood, and I have given it for you on the altar to make atonement for your souls, for it is the blood that makes atonement by the life." Here Moses specifically says that the blood is shed on the altar to make atonement.[56] The verb for atonement is *kipper* in the Hebrew and *hilaskomai* in Greek. Careful study demonstrates that the latter verb has to do with the appeasement or the satisfaction of God's wrath.[57] Such a definition fits the context here. We have seen above that God's wrath is provoked by human sin. Here we are told that the blood of the sacrifices atones for sin. Indeed, Leviticus 17:11 pauses to reiterate that blood atones because it contains life. Some scholars have defended the idea that blood atones because it designates the offering of life to God so that blood signifies the release of life instead of the giving up of life in death. More likely, the idea is that the spilling of blood signifies death since it is evident that animals and humans die when their blood is poured out.[58] The shedding of blood spells the death of the victim, and therefore atonement comes through the death of the one sacrificed. It is not difficult to see that the animal's blood is shed in place of the death of human beings. Wenham sees the "principle of substitution" here, for "animal life takes the place of human life."[59]

Animal sacrifices, of course, cannot ultimately save. As Hebrews clarifies,

---

[55]Geerhardus Vos, *Biblical Theology: Old and New Testaments* (Grand Rapids: Eerdmans, 1977), p. 163. I owe this citation to Nicole, "Atonement in the Pentateuch," pp. 26-27.

[56]For a thorough study of this text, see Rodriguez, "Substitution in the Hebrew Cultus," pp. 233-57. Milgrom admits that the Greek verb *kipper* refers to ransom from anger in some texts but denies that any notion of ransom from God's wrath is present in cultic texts (*Leviticus 1-16,* pp. 1082-83). His attempt to segregate cultic from noncultic texts is unsuccessful (see J. Alan Groves, "Atonement in Isaiah 53: 'For He Bore the Sins of Many,'" in *The Glory of the Atonement,* ed. Charles E. Hill and Frank A. James III [Downers Grove, Ill.: InterVarsity Press, 2004], pp. 65-68). The substitutionary character of the verb *kipper* is defended well by Nicole, "Atonement in the Pentateuch," pp. 47-50. See also Peterson, "Atonement in the Old Testament," pp. 10-12.

[57]For study of *hilaskomai,* see n. 40. The sacrifice of Noah after the flood communicates the idea that the sacrifice averted God's wrath (Gen 8:21). So Wenham, "Theology of Old Testament Sacrifice," pp. 80-81.

[58]See especially Morris, *Apostolic Preaching of the Cross,* pp. 112-28; Nicole, "Atonement in the Pentateuch," pp. 39-40, 46.

[59]Wenham, "Theology of Old Testament Sacrifice," p. 82; cf. Nicole, "Atonement in the Pentateuch," pp. 35-50, esp. 36-40.

they point to the death of Jesus Christ, for he fulfills what is anticipated ty-
pologically by Old Testament sacrifices (cf. Heb 9:1—10:18). One of the
most striking texts on the atoning work of Christ is Isaiah 52:13—53:12. Sacrificial language pervades the text: "sprinkle" (Is 52:15), "carried" (Is 53:4),
"lamb that is led to the slaughter" (Is 53:7), "offering for sin" (Is 53:10),
"bear" (Is 53:11, 12). The sacrificial character of the text is particularly evident with the reference to the guilt offering in Isaiah 53:10. We have a clear
indication that the guilt offering described in Leviticus finds its fulfillment in
Jesus Christ. All the elements of a substitutionary atonement are here.[60] All
without exception have sinned (Is 53:6). Jesus has taken the punishment deserved by sinners. He became a guilt offering, taking the punishment sinners
deserve (Is 53:10). He took our griefs and sorrows upon himself (Is 53:4).
He was pierced and crushed for our transgressions and iniquities (Is 53:5).
"The LORD has laid on him the iniquity of us all" (Is 53:6). He was cut off for
the transgression of the people, and they deserved such punishment rather
than he (Is 53:8). He bears their iniquities and is the means of their justification (Is 53:11). He was numbered with the transgressors, bore their sins
and intercedes specially for them (Is 53:12). Isaiah 53 is without doubt the
most important messianic text in the Old Testament: here the suffering of
the Messiah is clearly prophesied. The passage also teaches clearly and often
that Christ Jesus died in place of sinners, taking their penalty on himself. We
also see in verse 10 that it was God's will to crush him.[61] It was the will of
God for Christ to die in the place of sinners.[62] In his death Christ satisfied
the wrath of God.[63]

---

[60]In support of substitution, see Rodriguez, "Substitution in the Hebrew Cultus," pp. 276-301;
J. Alec Motyer, *The Prophecy of Isaiah* (Downers Grove, Ill.: InterVarsity Press, 1993), pp. 429-
43; John N. Oswalt, *The Book of Isaiah: Chapters 40-66,* New International Commentary on
the Old Testament (Grand Rapids: Eerdmans, 1998), pp. 385-408; Groves, "Atonement in Isaiah 53," pp. 61-89.

[61]Weaver rejects substitution because it insists that God satisfies God in the atonement (*Nonviolent Atonement,* pp. 72-74). I would argue that Isaiah 53 teaches that God, because of his
great love, sent Jesus to satisfy his own wrath, and that Jesus gladly submitted himself to his
Father's will and found it to be his greatest joy (cf. Heb 12:2). For the notion that Isaiah 53
teaches that God willed and planned Jesus' suffering, see Tidball, *Message of the Cross,* p. 106.

[62]Fiddes tries to wriggle out of what the Scriptures say about God directly planning the death
of Jesus. Note that he admits that Scripture does portray God as if he were the cause behind
the death of Christ (*Christian Idea of Atonement,* p. 92), but he dances away from the plain
meaning of the text to sustain his theory. For God's planning of Jesus' crucifixion, see Acts
2:23; 3:18; 4:27-28.

[63]Fiddes rejects the idea that God satisfied himself, but he operates by way of assertion rather
than argument (ibid., p. 70), thinking that the main effect must be on humans.

Romans 3:21-26 is a key text on penal substitution.[64] This paragraph functions as the hinge for the letter to the Romans and is one of the most important, if not the most important, in the letter. The placement of the text in the letter should be observed. Paul has finished arguing that all without exception sin and deserve judgment (Rom 1:18—3:20). He summarizes this truth in Rom 3:23: "For all have sinned and fall short of the glory of God." God demands perfect obedience, and all fall short of his standard. How then will people become right with God? Paul argues in Rom 3:21-22 that a right relation with God is not obtained by keeping the law, but through faith in Jesus Christ. All people who trust in Christ are justified by God because of the redemption accomplished by Christ Jesus (Rom 3:24).[65]

Romans 3:25-26 is of particular importance for our subject. God set forth Christ as a propitiatory sacrifice by virtue of Jesus' bloody death. The terms *hilasterion* and *haima* point back to the Old Testament cultus and sacrificial system. Discussion has centered on the meaning of the term *hilasterion*, whether it should be rendered expiation or propitiation. I would argue that those who defend the notion of propitiation have the better argument, for the term includes the sense of the averting of God's wrath—the appeasement or satisfaction of his righteousness. To be more precise the term includes *both* notions, expiation *and* propitiation.[66] This fits beautifully with Romans 1:18, where the wrath of God against sin is announced, and Romans 2:5, where the final judgment is described as the day of God's wrath. The line of argument in Romans 1:18—3:20 provokes us to ask how God's wrath can be averted. We discover in Romans 3:25 that God's wrath has been satisfied or appeased in the death of Christ.

---

[64]See the convincing exposition of Carson, "Atonement in Romans 3:21-26," pp. 119-39. Hengel demonstrates that the offering of sacrifices to avert the wrath of the gods was common in the Greco-Roman world (*Atonement*, pp. 1-32). Hence, Gentile readers would have no difficulty understanding the concept of a substitutionary atonement (so ibid., p. 32). The biblical view of the atonement, of course, corrects the pagan notions present in the Greco-Roman world, and hence cannot be identified with them in every respect. See Beckwith, "Sacrifice in the World of the New Testament," p. 106.

[65]Blocher correctly notes that the different "languages" of ransom and sacrifice are closely related to one another and therefore should not be segregated too strictly ("Sacrifice of Jesus Christ," p. 30).

[66]See Carson, "Atonement in Romans 3:21-26," p. 130; J. Ramsey Michaels, "Atonement in John's Gospel and Epistles: 'The Lamb of God Who Takes Away the Sin of the World,' " in *The Glory of the Atonement*, ed. Charles E. Hill and Frank A. James III (Downers Grove, Ill.: InterVarsity Press, 2004), pp. 114-15. For the importance of propitiation in biblical theology, see the very helpful exposition of Stott, *Cross of Christ*, pp. 111-32.

The words following "propitiation" in Romans 3:25 substantiate the inter-pretation offered here.[67] Paul explains that Christ was set forth as a propitia-tory sacrifice to demonstrate God's righteousness. The context reveals that by "righteousness" Paul refers to God's holiness or justice, for Paul immediately refers to the sins God passed over in previous eras. By passing over sins Paul means that sins committed previously in history did not receive the full pun-ishment deserved. Hence, they call into question God's justice or holiness, for how can a holy God tolerate sin without imposing immediate and full pun-ishment? Modern people tend to ask, "How can God send anyone to hell?" Paul asks a completely different question because he thinks theocentrically and not anthropocentrically. He asks how God can refrain from punishing people immediately and fully. His answer is that God looked ahead to the cross of Christ, where his wrath would be appeased and justice would be sat-isfied. Christ as the substitute would absorb the full payment for sin.

This interpretation is confirmed by Romans 3:26: "It was to show his right-eousness at the present time, so that he might be just and the justifier of the one who has faith in Jesus."[68] Christ's death as a propitiatory sacrifice, Paul repeats, demonstrates God's holiness and justice at the present juncture of salvation history. Thereby God is both "just and the justifier" of those who put their faith in Christ. God's justice is satisfied because Christ bore the full payment for sin. But God is also the justifier because on the basis of the cross of Christ sinners receive forgiveness through faith in Jesus. In the cross of Christ the justice and mercy of God meet. God's holiness is satisfied by Christ's bearing the penalty of sin, and God's saving activity is realized in the lives of those who trust in Christ.

Some object that retribution cannot be in view here, for the focus is on personal relationships rather than retribution. But personal relationships and retribution are not at odds with one another.[69] God's justice is not an at-tribute that can be separated from his person. The question about God's jus-

---

[67]Gathercole argues that the notion of propitiation should be anchored in the flow of thought of Rom 1—3 rather than the meaning of *hilastērion* ("Cross and Substitutionary Atonement," p. 161). I am inclined to think that *hilastērion* includes the notion of propitiation, but Gather-cole is correct in saying that penal substitution in Rom 1—3 doesn't depend solely on *hilastērion*. He also rightly argues that the common notion in Scripture that Christ died for our sins supports penal substitution (ibid., pp. 159-62).

[68]For further support of the interpretation offered here and interaction with the literature, see Thomas R. Schreiner, *Romans,* Baker Exegetical Commentary on the New Testament (Grand Rapids: Baker, 1998), pp. 176-99.

[69]Tidball, *Message of the Cross,* pp. 190-92.

tice that Paul answers here would not even be raised in the therapeutic, exemplary or Christus Victor views of the atonement.

The argument of Galatians 3:10-14 is remarkably similar to that of Romans 3:21-26. Galatians 3:10 teaches that God's curse comes upon all those who fail to keep God's law perfectly. How can such a curse be removed? Not by Christ's good example. Not merely by Christ defeating demonic powers. Not merely by God healing our damaged souls. Galatians 3:13 answers the question posed: "Christ redeemed us from the curse of the law by becoming a curse for us—for it is written, 'Cursed is everyone who is hanged on a tree.'"[70] The curse we deserve was borne by Christ.[71] He became our substitute.[72] The sinless One took upon himself the curse of God that weighed us down.[73] He freed us from God's curse "by becoming a curse for us."[74] Could substitution be expressed any more clearly? Christ took upon himself the curse that we deserve. He paid our penalty. He saved us from consequences of our sin.

Such a teaching is not an isolated theme in Paul. We find it especially in

---

[70]The preposition *hyper* denotes substitution here. Cf. the discussion of this preposition by Daniel B. Wallace, *Greek Grammar Beyond the Basics* (Grand Rapids: Zondervan, 1996), pp. 383-89.

[71]Contra F. F. Bruce it seems that the curse comes from God himself (*The Epistle to the Galatians,* New International Commentary on the New Testament [Grand Rapids: Eerdmans, 1982], pp. 165-66). See James D. G. Dunn, *The Epistle to the Galatians,* Black's New Testament Commentary (Peabody, Mass.: Hendrickson, 1993), p. 177; Morris, *Apostolic Preaching of the Cross,* pp. 57-58.

[72]For a powerful argument supporting substitution, see Timothy George, *Galatians,* New American Commentary (Nashville: Broadman & Holman, 1994), pp. 240-42. Also supporting a reference to substitution, Hans Dieter Betz, *Galatians,* Hermeneia (Philadelphia: Fortress, 1979), p. 151; Bruce, *Galatians,* p. 166; Morris, *Apostolic Preaching of the Cross,* pp. 56-59. Frank J. Matera summarizes Paul's argument concisely, "This Law could not bring us life because it operates on the principles of doing, not on the principle of Christ-faith, and no one perfectly fulfills the Law. The Christ in whom we believe, however, freed us from the Law's curse by assuming the curse of the Law for us" (*Galatians,* Sacra Pagina [Collegeville, Minn.: Liturgical Press, 1992], p. 124).

[73]Weaver argues that neither Gal 3:13 nor 2 Cor 5:21 teach that God acted directly in making Jesus a curse or sin (*Nonviolent Atonement,* p. 57). Gal 3:13 is debatable, but 2 Cor 5:21 explicitly says that God made Christ to be sin on our behalf. Furthermore, Is 53:10 says that "it was the will of the Lord to crush him," and thus it is clear that it was *God's* design that Christ die for sinners. Weaver also maintains that we must reject the idea that God's will was accomplished in the death of Jesus (ibid., p. 56), but Acts 4:27-28 demonstrates that Weaver is incorrect, for there we are told that the evil hatched and carried out by Pilate, Herod and the leaders of Israel was predestined by God (cf. Acts 2:23). The biblical writers hold in tension predestination with the responsibility of human beings for evil actions.

[74]Morris correctly argues that the preposition *hyper* denotes substitution here (*Apostolic Preaching of the Cross,* pp. 62-63).

theologically rich texts where the significance of Christ's death for our salvation is explained (cf. Rom 3:21-26; Gal 3:10-14). Surely 2 Corinthians 5:14-21 falls into this category as well. The saving and reconciling work of Christ is celebrated in these verses. Paul concludes with 2 Corinthians 5:21: "For our sake he made him to be sin who knew no sin, so that in him we might become the righteousness of God." The principle of substitution is again evident in this verse. Christ who was sinless was made to be sin on the cross; so the Father poured out on him the punishment and wrath we deserve.[75] God's holiness is satisfied in the cross of Christ so that our sins may now be forgiven. This has often been called "the great exchange." We receive God's forgiveness and righteousness, and Christ suffers in our stead and receives our punishment.

It might be objected that substitution is not taught by Jesus himself. But Mark 10:45 is a clear statement of substitution: "Even the Son of Man came not to be served but to serve, and to give his life as a ransom for many" (cf. Mt 20:28). The preposition *anti* ("for") often denotes "in place of" (Mt 17:27; Lk 11:11; Rom 12:17; 1 Cor 11:15), and it most naturally has that meaning here.[76] Christ in his death suffered in the place of others.[77] Furthermore, the text teaches penal substitution since Christ's death is described as a ransom *(lytron)*.[78] The term *ransom* indicates that Christ by his death paid the price

---

[75]Following a long line of interpreters Ralph P. Martin thinks the idea is that Christ was made a sin offering, drawing on Is 53:10 (*2 Corinthians,* Word Biblical Commentary [Waco, Tex.: Word, 1986], pp. 140, 157). He also maintains that substitution is in view in a qualified way (ibid., pp. 143-45). David E. Garland argues that reference to a sin offering is unlikely (*2 Corinthians,* New American Commentary [Nashville: Broadman & Holman, 1999], pp. 300-301), for such a view requires two different meanings for the word *sin* in the verse, and we would expect verbs like *offer* or *present,* which are typically associated with Old Testament sacrifices. Garland thinks the point is that Jesus was treated as a sinner on the cross just as he was cursed according to Gal 3:13. In any case, Garland also argues that substitution is in view in the text (ibid., pp. 301-2). For the substitutionary character of Christ's sacrifice in 2 Cor 5:21, see also Scott Hafemann, *2 Corinthians,* NIV Application Commentary (Grand Rapids: Zondervan, 2000), pp. 247-48.

[76]A. T. Robertson, *A Grammar of the Greek New Testament in the Light of Historical Research* (Nashville: Broadman, 1934), p. 573; Wallace, *Greek Grammar,* pp. 365-67.

[77]See also William L. Lane, *The Gospel According to Mark,* New International Commentary of the New Testament (Grand Rapids: Eerdmans, 1974), pp. 383-84; Robert H. Gundry, *Mark* (Grand Rapids: Eerdmans, 1993), pp. 590-91; Seyoon Kim, *The Son of Man as the Son of God* (Grand Rapids: Eerdmans, 1985), pp. 58-59. Donald A. Hagner concurs in seeing substitution in the parallel text in Mt 20:28 (*Matthew 14-28* [Dallas: Word, 1995], p. 583). See also Morris, *Apostolic Preaching of the Cross,* pp. 33-38.

[78]See the discussion in Peter G. Bolt, *The Cross from a Distance* (Downers Grove, Ill.: InterVarsity Press, 2004), p. 71-75.

necessary to liberate sinners from the dominion of sin.[79] By his death he freed us from the power of sin and death.[80] He paid the price that we owed, so that we might go free.[81] This fits with the narrative, for Jesus as a human being shrinks from taking the cup because the cup symbolizes the taking of God's wrath upon himself (Mk 14:36). The Old Testament background clarifies that the cup represents God's judgments poured out on the nations (cf. Is 51:17-22).[82] Furthermore, Peter Bolt has insightfully demonstrated that being handed over to human hands or the hands of sinners (Mk 9:31; 14:41) indicates that Jesus was handed over to God's wrath, for in the Old Testament those who were handed over to others were delivered over because they stood under God's wrath.[83] And it is quite clear that Jesus is handed over to God's wrath for the sake of the sins of his people, not his own sins. We should also observe that the teaching of the Lord's Supper supports substitution. The body and blood of Jesus represent his body that is broken for sinners and his blood that is shed for sinners (cf. Mt 26:26-29; Mk 14:22-25; Lk 22:19-20; 1 Cor 11:23-26).[84] I have already noted that Jesus' being handed over to the nations was an indication that he was under God's wrath. So too the darkness that came upon the land symbolized that Jesus stood under God's judgment (Mk 13:24), as the darkness in Egypt (Ex 10:21-22) and on the day of the Lord (Is 13:10; Joel 2:2, 31; 3:14-15; Amos 5:18, 20; Zeph 1:14-15) represented God's judgment.[85] In the same way, Jesus' cry that God had

---

[79]Peter M. Head observes that the term *lytron* refers to money paid as ransom for release of war prisoners or slaves ("The Self-Offering and Death of Christ as a Sacrifice in the Gospels and the Acts of the Apostles," in *Sacrifice in the Bible,* ed. Roger T. Beckwith and Martin J. Selman [Grand Rapids: Baker, 1995], p. 113). He points out that the substitutionary character of the ransom is clear also from Josephus, *Antiquities* 14.107.

[80]Head concludes that Mk 10:45 is "an important pointer to Mark's understanding of Jesus' death as a substitutionary ransom for many. It is difficult to conceive how such an idea can be entirely divorced from an association with sacrificial categories" ("Self-Offering and Death of Christ," p. 114).

[81]Gathercole demonstrates from the Old Testament (Ex 21: 23-24, 28-30; 30:12) that the notion of the ransom hearkens back to judicial contexts in which the payment of a price (a ransom), giving, and one's own life are brought together, demonstrating that Jesus gave his own life as the payment or ransom for human sin ("Cross and Substitutionary Atonement," pp. 163-64).

[82]Head, "Self-Offering and Death of Christ," p. 113; Bolt, *Cross from a Distance,* pp. 66-67.

[83]See Bolt, *Cross from a Distance,* pp. 52-54, 56-58. For some relevant Old Testament texts noted by Bolt, see Lev 26:25; Judg 16:23-24; Ezra 9:7; Ps 41:2; 106:41.

[84]Peter Stuhlmacher says, "In the cup saying, when Jesus speaks of his blood shed for the many, he has in mind his impending violent death and the substitutionary yielding up of his life 'for the many' contained in it" (*Jesus of Nazareth: Christ of Faith,* trans. S. Schatzmann [Peabody, Mass.: Hendrickson, 1993], p. 72). Cf. Bolt, *Cross from a Distance,* p. 105.

[85]See Bolt, *Cross from a Distance,* pp. 125-26.

forsaken him (Mk 15:34) and the mocking he receives confirm that he experienced the wrath of God.[86]

I should note here that the benefit of Jesus' death for sinners is often communicated by the preposition *for* (*hyper;* see e.g., Lk 22:19-20; Jn 6:51; 10:11, 15; 11:50-52; Rom 5:8; 1 Cor 11:24; 2 Cor 5:14-15, 21; Gal 3:13; 1 Pet 3:18). The preposition conveys the benefit that accrues to sinners because of Christ's death. But *how* does Jesus benefit sinners? He benefits them by taking the punishment and guilt they deserve, by dying in their place.

The substitutionary character of Christ's death is also proclaimed in Johannine literature.[87] Jesus is God's sacrificial "Lamb of God, who takes away the sin of the world" (Jn 1:29).[88] The prophetic words of Caiaphas demonstrate that John understood Jesus to die on behalf of and in place of the people (Jn 11:49-52). We learn from these two texts that Jesus was a sacrificial lamb, dying in the stead of his people. His flesh and blood constitute the basis of forgiveness of sins that are necessary for eternal life (Jn 6:51-59).[89] Furthermore, his death was propitiatory (1 Jn 2:2; 4:10). God's wrath was satisfied and appeased, so that forgiveness of sins was accomplished for his people.[90]

Space does not permit a full exposition of all the texts that teach substitutionary atonement, but two texts from 1 Peter should be noted.[91] "He

---

[86]Ibid., pp. 127-36.

[87]Cf. George L. Carey, "The Lamb of God and Atonement Theories," *Tyndale Bulletin* 32 (1981): 97-122; Bruce H. Grigsby, "The Cross as an Expiatory Sacrifice in the Fourth Gospel," *Journal for the Study of the New Testament* 15 (1982): 51-80.

[88]Some scholars argue that the notion of bearing away sins by an atoning death is not present here (Michaels, "Atonement in John's Gospel and Epistles," pp. 107-8). But Thielman suggests that John has Is 53:7 particularly in mind ("Atonement"). Charles E. Hill thinks both Is 53:7 and the Passover lamb are antecedents, and raises questions about the likelihood of the notion of a conquering apocalyptic lamb being in view ("Atonement in the Apocalypse of John: 'A Lamb Standing as if Slain," in *The Glory of the Atonement,* ed. Charles E. Hill and Frank A. James III [Downers Grove, Ill.: InterVarsity Press, 2004], pp. 196-99).

[89]D. A. Carson remarks that John conceived of Jesus' death as substitutionary in each of these texts (*The Gospel According to John,* Pillar New Testament Commentary [Grand Rapids: Eerdmans, 1991], pp. 295, 422). The notion of Jesus laying down his life for *(hyper)* his sheep (Jn 10:11, 15) or for *(hyper)* his friends (Jn 15:13) also supports substitution (see Thielman, "Atonement").

[90]In defense of this view, see Michaels, who correctly argues that both propitiation and expiation are in mind in these verses ("Atonement in John's Gospel and Epistles," pp. 114-16).

[91]For an interpretation of these texts in context and an interaction with alternate interpretations, see Thomas R. Schreiner, *1-2 Peter, Jude,* New American Commentary (Nashville: Broadman & Holman, 2003), pp. 144-46, 180-83.

[Christ] himself bore our sins in his body on the tree, that we might die to sin and live to righteousness. By his wounds you have been healed" (1 Pet 2:24). This section of 1 Peter 2 is suffused with allusions to Isaiah 53, which itself teaches us about Christ's death in place of sinners. Here Peter emphasizes that Christ on the cross bore our sins, that his suffering was the pathway to our healing, and here healing focuses on forgiveness of sins and a renewed relationship with God.[92] Surely this wording means that he died in our place, that he bore our punishment, that his death is the pathway to our life. First Peter 3:18 teaches the same truth: "For Christ also suffered once for sins, the righteous for the unrighteous, that he might bring us to God." Christ died in our place. As the righteous and sinless One he suffered for the sins of the unrighteous. He did this to provide access and entrance into God's presence.

Concluding Reflections

Penal substitution is the anchor and heart of the atonement, for it reminds us that God himself is central in the universe. What God has accomplished in Jesus Christ displays both the justice and love of God because God's holiness is vindicated in the cross, while at the same time his love is displayed in the willing and glad sacrifice of his Son. Penal substitution is not all that needs to be said about the atonement, but it is the anchor of all other theories of the atonement precisely because of its God-centered focus. As human beings we are prone to think first and foremost about ourselves, but Christ's propitiatory death points us to God's beautiful and awesome holiness, and his matchless saving love. The most important being in the universe is God, and penal substitution lifts our gaze from ourselves to God himself.

Yet it must also be said that penal substitution answers the most important question of human existence: How can human beings enjoy a right relationship with God? It explains how God as the holy and righteous judge can forgive sinners who have personally rebelled against their sovereign Lord. The fundamental character of penal substitution is supported by at least three strands of evidence: (1) the emphasis on human sin and guilt in Scripture, (2) the theme that God judges retributively sinners who disobey him and flout his law, and (3) the central texts in both the New Testament

---

[92]Thielman observes that the reference to the tree alludes to Deut 21:23 and supports substitution ("Atonement").

and the Old Testament that emphasize that sacrifice is necessary for the forgiveness of sins. We can confidently say that the texts in view are some of
the most important in Scripture, whether we think of the Day of Atonement
in Leviticus 16 or Christ's sacrifice as explained in John 1:29 and 11:51-52,
Galatians 3:10-14, Romans 3:21-26, 2 Corinthians 5:21, 1 Peter 2:21-25 and
3:18, and 1 John 2:2 and 4:10.

Does penal substitution matter? If what I have argued in this essay is correct, Christ's dying in our place is the only way we can be right with God.[93]
His death is the only means by which we avert God's holy and just wrath
on the day of judgment. The retribution we deserved was poured out on
Christ instead of us. In penal substitution, then, the mercy and justice of God
meet. God satisfies his perfect justice and holiness by punishing his Son—
Jesus the Christ. At the same time, he extends mercy to sinners by forgiving
the sins of those who trust in Christ. Penal substitution explains how God
remains God in forgiving us of our sins, for God would deny his very being
as God if he forgave us and violated his justice and holiness. In addition,
penal substitution emphasizes God's objective work *for* us as the basis for
his subjective work *in* us. Sinclair Ferguson correctly remarks that in our ex-
periential and subjective age we are prone to focus on God's work *in* us and
slight God's work *for* us. The latter is always the ground for the former, so
that the stress remains on what God has accomplished for us instead of our
response to him.[94]

Some object strenuously to the notion that God sent Christ to satisfy his
own wrath.[95] They worry that it pits God against Christ; thus Christ becomes
the abused victim and God the abusive and bloodthirsty Father who demands the death of his Son. Two things should be said in reply.[96] First, it is
contrary to the Scriptures to think of God as angry and Christ as loving, as

---

[93]Gathercole argues that assurance is integral to the gospel and tied to penal substitution
("Cross and Substitutionary Atonement," p. 153).

[94]Sinclair B. Ferguson, "Preaching the Atonement," in *The Glory of the Atonement*, ed.
Charles E. Hill and Frank A. James III (Downers Grove, Ill.: InterVarsity Press, 2004), pp.
431-32.

[95]We should be reminded when considering such objections that our task in doing Christian
theology is *not* to determine whether what is taught in Scripture conforms to our moral notions. Rather, we are to conform our moral worldview to the Scriptures because our minds
are also fallen.

[96]Christina A. Baxter rightly argues that many of the objections raised against penal substitution
are unpersuasive or are based on misunderstandings ("The Cursed Beloved: A Reconsidera-
tion of Penal Substitution," in *Atonement Today*, ed. John Goldingay (London: SPCK, 1995),
pp. 54-72.

if they were divided from one another.[97] I am not denying that God is angry, but the Scripture also teaches that God sent his Son because of his great love for sinners (Jn 3:16; Rom 5:6-10; 8:32; 1 Jn 4:10).[98] We must beware of simplistic and one-sided depictions of the biblical truth about God. Second, God did not compel Christ to die for sinners against his will. The Son gladly gave his life for sinners. It was his delight to do the will of God (Heb 10:5-10), and he surrendered his life voluntarily (Jn 10:18).

Some still object that the picture drawn here is inconceivable because it says that God sent Christ in his love, and that Christ willingly gave his life to satisfy the Father's anger (Eph 5:2; Heb 10:7, 9; 12:2).[99] The Father, some might say, cannot be filled with both love and wrath at the same time. The objection betrays a rationalistic worldview that restricts God to the parameters of human thinking. I am not claiming that my view is either irrational or contradictory. There is no inherent contradiction in the claim that God is both loving and wrathful at the same time. A contradiction only exists when we affirm A and non-A at the same time and in the same way. At the cross God's love is directed to the person of his Son, but his wrath is poured out on his Son insofar as he is bearing the weight of sin.[100] The previous observation does not exhaust the complexity and mystery of the person of God; he surpasses our understanding and comprehension.[101] Moreover, the doctrine of the Trinity forbids us from separating the persons of the Trinity too rigidly from one another, though, of course, there is also the danger of going to the other extreme and minimizing the dis-

---

[97]See Stott, *Cross of Christ,* pp. 150-51.

[98]See John Murray, *Redemption Accomplished and Applied* (Grand Rapids: Eerdmans, 1955), pp. 1-2; Peterson, "Atonement in the New Testament," pp. 43-45.

[99]The voluntary nature of Christ's sacrifice is brought out well by Colin E. Gunton, though he does not endorse the view of penal substitution defended here (*The Actuality of the Atonement* [Grand Rapids: Eerdmans, 1989], pp. 124-25).

[100]My thanks to Justin Taylor for this clarification.

[101]This theme is brought out well by Packer, "What Did the Cross Achieve?" pp. 86-94. Timothy George argues that Luther feared that human reason would domesticate Scripture and hence he called reason a "whore," but in doing so Luther was not embracing irrationalism but emphasizing that theology must conform to divine revelation and that the Scriptures rather than human reason must have priority ("The Atonement in Martin Luther's Theology," in *The Glory of the Atonement,* ed. Charles E. Hill and Frank A. James III [Downers Grove, Ill.: InterVarsity Press, 2004], pp. 269-70, 272). George also demonstrates that Luther clearly espoused a substitutionary atonement (ibid., pp. 263-78). Calvin also taught penal substitution, see Henri Blocher, "The Atonement in John Calvin's Theology," in *The Glory of the Atonement,* ed. Charles E. Hill and Frank A. James III (Downers Grove, Ill.: InterVarsity Press, 2004), pp. 279-303.

tinctions between the Father, the Son and the Spirit.[102]

Still, we must confess that ultimately the teaching on the atonement involves mystery, and no human analogy captures the dynamic of the Father sending his Son to die for our salvation. Some object that *mystery* is simply another term for nonsense, but such an objection is mistaken. There is the danger of crying out "mystery" before we explore adequately the entirety of the evidence. The appeal to mystery can be the lazy way out, and it can be used as an excuse to short-circuit our thinking. Our primary responsibility as Christians, however, is to listen and yield to the teaching of the biblical text. In some instances what Scripture teaches exceeds our human comprehension.

A common complaint is that penal substitution is sundered from ethics. J. I. Packer demonstrates, however, that Christ's atoning work is the foundation of faith, hope and love.[103] Surely faith, hope and love are eminently practical and relate to our daily lives as Christian disciples! It is also instructive that some of the texts that teach most clearly the substitutionary atonement of Christ also emphasize that we must follow Jesus as an example (cf. Mk 10:31-45; Jn 13:1-17; 1 Pet 2:21-25), and that our hearts should respond in love to the greatness of his sacrifice (cf. 1 Jn 3:16-18; 4:7-11).[104] The intermingling of exemplary and substitutionary themes suggest that New Testament authors believed that the substitutionary death of Christ, though it alone atoned for sin, also functioned as an example for believers. The love of God expressed in the reconciling and substitutionary work of Christ should motivate believers to live for Christ instead of themselves (2 Cor 5:15). Further, I'm not arguing that penal substitution is all that needs to be taught about the Christian life. Judicial and participatory themes, for example, in Pauline theology should not be separated from one another. Union with Christ and life in the Spirit are vital themes in Pauline theology and

---

[102]Cf. Bruce L. McCormack, "The Ontological Presuppositions of Barth's Doctrine of the Atonement," in *The Glory of the Atonement*, ed. Charles E. Hill and Frank A. James III (Downers Grove, Ill.: InterVarsity Press, 2004), pp. 364-66. McCormack argues that there is a sense, then, in which the Father also suffered in the death of the Son, for the Father is not only the subject of the action but also the object because what the Son experiences is not hermetically sealed from the Father.

[103]J. I. Packer, "The Atonement in the Life of the Christian," in *The Glory of the Atonement*, ed. Charles E. Hill and Frank A. James III (Downers Grove, Ill.: InterVarsity Press, 2004), pp. 417-25.

[104]This observation was pointed out to me by James Agan privately after I gave a lecture on the substitutionary atonement at Erskine Theological Seminary in Due West, South Carolina, on April 9, 2003.

foundational for ethics, but it is not the burden of this essay to explore every facet of biblical theology.

It is doubtless true that some have abused the teaching on penal substitution and separated it from a life of discipleship. The biblical teaching on God's grace can be abused as Paul warned long ago (Rom 6:1-23). As believers our focus is not to be on penal substitution but Jesus Christ himself as the crucified and risen One. And yet we should also note that Christ's substitutionary sacrifice has inspired countless hymns of praise and wonder for God's grace. And genuine praise and thanksgiving leads to a transformed life. True worship is never separated from ethics but is the foundation for it. Those who are stunned by God's gracious gift in Christ live in a radically different way. Do some doubt it? I myself have experienced it. Further, I have seen the same transformation in the lives of many believers who say the foundation of their changed life is Christ's substitutionary work. The proof of the pudding is in the eating, and the testimony of Scripture and the saints throughout history is that the substitutionary death of Christ leads to praise and to a transformed life.

I close with a recent song of praise that I have sung often with other believers. I have sensed how this truth has strengthened, comforted and empowered believers in worship. It is a powerful testimony to the transforming power of penal substitution, for true worship can never be separated from actions. Read the words and worship!

"Before the Throne of God Above"

Before the throne of God above
I have a strong, a perfect plea.
A great High Priest whose name is Love
Who ever lives and pleads for me.
My name is graven on His hands,
My name is written on His heart.
I know that while in Heaven He stands
No tongue can bid me thence depart.

When Satan tempts me to despair
And tells me of the guilt within,
Upward I look and see Him there

Who made an end to all my sin.
Because the sinless Savior died
My sinful soul is counted free;
For God the just is satisfied
To look on Him and pardon me.

Behold Him there! The risen Lamb,
My perfect, spotless righteousness;
The great unchangeable, I AM,
The King of glory and of grace!
One with Himself I cannot die.
My soul is purchased with His blood,
My life is hid with Christ on high,
With Christ, my Savior and my God![105]

---

[105]"Before the Throne," lyrics by Charitie Less Bancroft, 1863.

Christus Victor Response

GREGORY A. BOYD

I applaud Tom Schreiner's countercultural emphasis on God's holiness, on the severity of human sinfulness and on the central importance of Christ's substitutionary death. Moreover, I deeply respect his clear commitment to courageously adhere to Scripture, regardless of how counterintuitive and otherwise problematic his interpretation of its teachings may strike contemporary people. Yet I have significant reservations about certain aspects of Schreiner's penal substitution perspective.

First and most fundamentally, while Schreiner repeatedly asserts that the penal substitution motif of the atonement is the "foundation," "heart" and "soul" of everything else Scripture says about the significance of Jesus' life and death, he offers us little reason to accept this claim. In fact, after reading his essay I confess I remain unclear even as to how the penal substitution motif can be integrated with (let alone central to) most other aspects of Jesus' life.

For example, Schreiner asserts that the resurrection is necessary for us to be forgiven and thus is part of the penal substitutionary dimension of Christ's work. Unfortunately, Schreiner nowhere explains why this is so. An explanation would seem to be called for, however, for if the main problem needing to be addressed by Christ was that God's wrath needed to be appeased, and if the main solution to this problem consisted of God slaying his Son on the cross, one naturally wonders what could possibly be left to be done once this is completed. God may (and does) have other reasons for raising Jesus from the dead, but what reason could he have that would be *penal* in nature?

Beyond this we have to wonder how the penal substitution motif is foundational to our understanding of Jesus' radically countercultural life and, therefore, to his lifelong nonviolent opposition to the powers. And how is the penal substitution motif foundational to our understanding of Jesus' various kingdom teachings or his healing and exorcism ministry? Far from being foundational to every other aspect of Jesus' life and ministry, I frankly struggle to see how it's even relevant to any other aspect of Jesus' life and ministry. Thus, as an overarching motif within which all other aspects of Jesus' life and ministry can be best understood, it seems to me the penal substitution view is significantly inferior to the Christus Victor view which, as I suggested in my essay, is able to weave all aspects of Jesus' incarnation, life, ministry, death and resurrection together under one theme (and this in concert with the warfare motif that runs through Scripture).

Now, this criticism holds even if we grant Schreiner's penal interpretation of Christ's substitutionary death (which some adherents of the Christus Victor view have in fact done).[1] But, I shall now argue, the Christus Victor model of the atonement offers a much more compelling way of understanding the substitutionary dimension of Christ's ministry. One illuminating way to capture the heart of the Christus Victor view and relate it to the penal substitution view is by recalling a scene from C. S. Lewis's masterpiece (recently turned Hollywood movie) *The Lion, the Witch and the Wardrobe*.

As many readers will undoubtedly recall, an evil witch had illegitimately seized control of Narnia and brought it under a curse. At one point in Lewis's tale this wicked witch confronts Aslan—Narnia's rightful ruler—about the fate of a certain young man named Edmund. This irksome whiner had allowed himself to be taken captive by the Queen and had then maliciously betrayed his brother and two sisters. He had been rescued, however, and was now under Aslan's care. "You . . . know the Magic which the Emperor put into Narnia at the very beginning," the wicked witch says to Aslan. "You know that every traitor belongs to me as my lawful prey and that for every treachery I have a right to a kill. And so," the witch continues, "that human creature is mine. His life is forfeit to me. His blood is my property."

Aslan deeply loves Edmund and wants to protect him, but he cannot dispute the witch's legal claim. The Deep Magic set in place at the beginning of Narnia indeed stipulates that traitors become prey for this malevolent

---

[1]For example, while the Christus Victor view was the dominant understanding of the atonement for most early Anabaptists, some combined this with a penal substitutionary view. See Thomas Finger, *A Contemporary Anabaptist Theology* (Downers Grove, Ill.: InterVarsity Press, 2004), pp. 331-50. It should perhaps be added that historically almost all advocates of the Christus Victor model of the atonement have accepted, if not emphasized, the substitutionary dimension of Jesus' death. But they have not usually interpreted this substitution in *penal* terms.

Queen. Edmund is spared, however, because Aslan offers up his own life to the witch in Edmund's place. Since the Lion is obviously a much greater prize than Edmund, and since (she thinks) killing "the great Lion" would allow her finally to rule Narnia without opposition, she accepts Aslan's offer.

Later that night a lonely Aslan makes his way to the enemy's camp. The witch's minions mock and torture him, and then the witch gets her "kill." Aslan is slain on the Stone Table where the justice of the Deep Magic is always carried out. But the story is not over, for after a brief time of great mourning on the part of Edmund's two sisters, Aslan rises from the dead, splitting the Stone Table in two. Aslan then explains the meaning of what happened to the two surprised and overjoyed girls:

> Though the Witch knew the Deep Magic, there is a magic deeper still which she did not know. Her knowledge goes back only to the dawn of time. But if she could have looked a little further back, into the stillness and the darkness before Time dawned, she would have read there a different incantation. She would have known that when a willing victim who had committed no treachery was killed in a traitor's stead, the Table would crack and Death itself would start working backwards.

Tapping into the deepest and oldest magic there is, the power of self-sacrificial love, Aslan overcomes death, overturns the condemning justice of the law that the witch holds against Edmund, and leads his disciples in victory over the dreadful witch and her army, thereby freeing the inhabitants of her diabolical rule once and for all.[2]

This is a marvelous parable of the Christus Victor understanding of Christ's substitutionary role in redeeming humanity, and it perfectly illustrates the ways that it agrees and disagrees with the penal substitution understanding. Both Schreiner and Lewis agree there exists Deep Magic (the law), rooted in the Emperor's (God's) holy character, that is very good in and of itself (e.g., Rom. 7:12) and that cannot simply be waved aside (e.g., Heb 9:22). Both Lewis and Schreiner agree that, for this reason, only the innocent Aslan can save a guilty soul like Edmund from being justly executed and that he must do so by dying in his place.

For this reason both views can describe the significance of Aslan's action on behalf of Edmund using Scripture's substitutionary terminology. For ex-

---

[2]C. S. Lewis, *The Chronicles of Narnia* (1950; reprint, New York: Harper Collins, 2001), pp. 175-91.

ample, both views could affirm that Aslan's body was broken and that his blood was poured out (cf. Mt 26:26-29; 1 Cor 11:23-26) in order to ransom Edmund (cf. Mt 20:28; Mk 10:45). Both views could further affirm that Aslan offered himself up as an unblemished sacrifice in Edmund's place (cf. Is 53:10; Heb 9:14), that he bore Edmund's sin and punishment (cf. Is 53:4-6, 11-12; 2 Cor 5:21), suffered the curse required by deep magic that hung over Edmund's head (cf. Gal 3:13), and satisfied and set aside the just requirements of deep magic that would have had Edmund slain (cf. Rom 3:25; Col 2:14-15).

In fact, if we were to make Lewis's tale a bit more explicitly trinitarian by inserting into it the belief, shared by both views, that everything Aslan and the witch did fit into the Emperor's plan to save Edmund (cf. Acts 2:23; 4:27-28), we could find yet another profound agreement between these views. Both views would affirm that, while the witch maliciously killed Aslan, it is nevertheless also true that it pleased the Emperor to have Aslan punished in Edmund's place (Is 53:4; Rom 3:25). Both views would affirm that Aslan was sent by the Emperor to redeem Edmund (Jn 6:38; Tit 2:14). And both views could affirm that Aslan offered himself up to the Emperor on behalf of Edmund even as he offered himself up to the witch and her minions on behalf of Edmund (Heb 7:27; 9:14; 10:12).

Clearly, on the matter of Christ's substitutionary death, Schreiner and Lewis speak the same biblical language. But there are two closely related theological differences that lead them to very different understandings of what this substitutionary language means.

First and most fundamentally, Lewis believes that self-sacrificial love is a "deeper magic" than the law, while Schreiner, so far as I can see, does not. Whereas Lewis would understand God's wrath against sin as an expression of God's love, Schreiner seems to see them as equally "deep" in God. God's very nature requires that his wrath be satiated in order to love and redeem sinners. God's very nature forbids him from ever simply forgiving without payment. I suspect this is also why Schreiner construes the problems the atonement addresses and the solution the atonement expresses primarily in legal terms and, consequently, why he interprets the sacrificial and substitutionary language in Scripture primarily in legal, penal terms. Because law and love are both equally deep magic for Schreiner, the ultimate problem the atonement resolves is a legal conflict within the godhead. In contrast, for Lewis, God *expresses* holy rage, but "God *is* love" (1 Jn 4:8). Indeed,

God expresses holy rage *because* God is love.

This leads directly to a second profound difference. Because of their differing views on "deep magic," Lewis and Schreiner provide very different answers to the question, Who demanded that the deep magic of the law be satisfied with "a kill"? For Schreiner, it is God. For Lewis (and most advocates of the Christus Victor view) it is the devil. Here is where the rubber meets the road in terms of the difference between these two views, and thus I will flesh out my agreement with Lewis on this matter more fully.

In the Christus Victor view that I and Lewis embrace, Jesus' death was not centered on saving us from God's threatening wrath. It was rather centered on manifesting God's love in order to free us from the devil's wrath. God does not hold our feet to the fire of the law: Satan, the "accuser," the "Inspector Javert" of the spiritual realm, if you will, does (Rev 12:10; cf. Job 1—2; Zech 3:1).[3] To be sure, the Christus Victor view fully agrees that God's wrath burns against sin (Eph 2:3), as Schreiner makes abundantly clear in his essay. But the demand for a "kill" does not come from God to satisfy his otherwise insatiable rage: it comes from the cosmic accuser who preys on all who have forfeited their lives and put themselves under his authority by their treason. Satan, not God, has the witch's and Inspector Javert's character that insists that the wrath of the law must be vented! Satan, not God, holds that no one can be forgiven truly for free: someone or other must pay!

Perhaps no passage expresses the Christus Victor view more clearly than Colossians 2:13-15. Here Paul says that God "forgave us all our trespasses" by "erasing the record that stood against us with its legal demands." He "set this aside, nailing it to the cross." In Lewisian terms, he broke apart "the Stone Table" (cf. Mt 27:51)! In this way God "disarmed the rulers and authorities and made a public example of them, triumphing over them in [the cross]" (Col 2:13-15). The passage clearly proclaims that the cross disarmed Satan and his minions, just as in Lewis's tale. But it didn't disarm God! And the cross did this by taking away from our accusers the only thing they ever had on us—the "deep magic" of "the written code" (Col 2:14 NIV). Deep magic was overturned by a "still deeper" magic of self-sacrificial love.

---

[3]Javert is the police inspector in Victor Hugo's masterpiece *Les Misérables* who compulsively insists on carrying out the law in meticulous detail. Nothing, he insists, is more fundamental than the law, so forgiveness without punishment is impossible (which is to say, forgiveness is impossible). We might say that, like Lewis's wicked witch, Javert (like Satan) is hostile to any suggestion that there exists a magic deeper than the deep magic of the law.

So far as I can see, Lewis's Christus Victor understanding of Christ's substitutionary death is consistent with every piece of scriptural evidence Schreiner cited in support of the penal substitutionary view. But it has at least two significant advantages. First, it places Christ's substitutionary death in a much broader context that allows it to be integrated with everything else Jesus said and did, and with the whole of Scripture. It thus brings a coherence to this (and every other) dimension of Jesus' life that would otherwise be missed.

Second, this understanding of Christ's substitutionary death has the advantage of completely avoiding a host of insurmountable difficulties that plague the penal substitutionary view. For example, how are we to understand sin and guilt literally being transferred from a guilty person to an innocent person (or to innocent animals with the Old Testament sacrifices)? What sort of justice is it that punishes an innocent person (or animals) for what another person did?[4] How are we to reconcile the idea that the Father needs to exact payment from or on behalf of his enemies with Jesus' teaching (and example) that we are to love unconditionally and forgive without demanding payment?

Along these same lines, how are we to reconcile the idea that God cannot be reconciled with sinners without his wrath being satisfied with blood with the pervasive scriptural depiction of God forgiving people without needing his wrath appeased (e.g., Lk 15:11-32)? If God must always get what is coming to him in order to forgive (namely, "a kill"), does God ever really forgive? And how is the view that God requires a kill to have his rage placated essentially different from the pagan or magical understanding of divine appeasement found in primordial religions throughout history?

These are a few of the significant problems that plague the penal substitutionary view, and I frankly found nothing in Tom Schreiner's essay that assuaged or even seriously addressed these problems. But none of these problems arise if we accept Lewis's view that love is a "deeper magic" than the law and, therefore, that it is the devil, not God, who demands a "kill." God is "satisfied" not in killing but in allowing himself to be killed for the

---

[4]Space permitting, I would flesh out a nonpenal interpretation of the Old Testament sacrifices that Schriener relies so heavily on in his defense of the penal substitutionary view of the atonement. For a succinct and insightful nonpenal perspective of Old Testament sacrifices, see John Goldingay, "Old Testament Sacrifices and the Death of Christ," in *Atonement Today,* ed. John Goldingay (London: SPCK, 1995), pp. 3-20.

sake of expressing a love that is deeper than law. God's "satisfaction" is found in thereby overthrowing all evil, setting his children free from evil's oppression and enthroning them to reign with him in Narnia—like Peter, Lucy, Susan, and (yes) even Edmund—which was his plan for humans from the very start (Gen 1:26-28; 2 Tim 2:12; Heb 2:6-9; Rev 5:10; 22:5).

Healing Response

BRUCE R. REICHENBACH

Tom Schreiner's presentation of the penal substitution view as *one* approach to interpreting the atonement is convincing. Although it is *de rigueur* today to critique the penal substitution view,[1] Schreiner marshals ample scriptural evidence to support it. It is not that the individual passages he invokes are indisputable (what interpretations of scriptural passages are not disputed by scholars somewhere?), but taken as a whole, he shows that such a model has biblical roots.

That said, I want to reflect on one of Schreiner's claims that often lies at the heart of formulations of the penal substitution view. He writes, "for God would deny his very being as God if he forgave us and violated his justice and holiness" (p. 94). Before I respond in detail to this statement, it is important to note what I will and will not argue. I will not argue that the penal substitution view is not an important scriptural motif. What I will critique in the claim is that this is *necessarily* the way God had to bring about our reconciliation with him. Whereas the first is a factual claim about interpretations found in the Scriptures, the second is a modal claim detailing the necessity of a particular event occurring, and this is far more difficult to defend. Critiquing the modal claim of necessity does not falsify the factual claim. It might be that the penal substitution view provides one way to properly understand the atonement. But contrary to Schreiner, the atonement need not have happened that way.

Suppose God merely decided to forgive our sins without requiring someone's death, in this case, Christ as our substitute. We would have forgiveness without death. Christ would neither have to voluntarily take on our punishment nor have to die. It still might be the case that God would decide that

---

[1]See especially Joel B. Green and Mark D. Baker, *Recovering the Scandal of the Cross* (Downers Grove, Ill.: InterVarsity Press, 2000).

punishment is appropriate and consequently that Christ would die for us. God can still rightly determine that the wages of sin are death (Rom 6:23). But the punishment of death is not necessary for salvation where forgiveness reigns, for forgiveness where offered can substitute for the punishment.

Tom Schreiner contends that justice and holiness preclude simple divine forgiveness of sins. But the New Testament suggests another story. In the New Testament three different conditions—faith, repentance, and the forgiveness of others—are connected with divine forgiveness. With regard to faith, Jesus sees the faith of the paralytic man and those who brought him to Jesus (Mt 9:2-6) and the faith of the woman who anointed his feet (Lk 7:44-50) as conditions for forgiveness of their sins. But in these two cases the texts do not treat faith as a necessary condition for forgiveness, only as a sufficient condition. "Your sins are forgiven. . . . Your faith has saved you." Repentance too is treated as a condition of forgiveness (Mk 4:12; Lk 17:3-4; Acts 8:22; Jas 5:13-16). Paul writes that "godly sorrow brings repentance that leads to salvation" (2 Cor 7:10; see also Ps 51). But again, confession and godly sorrow are treated not as a necessary condition for the forgiveness of sins but only as a sufficient condition. In 1 John 1:9, the author writes, "If we confess our sins, he is faithful and just and will forgive us our sins;" he does not proclaim, "Only if we confess our sins will he forgive us our sins."

This is not to diminish the importance of confession, which is necessary to bring about a change of attitude and lifestyle in the offender. Confession helps persons come to grips with their sins as acts they are responsible for. And it helps restore the persons to the community by putting them in communicative touch with those whom they offended. Thus, if the purpose of forgiveness is to restore the sinner to fellowship, then repentance is necessary. A sinner who did not repent would probably reject the forgiveness, for in its teleology repentance requires the offender to again enter into community with the forgiver who was offended. So from a teleological perspective, where forgiveness leads to a greater end, repentance is a necessary condition. But that repentance is necessary for restoring the person to the community does not make it necessary for forgiveness per se.

The third condition found in the New Testament is our forgiveness of others. Jesus states that if we forgive others, God will forgive us. But if we do not forgive others, God will not forgive us (Mt 6:14-15). This point is well illustrated by Jesus' parable (Mt 18:23-35) where the servant, begging for mercy, is forgiven of his debt but then goes out and ruthlessly claims what is owed him despite his debtors' similar pleas for mercy. The master then changes his mind and not only has the servant's debt reinstated but severely punishes him. Here our forgiveness of others is presented as both a necessary and a sufficient condition of receiving God's forgiveness.

In short, other than the requirement that we forgive others, there are no necessary conditions put on God's forgiveness of our sins. When discussing how many times we should forgive, Jesus says nothing about imposing necessary conditions (Mt 18:21-22), only that there is no limit to our forgiveness of others. Jesus himself forgives his executioners despite the fact that they apparently did not repent but continued, beneath his cross, casting lots to divide his clothing (Lk 23:34).

Notice that in none of the above is punishment mentioned as a necessary condition for forgiveness. In fact, in the New Testament passage that connects punishment with forgiveness (2 Cor 2:6-10), forgiveness follows punishment but is not made conditional on punishment. Hence, that God chose to present his Son to be punished in our place is not a logical necessity or even a moral necessity that follows from the nature of God. Rather, that God required punishment for sins is a determination by God's will; he chooses a method that requires death as a penalty for sin—the penalty he imposes for the sin committed in the Garden of Eden—and offers his Son as the substitution for that penalty.

Anselm presents three arguments in reply to our contention. First, he argues that to forgive without compensation or punishment is "not right."[2] And it is not right because one should not cancel sin without compensation or punishment. This argument, unfortunately, begs the question and hence fails to advance the cause. The second argument is more interesting. Anselm argues that failing to punish leads to indifference between the guilty and the not guilty. They are both in the same condition: unpunished. But this is not the case. The guilty one has performed an act that, though not punished, he is guilty of performing, whereas the other one has not. Punishment appropriately *may* be imposed on the guilty, but not on the innocent. The one is liable to punishment; the other not. Moreover, the very doing of the act has consequences for the character of the agent. Even were only forgiveness but no punishment administered, doing or not doing the sin has lasting effects. With forgiveness, sinning may not be held to the person's account, but sins

---

[2]Anselm *Cur Deus Homo* 12.

stain the character. The effects of the sin remain in the sinner. Anselm's third argument is that, without punishment, we have made the law null and void. But forgiveness does not negate the law; rather, forgiveness is only possible where the law—divine, civil or moral—is in effect. Otherwise there would be no violation to forgive. Forgiveness does not dispense with but presupposes the law. In effect, none of Anselm's arguments succeed in defending the thesis that forgiveness by itself, without punishment, is inadequate and violates the nature of God as holy and just.

If justice were God's only or primary characteristic, one would have grounds for the claim that punishment for sins is necessary. But Scripture portrays God as being both just and merciful, as both protective of his holiness and loving even to those who might besmirch his holiness. And it is out of this tension that forgiveness arises. Justice does require punishment; but the punishment might not be invoked because of mercy. Despite the fact that Israel continues to sin, God "blots out [our] transgressions, for [his] own sake, and remembers [our] sins no more" (Is 43:25; see Jer 31:34). And interestingly enough, God takes this action for his own sake.

At the same time, our reflections on forgiveness do not mitigate the penal substitution theory of atonement. That one forgives a wrongdoer does not automatically free the guilty from punishment. Considerations of justice may still be invoked. Punishment is not inconsistent with forgiveness, as 2 Corinthians 2 shows. One might forgive another but still require punishment in the name of justice. It is merely that justice tempered with mercy does not require it.

What the penal substitution view emphasizes is justice; sin when judged merits punishment (Is 40:2). What it allows for is grace, in that God himself initiates the atoning act. God presents Christ as the willing sacrifice (Rom 3:25). But what the penal view misses is that God's grace can be manifested in other ways. His mercy is so great that his forgiveness can be sufficient. God chooses the particular method of atonement for his own reasons, not out of necessity. The method God chose is consistent with diverse divine metaphors; it fits well with the rest of the story of God's interaction with humans. But penal substitution is not the whole or necessary story: it is one way to understand God's chosen story.

Kaleidoscopic Response

JOEL B. GREEN

Tom Schreiner has provided a robust defense of the penal substitution model of the atonement. In doing so, he makes two major, interrelated claims—namely, that this model is biblical, and that this model is the foundation of all other understandings of the atonement.

Before sketching a series of more particular concerns about these claims, I want to make two remarks. First, Schreiner claims for evangelical faith the centrality of the theory of penal substitution. It would be more accurate to claim that the atonement is central to evangelical faith, and that the penal substitutionary model is central to one strand of evangelicalism. Of course, Schreiner might wish to deny the label "evangelical" to ecclesial traditions that claim to be evangelical but which make no such claims regarding penal substitutionary atonement. I am thinking, for example, of Anabaptists (who are drawn more to the Christus Victor model) or Wesleyans (who have inherited from the founder of their movement an eclectic atonement theology) or African American evangelicals (at least some of whom worry that a theory like the one Schreiner espouses has faltered when it comes to calling Christians to reconciling action based on justice).[1] Moreover, many contemporary evangelical institutions affirm "substitution" in their faith statements without adding the modifier "penal." Many evangelicals are unready to surrender the term *evangelical* to the requirement of affirming this particular model of the atonement.

Second and more generally, I draw attention to the fact that the classic

---

[1] Harold Greenlee, a Wesleyan and an evangelical, provides a helpful illustration: "Reformed theology (Calvinism) says that Christ actually paid the penalty for sins. . . . Arminianism says that Christ's death provided an alternative to the penalty. This is a profound difference. If Christ actually paid the penalty for sins, then God cannot require a second payment. So either everyone is saved, or (as Calvinists would choose) the atonement is limited. From this, the necessary sequence is irresistible grace and eternal security of the elect believer. . . . Instead, Christ's atonement provided an alternative to paying the penalty. It is therefore open to as many or as few as will accept it" (Letter to the editor, *Good News* 38, no. 3 [November-December 2004]: 4).

creeds of the church are silent regarding the mechanics of the atonement. Similarly, the "rule of faith," as this was articulated variously in the ante-Nicene period, leaves undeveloped, or at least underdeveloped, how best we might construe the soteriological ramifications of the cross of Christ. From this I draw the self-evident corollary that one can inhabit the land of Christian orthodoxy, classically defined, without embracing a particular theory of the atonement. Moreover, though I am certain that there can be no Christianity apart from the cross,[2] I claim that debates regarding the best way(s) to articulate the saving message of the cross of Christ comprise an intramural conversation, and not one that can serve to distinguish Christian believer from nonbeliever or even evangelical from nonevangelical.

I will now move forward to address more fully the substance of Schreiner's chapter by raising a series of questions about the penal substitutionary theory.

With respect to *theological method,* how adequate is Tom Schreiner's presentation of the model of penal substitutionary atonement? I have two concerns. First, it is surprising that Schreiner has nothing to say about the development of this theory within the history of the church. Although proponents of this view typically refer to Anselm, Anselm himself did not articulate a penal view, and Schreiner was wise to avoid tying his wagon to Anselm's horse. Given Schreiner's claim that this view is foundational to all others, however, it would be surprising if we were not able to speak of its strong and pervasive representation in the theological tradition—indeed, if its centrality to Christian faith could not be traced from the second century to the present.

Second, Schreiner outlines a narrative of God-human relations that he apparently regards as self-evident in the Bible. That others might narrate the story differently and yet have an equally strong claim to be biblical does not factor in his presentation. In fact, Schreiner's reading of the canonical narrative is itself shaped by a theological tradition, the Reformed tradition—which, though a defensible tradition, is itself open to criticism from other Christian traditions.[3] Dis-

---

[2]See Joel B. Green, "No Cross, No Christianity?" *Circuit Rider* 29, no. 1 (2004): 4-6.

[3]Interestingly, when Craig G. Bartholomew and Michael W. Goheen, themselves working from within the Reformed tradition, turn to the atonement in their narration of *The Drama of Scripture* ([Grand Rapids: Baker Academic, 2004], pp. 164-65), they turn to an Anabaptist, John Driver (*Understanding the Atonement for the Mission of the Church* [Scottdale, Penn.: Herald, 1986]) for "images" of the atonement: victory, sacrifice and representation. See further, e.g., Herman-Emiel Mertens, *Not the Cross, But the Crucified,* Louvain Theological and Pastoral Monographs 11 (Louvain: Peeters, 1992); C. Norman Kraus, *Jesus Christ Our Lord,* rev. ed. (Scottdale, Penn.: Herald, 2000).

cussion of atonement theology in general would be helped if we were more transparent about the theological presuppositions that guide our biblical work.

With respect to the *theological narrative* Schreiner assumes, I have three questions. Let me first identify a puzzle related to the penal substitutionary theory, which presumes that the penalty due us on account of our status as sinners is death and this penalty was an expression of divine wrath. By what logic can it be assumed that anger is quenched by acting on it in this way? That is, even if we grant these two claims regarding the divine "penalty," on what basis does it follow that Jesus' dying quenches the anger directed at us by God? Does the transfer of guilt satisfy the demands of justice? Given the anthropathy at work in attributing this sort of anger to Yahweh, can we so easily escape the reality that redirecting anger at an innocent party does not (or at least need not) return the guilty party to good graces? If this logic is explanatory of the divine economy, how are we to understand those biblical accounts in which forgiveness is extended apart from the satisfaction of wrath (e.g., Mk 2:1-11)?

In any case, it is far from self-evident that we must follow Schreiner in claiming that the central need in the atonement is to address the wrath of God against human sin. Since he has criticized Mark Baker and me on our discussion of wrath in our book *Recovering the Scandal of the Cross*, let me focus there.[4] Mark Baker and I have been charged with holding to a one-sided view of the wrath of God—either (as in Schreiner's comments) because our view allegedly renders God's wrath as impersonal and passive or (more typically) because our view allegedly treats God's wrath in the present without reference to final judgment. I think that the problem actually lies elsewhere, in the rather narrow focus of our comments. We sought not to develop a theology of divine wrath but rather to explain God's wrath as this is represented in Romans 1. As Paul develops the concept in that chapter, we argued, "wrath" is the active presence of God's judgment toward "all ungodliness and wickedness" (v. 18). The wrath of God is not vindictive indignation or the anger of divine retribution but the divine response to human unfaithfulness. In Romans 1, wrath is not an anticipated future threat but is already present, for God is now handing people over to experience the consequences of the sin they choose (vv. 18, 24, 26, 28). That this is so is underscored by our recognition that, in sculpting his representation of the

---

[4]Joel B. Green and Mark D. Baker, *Recovering the Scandal of the Cross* (Downers Grove, Ill.: InterVarsity Press, 2000).

human situation in Romans 1:18-32, Paul is working with the portrait provided in Wisdom of Solomon 13:1—15:6.[5]

This is not to say that wrath for Paul is merely imminent or confined to the present, as Romans 2:5-10 already demonstrates.[6] Nor do we identify wrath with an impersonal set of "rules of the game of the universe," as though by doing so we might segregate God from wrath. Instead, in our narrow focus on Romans 1 we were recognizing that wrath is being worked out as divine action in the present world. From the human side, ungodliness and unrighteousness are identified with a general disposition to refuse to honor God as God and to render him thanks. Sin—that is, the proclivity to act as though things created, including ourselves, were the Creator—and such expressions of sin as lust, gossip, envy, deceit, same-sex relations, rebelliousness toward parents, and the rest *are themselves already expressions of the wrath of God.* They evidence the moral integrity of a God who takes sin seriously.

It is this, God's moral character, that Paul is defending here, and he does so by showing the progression from the human refusal to honor God, with its consequent denial of the human vocation to live in relation to God, to God's giving humanity over to its own desires—giving humanity, as it were, the life it sought apart from God—and from this to human acts of wickedness. In this economy, wicked acts do not stir up the wrath of God but are themselves already the consequences of the active presence of God's wrath. To crib the language of Wisdom of Solomon, God "torments" those who live unrighteously by allowing them their own atrocities (Wis 12:23). In Paul's own words the wrath of God is revealed in God's giving humanity over to their lusts, degrading passions and debasement of mind (Rom 1:18, 24, 26, 28). Our sinful acts do not invite God's wrath but prove that God's wrath is already active. What is needed then is not a transformation of God's disposition toward the unrighteous and the ungodly but rather a transformation on the human side of the equation.

In short, we put the emphasis quite differently than Schreiner does. Following Paul's statement in 2 Corinthians 5:19—"God was in Christ reconcil-

---

[5]On Paul's engagement with this Jewish text, see Francis Watson, *Paul and the Hermeneutics of Faith* (London: T & T Clark, 2004), pp. 405-8.

[6]In what sense then can Paul speak of the "wrath to come"? What does it mean for human beings to be rescued from the coming wrath (1 Thess 1:9-10)? This is the climactic, end-time scene of judgment when those who prefer to worship idols rather than the living God receive from God the fruits of their own misplaced hopes and commitments.

ing the world to himself"—we urge that it was the world that needed reconciling to God, not the other way around. The human family, not God, needs
transformation, a reading that does not mesh well with this emphasis on the
atonement as assuaging God's anger.

Second, though he protests against this criticism, Schreiner has not addressed one of the principal questions raised against the model of penal
substitutionary atonement, namely, that it presumes a breakdown of the
inner-trinitarian life of God. Not least given the doctrine of perichoresis (i.e.,
the Father gives himself to Son and Spirit, holding nothing back; the Son
gives himself to the Father and the Spirit, holding nothing back; and the
Spirit, likewise, gives himself to the Father and the Son, holding nothing
back), how can one claim that the Son had to die on the cross in order to
propitiate God's anger?[7]

Third, in spite of Schreiner's comments, I am unsure how the model of penal substitutionary atonement generates transformed life. Focused as it is on
the individual, on forensic judgment and on the moment of justification, how
can this model keep from undermining any emphasis on salvation as transformation and from obscuring the social and cosmological dimensions of salvation? If the purpose of God will be actualized in the restoration of all things,
then how is this purpose served by a theory of penal substitution? How does
the model of penal substitutionary atonement carry within itself the theological resolution of racism? What becomes the soteriological motivation for engaging in the care of God's creation? Against the backdrop of texts like Colossians 1:15-20 and Ephesians 2, these are not peripheral questions.

Schreiner might reply that on its own the model of penal substitutionary
atonement need not address concerns with holy life, personal and social,
and that penal substitutionary atonement, with its emphasis on the objective
side of Christ's saving work, needs to be supplemented with other models
of the atonement, including those that emphasize its subjective side. Such a
response raises a question and a concern. First the question: In what sense
then is it appropriate to insist, as Schreiner does, that the theory of penal
substitution is the heart and soul of evangelical faith? A faith, evangelical or
otherwise, that does not inherently address the cosmos or that does not pro-

---

[7]For recent attempts to tie atonement theology more fully into the larger theological enterprise,
see, e.g., Kathryn Tanner, "Incarnation, Cross, and Sacrifice: A Feminist-Inspired Reappraisal,"
Anglican Theological Review 86 (2004): 35-56; Leanne Van Dyk, "The Three Offices of Christ:
The *Munus Triplex* as Expansive Resources in Atonement," *Catalyst* 25, no. 2 (1999): 6-8; Robert Sherman, *King, Priest and Prophet* (London: T & T Clark, 2004).

mote human transformation in all of its fullness has little by way of heart or soul. The concern: In spite of the claim that the penal substitutionary view might be regarded only as one view among several, all of which are important and necessary for theological balance, it remains the case that penal substitutionary atonement has been represented in the Western church as *the* way to apprehend the saving work of the cross. My own experience is that, without exception, questions raised against the theory of penal substitution invite the response, "So, you don't believe in the atonement?" Of course I am not faulting Schreiner for this but am, rather, observing that appeals to greater balance in theological textbooks do not overcome the reality of what is conceived and articulated at the popular level by Sunday school teachers, Christian camp counselors, preachers, and evangelists, and in sermons, in praise songs, around campfires, and in small group Bible studies.[8]

Is the model of penal substitutionary atonement really the heart, soul, anchor and foundation of all other atonement models? Tom Schreiner seems to recognize that he is on thin ice here when, with reference to Christus Victor, he drops the metaphor of "foundation" in favor of the image of a "tether"; apparently these two models stand next to each other, joined at the wrist, rather than one on top of the other. This is because, whatever else they do, the models of penal substitution and Christus Victor each address the *objective* work of the cross, but do so in different ways. Penal substitution saves by assuaging the wrath of God. Christus Victor saves by conquering evil. Having diagnosed the problem differently, they each name different solutions.[9]

Other models are not easily fitted into the superstructure that has as its foundation a penal substitutionary model. The revelatory model of the atonement requires no such foundation, for example. But neither does the model of sacrifice, on which Schreiner spends a good deal of energy. Without repeating here the comments on sacrifice I make in my own chapter, let me say, simply, that (1) the drama of sacrifice as this is presented in Scripture

---

[8]For the beginnings of an attempt to reflect critically on how atonement theology is reflected in contemporary cultural products, see Howard Worsley, "Popularized Atonement Theory Reflected in Children's Literature," *Expository Times* 115, no. 5 (2004): 149-56.

[9]I presume that Schreiner's prose suffers an unintended lapse when, on page 68 he writes, "we ourselves are radically evil" (which I take to mean that we are "evil to the core") but on page 80 insists that "[God] . . . hates what is evil," for the effect of this would be to claim that God hates us! If this were accurate, then it would make sense to say that, in the atonement, God declares war on the human family.

is not oriented toward assuaging God's wrath,[10] (2) the drama of sacrifice does turn on the notion of representation (or substitution), but (3) this is an economic metaphor, not a penal one.

More could be said on any number of details, including the ease with which Tom Schreiner concludes that ὑπέρ (*hyper,* "on behalf of") refers to Jesus' bearing the punishment and guilt of others by dying "in [their] stead" (p. 92), when "for the sake of" is capable of a wider range of connotations; or the difficulties inherent in reading Mark 10:45 ("to give his life a ransom for many") as a reference to "substitution" (p. 90) rather than "price of deliverance."[11] Hopefully, however, this is enough to promote further conversation on these important issues.

---

[10]In his essay "The Theology of Old Testament Sacrifice," Gordon Wenham points to a single term for evidence that sacrifice appeases God's wrath: נִיחֹחַ; he writes, "The word suggests divine uneasiness which is quieted by sacrifice" (in *Sacrifice in the Bible,* ed. Roger T. Beckwith and Martin J. Selman [Grand Rapids: Baker, 1995], p. 80). Even if this reading of נתן is adopted, however, this idea would relate only to the burned offerings, as opposed to the "purification (or sin)" or "restitution (or guilt)" offerings which provide better analogs for the New Testament presentation of the sacrifice of Christ.

[11]See, e.g., Scot McKnight, *Jesus and His Death* (Waco, Tex.: Baylor University Press, 2005), p. 357.

THREE

Healing View

BRUCE R. REICHENBACH

In the Trisagion Prayers of the Orthodox Christian liturgy, believers pray, "All-Holy Trinity have mercy on us. Lord, forgive our sins. Master, pardon our transgressions. Holy One, visit and heal our infirmities for Your namesake. Lord have mercy." The prayer envisions the Lord's response in Isaiah.

'I was enraged by their sinful greed;
    I punished them, and hid my face in anger,
    yet they kept on in their willful ways.
I have seen their ways, but I will heal them;
    I will guide them and restore comfort to them. . . .
Shalom, shalom to those far and near,'
    says the Lord. 'And I will heal them.' (Is 57:17-19, modified TNIV)

Shalom—well-being, wholeness, peace—is what God envisions for his people. But humans are without well-being.

From the least to the greatest,
    all alike are greedy for gain;
prophets and priests alike,
    all practice deceit.
They dress the wound of my people
    as though it were not serious.
"Shalom, shalom," they say,
    when there is no shalom. (Jer 6:13-14, modified TNIV)

Restoration to well-being will occur when the rebellion is ended, when people no longer have "forsaken the commands of [their] God," when "the chains of injustice" are loosed, the oppressed set free, the hungry fed, the naked clothed (Is 58:2, 6-7).[1]

---

[1]Unless otherwise indicated, Scripture quotations are from the New International Version.

Then your light will break forth like the dawn,
    and your healing will quickly appear;
then your righteousness will go before you,
    and the glory of the LORD will be your rear guard. (Is 58:8)

In the days of Israel God provided the means for this well-being in the annual Day of Atonement ritual, in repeated merciful acts of forgiveness and restoration, and later once and for all through the Son's atonement, which begins with God the Father sending the anointed One (Jesus the Christ)

to preach good news to the poor . . .
to proclaim freedom for the prisoners
and recovery of sight for the blind,
to release the oppressed,
to proclaim the year of the Lord's favor. (Lk 4:18-19; Is 61:1)

As physician, Jesus takes up the task of restoration (Lk 4:23). Dramatically announcing his vocation in his hometown synagogue, he launches his teaching and healing ministry, which several years later culminates in his death by crucifixion.

I will unfold this biblical structure as we look at the atonement as healing or restoration, where God takes the initiative on our behalf. To get to our end we will travel a path that for many is uncomfortable because it challenges our modern sensibilities about God. God truly is held to be beneficent and loving, but the love envisioned often is shallow. As C. S. Lewis writes:

By the goodness of God we mean nowadays almost exclusively His loving-ness; and in this we may be right. And by Love, in this context, most of us mean kindness—the desire to see others than the self happy. . . . What would really satisfy us would be a God who said of anything we happened to like doing, "What does it matter so long as they are contented?" We want, in fact, not so much a Father in Heaven as a grandfather in heaven, . . . whose plan for the universe was simply that it might be truly said at the end of each day, "a good time was had by all."[2]

Lewis continues, "Love is something more stern and splendid than mere kindness."

In seeking our well-being, God demands the perfecting or maturing of the beloved. Anything less fails to take into account God's whole intent

---

[2]C. S. Lewis, *The Problem of Pain* (New York: Macmillan, 1962), p. 39.

to restore us. To accomplish this he employs many means, including punishment, discipline and ultimately even Jesus' death. God is impatient and patient, angry and gentle, judging and forgiving, occasioning calamity and restoration. Thus at the end of our journey we catch a vision of a good God whose benevolence is much more complex, manifested through his love in both justice and mercy, and above all in our salvation and restoration.

The Human Condition

We hardly get going in the biblical narrative before meeting up with the sorry state of the human condition. From the outset, in the story of the Fall, humans express the desire to be like God, taking charge and determining by their experience what is good and what is evil (Gen 3:1-6). The continuing narrative portrays the human condition as it regresses from bad to worse. "The LORD saw how great the wickedness of the human race had become on the earth, and that every inclination of the thoughts of the human heart was only evil all the time" (Gen 6:5 TNIV). Humans manifest the desire to displace God, among other ways, in disobeying God and in seeking other gods. The opening chapter of Isaiah sets the charge.

> I reared children and brought them up,
>> but they have rebelled against me. . . .
> Israel does not know,
>> my people do not understand.
>
> Ah, sinful nation,
>> a people loaded with guilt,
> a brood of evildoers,
>> children given to corruption!
> They have forsaken the LORD;
>> they have spurned the Holy One of Israel
>> and turned their backs on him. (Is 1:2-4)

In the New Testament, Paul sums up the human condition: all are sinful.

> There is no one righteous, not even one;
>> there is no one who understands,
> no one who seeks God. (Rom 3:10-11, quoting Ps 14:1-2)

What makes the picture so bleak is our inability to rectify the situation. We are inveterate covenant breakers. And even when instructed by the law, we often fail to keep it. So the New Testament sees the law as a preamble, not as salvific. "No one will be declared righteous in his sight by observing the law; rather, through the law we become conscious of sin" (Rom 3:20). We stand helpless, unrepentant, fixed in our human condition, separated from God and from others, sin-sick as it were.

Sickness describes not only our spiritual condition but our physical, economic, political, social and environmental conditions. In the Isaiah 1 passage, Isaiah continues to record the fruits of sin. The human predicament is written large in the communal life and history of the nation.

Your whole head is injured,
    your whole heart afflicted.
From the sole of your foot to the top of your head
        there is no soundness—
only wounds and welts
        and open sores,
not cleansed or bandaged
        or soothed with oil.

Your country is desolate
    your cities burned with fire;
your fields are being stripped by foreigners,
        right before you,
        laid waste as when overthrown by strangers. (Is 1:5-7)

Restoration is needed—of the people (Is 10:21), their land (2 Chron 7:14; Joel 2:25), their institutions (Hos 6:6—7:1), and their health (Ps 41:3-4, 8). The sufficient condition is to turn to God who restores—"I am the LORD, your Healer" (Ex 15:26 ESV).[3]

Sin and Sickness

Have you rejected Judah completely?
    Do you despise Zion?
Why have you afflicted us
    so that we cannot be healed?

---

[3]Michael Brown argues convincingly that the word most frequently connected with healing, *rāpāʾ*, should be understood in a broader sense of restoring or making whole. The word is used not only of the healing of sick bodies (2 Kings 20:5) but also of restoring of broken alters (1 Kings 18:30), restoring the land (2 Chron 7:14), making water potable (2 Kings 2:21-22), and even fixing smashed pottery (Jer 19:11) and restoring a mildewed house (Lev 14:48). (Michael Brown, *Israel's Divine Healer* [Grand Rapids: Zondervan, 1995], pp. 28-31).

> We hoped for shalom
> > but no good has come,
> for a time of healing
> > but there is only terror.
> We acknowledge our wickedness, LORD,
> > and the guilt of our ancestors;
> > > we have indeed sinned against you. (Jer 14:19-20, modified TNIV)

The importance of healing as a form of restoration follows from the biblical affirmation of the close connection between sin, sickness and well-being. As Brown notes, though "shalom is rarely part of the Old Testament vocabulary of healing," to be healed is part of being in the state of shalom.[4] The psalmist writes, "Have mercy on me, LORD; heal me, for I have sinned against you" (Ps 41:4 TNIV).

Restoration is necessary because God, directly or indirectly, brings calamities. The Lord sends the plagues Moses promised on the Egyptians, their livestock and their land. He heads the locust army that as a plague literally destroys the harvest but also is symbolic of the political devastation that God brings on the land through his servants, the nations under his command who are ranged against Israel (Jer 25:9; Joel 2). God subjects not only Israel but all nations who resist him (Deut 7:15) to disaster (Jer 25:29).

Unlike the Mesopotamian gods, however, Yahweh does not cause or allow calamities willy-nilly.[5] Calamities result from our sin, from our failure to keep the covenant made with God. "If you listen carefully to the voice of the LORD your God and do what is right in his eyes, if you pay attention to his commands and keep all his decrees, I will not bring on you any of the diseases I brought on the Egyptians, for I am the LORD, who heals you" (Ex 15:26; Deut 7:12, 15). However,

> If you do not obey the LORD your God and do not carefully follow all his commands and decrees, . . . the Lord will afflict you with the boils of Egypt and with tumors, festering sores and the itch, from which you cannot be cured. The LORD will afflict you with madness, blindness and confusion of mind. (Deut 28:15; 27-28; also Lev 26:14-16)

The message is clear: displacement of God and disobedience to his com-

---

[4]Ibid., p. 36.
[5]Hector Avalos, *Illness and Health Care in the Ancient Near East* (Atlanta: Scholars Press, 1995), pp. 242-43.

mands result in punishment of persons, community and land; honor of God and obedience to him result in God's blessing. Here the complexity of God is manifested in a way that might make it difficult for some to comprehend. God functions sometimes as the direct and other times as the indirect cause or occasion of illnesses (depending on how the punishment is afflicted). Yet at the same time he also is our healer: "I have wounded and I will heal" (Deut 32:39).

The theme that God punishes sin by bringing sickness, devastation and death to person, nation, and land runs consistently through the Old Testament. God smote the Philistines with tumors when they seized the ark of the covenant (1 Sam 5:6-12), brought a plague on Israel (2 Sam 24:13), and blinded and then healed the Aramaean army (2 Kings 6:18-20). God brings calamities and destruction not only on nations, primarily in view in the Old Testament, but also on individuals. He punished Miriam with a skin disease when she complained about Moses' recent marriage and his failure to share power (Num 12:10-16). Elisha's servant Gehazi and his descendants contracted a skin disease because of Gehazi's greed (2 Kings 5:27). God brought a fatal illness on the newborn son of David and Bathsheba for David's adultery and murder of Uriah (2 Sam 12:13-18) and caused Jeroboam to have a withered hand (1 Kings 13:4). The Lord afflicted Uzziah for his failure to remove the high places (2 Kings 15:4-5) and struck Jehoram with an incurable bowel disease for taking Judah into idolatry and for murdering his brothers (2 Chron 21:11-18).

This linkage of calamities with sin occurs not only in the Old Testament but is prevalent in the New Testament as well, though on a more personal basis. Jesus tells the leper whom he heals to offer the atonement offering upon his certification of being clean (Mt 8:4; also Lk 11:14). He commands the healed paralytic, who likewise went to the temple (probably to offer the atonement offering), to "stop sinning or something worse may happen to you" (Jn 5:14). In the story of the paralytic (Mt 9:1-8), Jesus makes "you are healed" synonymous with "your sins are forgiven." The lives of Ananias and Saphira are taken as a result of their sin (Acts 5:1-10), while in the Epistles James makes the clearest connection between sin and suffering. Since some sickness results from sin, prayers of confession are "powerful and effective" with the Lord who can bring about healing (Jas 5:13-16; see also 1 Cor 11:27-32).

Although both the Old and New Testaments claim that sin begets suffering and calamity, both likewise emphasize that not all suffering results from sin. The book of Job is an oft-cited case in point. Eliphaz links Job's suffering with his sin:

> Is it for your piety that he rebukes you
>> and brings charges against you?
> Is not your wickedness great?
>> Are not your sins endless? (Job 22:4-5)

But Job protests his own innocence:

> But he knows the way that I take;
>> when he has tested me, I will come forth as gold.
> My feet have closely followed his steps;
>> I have kept to his way without turning aside.
> I have not departed from the commands of his lips;
>> I have treasured the words of his mouth more than my daily bread.
>> (Job 23:10-12)

Moreover, the Levitical laws for atonement did not require a sin offering for every illness, boil or swelling, only for illnesses that were prolonged (and hence possibly contagious) or when a person abnormally emitted fluids like blood that could spread contagion. Indeed, not every physical healing by the Lord required confession; the request of a righteous Hezekiah was sufficient for God to change his mind (Is 38:16).

Similarly in the New Testament: When Jesus' disciples encounter a man blind from birth, they inquire whose sin caused his condition, his own or his parents'. Jesus replies that in this case sin had nothing to do with the man's condition; other factors were at work (Jn 9:1-3). James also carefully qualifies his connection between sin and sickness with the hypothetical "if." Consequently, we must be very careful about linking sin and sickness. Though sin can be divinely punished by sickness and other calamities, it by no means follows that all sickness and calamities are due to sin.

In short, Old Testament Israelites and New Testament Jews viewed calamities of all sorts, including illness, diseases, natural disasters and political conquest, as symptomatic of their spiritual condition. Serious illness was more than a physical phenomenon; it had moral and spiritual dimensions that made it appropriate to petition the Lord for deliverance (Ps 91:1-10).

God as Healer

One of the unusual dimensions of Israelite culture was the apparent absence of a class or group of individuals dedicated to healing. The Israelites apparently had no healing occupations parallel to those in Egypt and Mesopotamia.[6] This is not to say that physical/magical practices were non-existent in Israel. But with the exception of Job 13:4 and Jeremiah 8:22, the relative silence about physicians in Israel suggests that they, at least formally, played at most only a minor role in the healing structure of Israelite life. (Though any argument from silence needs to be recognized as such.)[7] Healing was not the function of the priests. They were overseers of the health of the community, removing from the community those who were contagious and certifying their cleanliness (healing and acceptance) upon return (Lev 13—14). The prophets' role in healing was more ambiguous. Though Elijah and Elisha occasionally healed (1 Kings 17; 2 Kings 5), and Ahijah, Elisha and Isaiah foretold what would happen to the ill (1 Kings 14:3; 2 Kings 8:8-10; 20:1), healing apparently was not a continuous or expected prophetic function. The key point is that since God brought about the Israelites' sickness because of their sins, it is only appropriate that the Israelites petition and rely on God for healing.

The sad fact was that Israel had turned for national healing elsewhere than to their God.

> When Ephraim saw his sickness,
>   and Judah his sores,
> Then Ephraim turned to Assyria
>   and sent to the great king for help.
> But he is not able to cure you,
>   not able to heal your sores. (Hos 5:13)

But whereas the kings of the earth cannot heal the people of Israel, the Lord can heal if they repent.

---

[6]Three kinds of medical practitioners are identified in ancient Egypt, although one person could play several roles. The role of the *wabw,* who served Sekhmet, a goddess of healing, is unclear. The *sa.u* attended to the ill, using magic, charms and incantations. The *swnw,* worshipers of their patron deity Thoth, practiced herbal medicine or surgery along with their prayers. In Mesopotamia one can find a division between magicians/priests (the *ašipu*) who discerned and treated diseases as being under supernatural influence and the *asû,* who perhaps took a more practical approach to medical problems. Whereas the former employed prayers, libations and incantations, the latter concentrated on ways to relieve the symptoms. See Darrell W. Amundsen and Gary B. Ferngren, "Medicine and Religion: Pre-Christian Antiquity," in *Health/Medicine and the Faith Traditions,* ed. M. E. Marty and K. L. Vaux (Philadelphia: Fortress, 1982), pp. 58-61.

[7]Gerhard F. Hasel, "Health and Healing in the Old Testament," *Andrews University Seminary Studies* 21, no. 3 (1983): 200.

Come, let us return to the LORD.
> He has torn us to pieces, but he will heal us;
>> he has injured us, but he will bind up our wounds.
> After two days he will revive us;
>> on the third day he will restore us,
>> that we may live in his presence. (Hos 6:1-2)

Of course their sickness is not merely physical but also deeply spiritual. God proposes to heal Israel not only as a political entity, but spiritually, healing their waywardness (Hos 14:4).

God not only heals but also protects. "If you listen carefully to the voice of the LORD your God and do what is right in his eyes, if you pay attention to his commands and keep all his decrees, I will not bring on you any of the diseases I brought on the Egyptians, for I am the LORD, who heals you" (Ex 15:26). In the Old Testament, God is the supreme prophylactic, keeping his people "from the deadly pestilence (Ps 91:3, 6).

> If you make the Most High your dwelling . . .
> then no harm will befall you,
>> no disaster will come near your tent. (Ps 91:9-10)

One should be careful not to read the affirmation that God is the healer to say that we should be suspicious of or avoid medical practice. It is true that Jeremiah expresses some skepticism about the ability of the physicians who practice in Gilead (Jer 8:22). It may also be thought that we could cite 2 Chronicles 16:12 as a prohibition against using physicians and their healing practices. The story concerns king Asa, who initially heeded the prophet's warning not to rely on any but the Lord for his kingship and victories over his enemies, but in the final years of his reign he turns for support even from his enemy, the king of Aram. In the end, when severely ill with disease in his feet (gangrene?), he fails to seek the Lord and consults only the physicians. In regard to the implied textual disapproval of this, some suggest that since pagan physicians were associated with pagan deities and their temples, and thus detracted from the true source of healing, it was inappropriate and hence censurable for Asa to consult them at all, let alone conjointly with consulting Yahweh.[8] Others explain this text by maintaining that "it is not the mere inquiring of the physicians which is here censured, but only the godless manner in which Asa trusted

---

[8]Avalos, *Illness and Health Care,* pp. 291-93.

in the physicians,"[9] an act parallel to his trust in the king of Aram. At the same time, we find no general biblical prohibitions against, for example, treating wounds or even physicians. Israelites had medicinal herbs for wounds (Jer 6:14; 46:11).[10] Remedies or balms were present (Jer 8:22; 46:11; 51:8), fractures set and wounds bandaged (Jer 6:14; Is 1:5-6; Ezek 30:21). Isaiah unperjoratively indicates that wounds and sores were "cleansed or bandaged or soothed with oil" (Is 1:6). The role of physicians is more fully clarified later in the second century B.C. in the *Wisdom of Jesus Ben Sirach,* where physicians are deemed important and respectable. Their activity is condoned because healing comes from the Lord, whose ministers they are.[11]

God's healing is both physical (including bodily, mental and emotional) and spiritual.

> Praise the LORD, . . .
> who forgives all your sins
> and heals all your diseases. (Ps 103:2-3)

Of course, sin and sickness are not identical. The first is the condition, the second is the result. So we need a healer who will address both the condition and the result. Though addressing the sin is central, at the same time only by addressing the complete human condition—physical, economic, political and environmental—can we attain well-being.

---

[9]C. F. Keil, *The Books of the Chronicles* (Edinburgh: T & T Clarke, 1872), p. 370. For further discussion, see Brown, *Israel's Divine Healer,* pp. 48-53.

[10]"Even though in the Old Testament, God is represented as the only healer and God's people are to refrain from resorting to magical or pagan healing practices, the use of natural or medicinal means is not only not precluded but even employed in ostensibly miraculous healings. Medical knowledge was probably limited to folk remedies . . . and there were very likely no systematized therapeutics, much less a distinct medical profession similar to what . . . existed elsewhere in the Ancient Near East. Not until the intertestamental period do we have evidence for a Jewish medical profession" (Amundsen and Ferngren, "Medicine and Religion," p. 68).

[11]"Honor the physician with the honor due him, according to your need of him, for the Lord created him; for healing comes from the Most High, and he will receive a gift from the king. The skill of the physician lifts up his head, and in the presence of great men he is admired. The Lord created medicines from the earth, and a sensible man will not despise them. . . . And he gave skill to men that he might be glorified in his marvellous works. By them he heals and takes away pain; the pharmacist makes of them a compound. His works will never be finished; and from him health is upon the face of the earth. My son, when you are sick do not be negligent, but pray to the Lord, and he will heal you. Give up your faults and direct your hands aright, and cleanse your heart from all sin. . . . He who sins before his Maker, may he fall into the care of a physician" (*Sirach* 38:1-10 RSV).

Sin, Healing and the Old Testament Sacrificial System

The Levitical sacrificial system was not designed to provide healing for persons afflicted with infectious diseases (Lev 13—14). Diseased persons were brought to the priest for examination. After sequential periods of isolation, if upon further inspection signs of infectious disease remained, the sick were removed outside the camp until they could show they were healed. If eventually the diseased persons thought healing had occurred, the priest was summoned to certify that they were clean. The priest who visited the ill did not bring healing, only certification that healing had occurred. When healed, the ill were then invited back into the camp (the community) and the priest atoned on their behalf by presenting the sin or the guilt offering.

Though sacrifice atoned for the sin of the person now certified as healed, it did not cure the ailment. Perhaps somewhat ironically, the sin and guilt offerings were generally for unintentional sins, where the person committed some fault such as mistakenly touching something ceremonially unclean (Lev 4:13-21; 5:2-6, 14).[12] The sacrifice was the penalty for the sin (Lev 5:7) and brought forgiveness. More serious malicious or deliberate sins were not individually atoned for but punished. Instead of having atonement available, persons who committed these sins often were cut off from the community (Lev 18:29; 20:1-6; Num 15:30). Atonement for all our sins was needed.

For the intentional, grave, national sin of rebellion[13] God instituted the Day of Atonement, a yearly event that involved the sacrifice of animals and the sending out into the desert a goat who bore the confessed sins of the nation. But since atonement for the sins of the people needed to be done annually, a more permanent atonement was needed (Heb 10:1-4, 10-12).

In effect, then, the instituted system of sacrifices was inadequate. It failed to provide atonement for all sins, including intentional, serious sins, and it required repetitive sacrifices. A better way was needed to address the human predicament.

---

[12]Megory Anderson and Philip Culbertson suggest that ancient Judaism had three categories of sin indicating varying degrees of severity. Inadvertent sin *(ḥaṭṭāʾ)*, though less serious, still is sin in that God's commandments are broken and hence requires a sin or guilt offering for its atonement (Lev 4:1—5:19; Num 15:22-29). *'Awōn* refers to advertent sin (1 Sam 25:24), while *peśaʿ* is demonstrative or defiant sin—rebellion against God. In the last case, no atonement was available; "the only provision for dealing with *peśaʿ* is through both confession and the scapegoat" (p. 314). ("The Inadequacy of the Christian Doctrine of Atonement in Light of Levitical Sin Offering," *Anglican Theological Review* 68, no. 4 [1986]: 308-9.)

[13]Lev 16:16, 21 is the only place *peśaʿ* is used in Leviticus.

The Suffering Servant

> He was despised and rejected by men,
>> a man of sorrows [suffering], and familiar with pain [sickness]. . . .
> Surely, he took up our pain [sickness]
>> and carried our sorrows [suffering]. (Is 53:3-4)

The key Old Testament passage announcing this more permanent divine atoning activity is Isaiah 52:13—53:12 (hereafter Is 53 for short). Although the word *atonement* does not occur in this passage, atonement is definitely in view. For example, Isaiah 52:15 recalls the sprinkling of the blood of the bull and the goat on and in front of the atonement cover and on the horns of the altar on the Day of Atonement, thereby "cleans[ing] it and . . . consecrat[ing] it from the uncleanness of the Israelites" (Lev 16:19). In Isaiah the atonement stretches beyond the confines of the Israelite sacred place to "many nations."[14]

Isaiah describes the human predicament. We suffer from sickness (pain) and sorrows (mental and physical suffering) brought on by our sins and transgressions. We are sinners who because of our punishment need to be made well (shalom—Is 53:5): our sins removed and our sickness healed.

The Servant was noteworthy neither in lineage nor in appearance. He was an unwanted shoot from a desert bush, possessing nothing to attract people to him. He was despised and rejected and so intimately acquainted with pain and suffering that people shunned him. Yet what is noteworthy about this Servant is his atoning work, wherein he assumes the dynamic role of taking on both our sins and their result—our sickness and pain. The observers rightly see the Servant's suffering as coming from God, but they mistake it as punishment for the Servant's own sins. The real truth is that the Servant was innocent—"he had done no violence, nor was any deceit in his mouth" (Is 53:9). Rather, the Servant suffers for our sins.

> But he was pierced for our transgressions,
>> he was crushed for our iniquities; . . .

---

[14]It should be noted that the translation of the Masoretic Text *hizzâ* as "sprinkle" is not without dispute, especially in light of the context. The alternative "startle," from the Arabic, has been suggested as a more appropriate alternative to parallel the claim that the kings will be silent because of him. See John N. Oswalt, *The Book of Isaiah: Chapters 40-66* (Grand Rapids: Eerdmans, 1998), pp. 374, 380. This would affect the interpretation suggested in the text. For a defense of the more cultic "sprinkle," see Alec Motyer, *The Prophecy of Isaiah* (Downers Grove, Ill.: InterVarsity Press, 1993), pp. 425-26.

For he was cut off from the land of the living;
　　for the transgression of my people he was stricken. (Is 53:5, 8)

The Servant's punishment and accompanying suffering has a healing effect.

The punishment that brought us peace (shalom) was upon him,
and by his wounds we are healed. (Is 53:5, modified NIV)

Not only does he bring healing, but he addresses our sins, justifying us before God.

By his knowledge my righteous servant will justify many,
and he will bear their iniquities. (Is 53:11)

The passage is complex because of the many verbs describing the action of the Servant. He takes up sickness, bears our sorrows (suffering), brings us well-being and heals us by his wounds. He is a guilt offering (for he did not intentionally sin, but substitutionally[15] took on the sins of others) who thereby takes on the penalty for our sins (Lev 5:7, 15), was pierced for our transgressions and crushed for our iniquities, justifies many, bears their sins, and makes intercession for sinners. But what is clear is that the suffering, death, resurrection ("he will see the light of life," Is 53:11),[16] knowledge, and intercession of the Servant address both our sins and the resulting sickness.

Isaiah is not alone in seeing the Messiah as a healer. Malachi records that in the midst of terrible punishment, for those who honor God "the sun of righteousness will rise with healing in its wings. And you will go out and leap like calves released from the stall" (Mal 4:2).

What then is atonement as healing? On the one hand, and most basically,

---

[15]That the Servant acts as a substitution for others is disputed by Morna Hooker ["Did the Use of Isaiah 53 to Interpret His Mission Begin with Jesus?" in *Jesus and the Suffering Servant,* ed. William Bellinger Jr. and William Farmer (Harrisburg, Penn.: Trinity Press International, 1998), p. 101], who suggests that he represents us (insofar as we are in him) rather than is a substitution for us. The atonement is not a matter of place-taking; rather, "Christ shares our condemnation in order that we might share his vindication by God" (ibid.). But this radically breaks the connection of Isaiah 53 with the guilt offerings in Leviticus.

[16]This phrase is in the Dead Sea Scrolls and Septuagint but not in the Masoretic Text. "He will see his offspring and prolong his days" (v. 10) may suggest a similar view. However, scholars dispute whether a resurrection is in view here. Those who envision an actual seeing of offspring imply a resurrection to victory and prosperity; those who take it metaphorically emphasize the continued impact of the Servant's atoning work on those for whom he died and who perceive its significance.

it addresses the human predicament in that the relationship between humans and God is restored (healed). The central piece in this restoration is that God, through the Servant who personally takes on all our iniquities, grants forgiveness for sins. Atonement brings the healing of forgiveness and reconciliation. No additional sacrifices are necessary. On the other hand, the punishment for our sins, which was often meted out in terms of suffering, sickness and calamity, has also been taken on by the Servant. His absorption of both the sin and its punishment is the means to our healing and restoration, by grace bringing us shalom or well-being in all its richness. When the king comes, "No one living in Zion will say, 'I am ill'; and the sins of those who dwell there will be forgiven" (Is 33:24).

Jesus the Physician

The New Testament picks up both healing themes: the healing of our infirmities and the healing of our broken relationship with God, by Christ taking on and forgiving our sins. The Gospel writers portray Jesus as the physical healer. Whereas the Old Testament presented no role for a physician, in the very initiation of his ministry Jesus announces himself as the physician (Lk 4:23). Jesus goes "through all the towns and villages, teaching in their synagogues, preaching the good news of the kingdom and healing every disease and sickness" (Mt 9:35). His healing ministry is prevalent and central: almost a third of the Gospel of Mark is devoted to Jesus' healing ministry. Even when we include the more theologically laden John, almost 20 percent of the four Gospels deal with healing. We "cannot help but feel that the floodgates of healing have opened in the pages of the New Testament. The trickle has become a deluge, the exceptional has become the norm."[17]

Jesus as the divine healer does not pray to the Father to heal but directly and immediately heals. The lame are told to get up, lepers are made clean, the woman with persistent bleeding no longer suffers, blind people see, dead are commanded to rise and demons are displaced. By this Jesus shows his continuity with the divine healer of the Old Testament. There is no break, except that now the divine healer has come incarnate to earth with the power to directly perform this ministry of spiritual and physical healing.

For Matthew, physical healing is certainly in view when he sees Jesus'

---

[17]Brown, *Israel's Divine Healer*, p. 208.

healing ministry—driving out the demons and healing the sick—as directly fulfilling Isaiah's prophecy. In this regard he quotes Isaiah 53:4: "He took up our infirmities and carried our diseases" (Mt 8:17). There is no spiritualizing here. Jesus himself takes on *(lambanō)* and bears *(bastazō)* the infirmities of those he heals. Moreover, Matthew sees sin and sickness as connected. The subsequent story of the healing of the paralyzed man in Matthew 9 makes clear that Jesus does not differentiate between the paralytic's physical healing and the spiritual treatment of his sins. Seeing the paralytic, Jesus tells him that his sins are forgiven. When questioned, he turns to the physical dimension of the illness, telling the paralytic to "Get up, take your mat and go home" (Mt 9:6). One is as easy to say as another, he comments. The healing of the paralysis comes from the same power and authority that Jesus has to forgive sins.

Objectors contend that Matthew cannot be thinking of the atonement when he quotes Isaiah. For one thing, they affirm, Jesus did not actually take on the illnesses of those he healed. In particular, he did not let himself be inhabited by the demons he dispossessed, something that "is unthinkable for the Son of God."[18] For another, Christ has not yet suffered and died on the cross. The connection between healing disease and atonement is found only in Jesus' power to accomplish both, not in any intrinsic connection. Yet interestingly enough, Matthew bypasses the Septuagint's rendering of Isaiah 53 ("this one bears our sins and suffers for us") that closely connects verses 3 and 4 with the verses in Isaiah 53 that address sin and justification with a Greek translation of the Masoretic Text that directly connects Jesus' healing ministry with his taking up of our pains and sufferings. We are hard-pressed not to see Matthew intentionally referring to the healing dimension of the atonement. Regarding what Jesus takes on or assumes, though Jesus does not assume the demonic powers, there is reason to think that taking on our sins affected him physically, especially in light of Luke's statement that the agony in the garden brought "sweat . . . like drops of blood falling to the ground" (Lk 22:44).

It is true that healing flows from Jesus' power. But healing connects also with his power and authority to forgive sin. We should not so easily bifurcate Jesus' life, cutting off his healing and teaching ministry from his passion and death. Christ's atoning work should not be restricted merely to his

---

[18]John Wilkinson, "Physical Healing and the Atonement," *The Evangelical Quarterly* 63 (1991): 159.

death event. Rather, we should treat this healing ministry as part of the entire incarnational event. As Paul notes in his incarnational-glorification hymn (Phil 2:6-11), the "mind of Christ" begins with the incarnation and extends throughout his entire ministry.[19] Even the demons are reported as recognizing the connection between Jesus' healing ministry and the fact that he is the Christ (Lk 4:40-41). "If the healings done by Jesus presuppose the invasion of the kingdom of God into the realm of suffering caused by evil [as can most graphically be seen in the demon exorcism of the preceding passage (Mt 8:28-34)], then the healing of diseases is only a part of a much larger picture, wherein sin itself, and not just its symptoms, is dealt a final blow."[20]

The kingdom of God, which is made possible by the atonement, begins with the preaching of good news. "If it is by the Spirit of God that I drive out demons, then the kingdom of God has come upon you" (Mt 12:28 TNIV). When Jesus sends out the Twelve, he instructs them to preach that the "kingdom of heaven is near." They are to "heal the sick, raise the dead, cleanse those who have leprosy, drive out demons" (Mt 10:7-8). Their preaching is joined with their healing ministry (Lk 9:6). And when Jesus welcomes them back, he again speaks to them "about the kingdom of God, and [he] healed those who needed healing" (Lk 9:11).

At the same time, the New Testament writers see the healing atonement as fundamentally addressing our sinfulness (e.g., Lk 22:37). Although John 12:37-40 links physical and spiritual healing by noting that Jesus' miraculous healings, signs of God's revelation, fail to bring observers to belief (Is 53:1), the writer's emphasis clearly rests on the spiritual when he then recalls Isaiah's statement (Is 6:10) that God would not heal those who because of their blindness and moribund hearts refused to believe in Jesus. Paul's similar quote of Isaiah 6 in Acts 28:26-27 emphasizes only the spiritual healing of salvation.

Christ's atonement heals our fundamental human predicament, that is, our alienation from God due to our disobedience and attempts to displace him. As one-time enemies of God, we are restored by Christ's atonement to a right relationship with God, with whom we are now reconciled (Rom 5:10-11). Our sins are forgiven, no longer to be held against us (2 Cor 5:18-19). Christ takes on not only our punishment but our very sins (2 Cor 5:21) and intercedes on our behalf (Rom 8:34). In this act of restoration we are given

---

[19]Even Isaiah 53:2 begins with the Servant's "growing up."

[20]Donald A. Hagner, *Matthew 1-13*, Word Biblical Commentary 33a (Dallas: Word, 1993), p. 232.

shalom by the mercy of God the Father and the painful death of his Son.

In short, the healing ministry of Jesus encompasses both the physical and spiritual. The arrival of the new covenant does not break the link between sin and suffering as punishment. Sin can bring sickness. (Though again, not all sickness is due to sin. Such a connection, for example, is never made with Jairus's daughter, Lazarus or a host of others.) Thus, in simultaneously addressing both sin and sickness, Jesus' ministry is holistic. In a holistic way Jesus saves. He saves from sickness (Lk 8:48), he saves from death (Lk 8:49) and demons (Lk 8:26-28), and he saves from sin (Lk 7:50). Again, the last is crucial in that it addresses a root of the others.

We might interpret atonement using the model of the traditional healing process, a model with which ancient Israel would have been familiar. We are sick with sin that we ourselves cannot cure. Exiled from the covenant camp, we await death. God calls us to repent of our sinful ways and in response to our need provides healing in a dramatic fashion. The healing is *curative* in that it deals with our fundamental human predicament of sin, removing our sin from us. It is *restorative* because it returns us to wholeness: to the wholeness of our relation to God from whom we have been cut off because of our sin in rejecting his covenant and his forgiving attempts to reconcile us, to the wholeness of our person from which sickness has been removed, and to the wholeness of God's community from which we were ostracized. God, the great Healer who addresses not merely the symptoms but the root cause of the human predicament, initiates and implements atonement healing holistically to bring us shalom.

Jesus the Suffering Servant

There is a long tradition that sees Jesus as the suffering Servant of Isaiah 53. In the first half of the second century A.D., Justin Martyr, in his *Dialogue with Tryphon the Jew,* viewed Jesus as assuming the role of the Servant. But the identification is even earlier. First Peter, in a passage that commences by treating Christ's suffering as an example of patient perseverance, digresses to a forceful presentation of the atonement as addressing our sins, using phrases from Isaiah 53.

> He himself bore our sins in his body on the tree, so that we might die to sins and live for righteousness; by his wounds you have been healed. For you were like sheep going astray, but now you have returned to the Shepherd and Overseer of your souls. (1 Pet 2:24-25)

Despite this history of identification, critics have discussed the extent to which the New Testament discussion of Jesus' vicarious death is shaped or influenced by Isaiah 53. In her important book *Jesus and the Servant,* Morna Hooker argued that, with the exception of 1 Peter, the New Testament passages that clearly quote Isaiah 53 do not address the atoning significance of the Servant's suffering.[21] Matthew 8:17, as we have seen, stresses physical healing, not atonement for sin. Mark 15:28 (a probable later addition) and Luke 22:3 use Isaiah 53 as a prophetic proof text for passion events. John 12:38, Romans 10:16 and Romans 15:21 appeal to Isaiah 53:1 and Isaiah 52:15 to establish the anticipated rejection or acceptance of Jesus and the gospel. Acts 8 describes Christ's suffering but omits the preceding and succeeding parts of the passage that interpret it in terms of atonement for sin. It is not until 1 Peter that the meaning of the Servant's atonement is definitely linked with the atoning work of Christ.

Even if Hooker's argument stands, however, this does nothing to undermine the view of the atonement as healing, nor does it mean that the atonement cannot be rooted in the Servant Song of Isaiah 53. It only means that this connection gradually develops as the church theologically reflects on the person and work of Christ. The view of atonement as healing remains.

But is Hooker's argument sound? This is not the place to undertake a critique, but three points might be noted. First, this argument overlooks the connection between the healing of physical suffering and the healing/forgiveness of sin that we have already noted characterizes Matthew 8—9. Only a narrow approach that looks for specific textual quotes will miss the connection between the healing Jesus in Matthew 8 and the healing/forgiving Jesus in chapter 9, and between these passages and the identification of Jesus with the healing and victorious Servant in Matthew 12:15-21.[22]

Furthermore, it is clear that Jesus had a good sense of the contents of Isaiah. From the very outset of his ministry the restorative words of Isaiah are in view. In the passage, part of which Jesus read in the synagogue (Lk 4:18-19), Isaiah sees the anointed One as the liberator and restorer (Is 61:1-6). As Jesus interprets it, the liberation and restoration are not merely the political or spiritual liberation of a *nation* but *personal* restoration as well: political

---

[21]Morna Hooker, *Jesus and the Servant* (London: SPCK, 1959).
[22]Note again that the identification of Jesus as Servant occurs in the context of his healing of physical ills and demon possession.

freedom for prisoners, recovery of sight for the blind and, as the events that follow Jesus' reading from the scroll in the synagogue show, the liberation from the bonds of demon possession and illness.

At the end of his ministry Jesus explains to his companions on the road to Emmaus, "beginning with Moses and all the Prophets, . . . all the Scriptures concerning himself" (Lk 24:25-27). The passage does not specifically name Isaiah 53 among those passages, yet in a closely precedent passage, Jesus in the Garden quotes from Isaiah 53 (Lk 22:37). Here Jesus identifies himself with the Servant and with what happens to the Servant. Putting these passages together suggests that at the very least, though we do not actually have the words of Jesus fleshing out the theology of Isaiah 53, we have good reason to think that not only did Jesus identify with the role of the Servant, but that this motif helped shape his view of his person as Messiah and his healing/salvific work.[23]

Finally, even though Paul in Romans 10 and Luke in Acts 8 do not develop a theology of the suffering Servant, the Servant is identified by them with Jesus in the context of the good news (Acts 8:34; Rom 10:16). It is the same good news of the coming of the kingdom of God that Matthew speaks about as accompanied by Jesus' healing and restorative work. It is the good news of those

> who proclaim peace [shalom],
>> who bring good tidings,
>> who proclaim salvation,
> who say to Zion,
>> "Your God reigns!" . . .
> The LORD will lay bare his holy arm
>> in the sight of all the nations,
> and all the ends of the earth will see
>> the salvation of our God. (Is 52:7, 10)

That salvation, revealed by the arm of the Lord, is the very work of the Servant in Isaiah 53:1, the one about whom both Philip and Paul preach.

---

[23]Indeed, that Luke understands the Isaianic context of Jesus and his salvific ministry is evidenced not only by Jesus' own introduction in Luke 4 but also by the introductory salvo to his ministry in John the Baptist's quotation from Isaiah 40 (Lk 3:4-6). For the contention that an Isaianic perspective also underlies Mark, see Rikki E. Watts, "Jesus' Death, Isaiah 53, and Mark 10:45," in *Jesus and the Suffering Servant,* ed. William Bellinger Jr. and William Farmer (Harrisburg, Penn.: Trinity Press International, 1998), pp. 125-51.

How Might Atonement as Healing Be Understood?

Isaiah does not tell us exactly how Christ took on our illness, pain and sin. The Vulgate translates Isaiah 53:4 as saying that the Servant became a leper, actually manifesting physical disease or illness. Other writers suggest, more weakly, that Christ understood or knew what it was to be diseased, but not that he was diseased.[24] Yet none of this does justice to Isaiah's emphasis that the Servant was familiar with or experienced pain, indeed to such an extent that people turned away from him and "held him in low esteem." The traditional methods of healing found in the surrounding cultures frequently contained symbolic dimensions. Features like shape (analogous to the ailing organ),[25] texture and color often defined the use of the plant or amulet in healing. Both Isaiah 53 and Romans 8:3 make a symbolic connection of Christ's atonement with Israel's national atonement ritual (Lev 16). The sacrifice had two steps. One was the slaughter of animals for the sin offering; the other was the release of the sin-laden goat into the wilderness. The first brings atonement through suffering and death; the blood symbolically purifies the community, consecrating it from its state of uncleanness. The second symbolically bears the sins of the community away from the community. Both of these symbolic motifs are found in the Servant's atonement act. Christ's suffering and death cleanses those who have strayed from the covenant, and being made "to be sin for us" (2 Cor 5:21) he personally bears away the sins (Is 53:11), as the goat takes them into the desert. In this he restores us as cured (righteous) to God and to the community. But, as we might expect, the symbolism does not provide a description of the literal "how."

Traditional cultures treat healing as both symbolic and actual. Shamans bring about healing through the removal of the (usually external) cause of the illness that somehow has penetrated the sick person. By allegedly sucking out or removing the foreign substance or in some other way transferring the illness to themselves, shamans briefly take on the illness and suffer until they can get rid of it.[26] Indeed, if the illness is great, it's possible that the shaman will lose his or her own life in the healing process. The risk can be that great. I have not determined whether such practices were known to the

---

[24]Wilkinson, "Physical Healing and the Atonement," p. 158.

[25]Liver models from the Late Bronze Age I were found in an area in Hazor where a bronze serpent, possibly used in healing, was discovered. B. Landsberger and H. Tadmor, "Fragments of Clay Liver Models," *Israel Exploration Journal* 14 (1964): 201-18.

[26]Doug Boyd, *Rolling Thunder* (New York: Random House, 1974), pp. 20-21.

Israelites or surrounding cultures, but shamanistic healing rituals suggest a cultural motif that has provocative parallels with the Isaiah passage, where the Servant takes up, carries and heals by his wounds.

The Death of the Servant/Physician

Why is the death of the Servant or Physician necessary? For most atonement theories this is the heart of the problem. If God is omnipotent and merciful, why demand a route to salvation that exacts the price of the death of God's Son?

Our response can be traced to the virulence of our disease borne by the Servant. What he takes on is no trivial matter; the wages of sin are death (Rom 6:23). Death, in some form, came into the world through sin (Rom 5:12). Christ voluntarily assumes this virulent poison, so strong that it brings death, ours and his, but at the same time not so strong that death can permanently hold the Physician. The death is in the sin. Our sin, not God, kills the Physician. God's part is in mercy to send his Servant/Physician to heal and then to restore him to life and power.

Questioning the Connection

Some object that connecting suffering with healing is a perversion, that it sanctions causing suffering in others. For example:

> Christianity has been a primary—in many women's lives *the* primary—force in shaping our acceptance of abuse. The central image of Christ on the cross as the savior of the world communicates the message that suffering is redemptive. If the best person who ever lived gave his life for others, then, to be of value we should likewise sacrifice ourselves. . . . Our suffering for others will save the world.[27]

The argument is that suffering is oppressive, not redemptive and curative. It glorifies the victim, encouraging people to make others to be victims for their salvation, and encouraging victims to welcome their suffering for others' salvation. Since frequently women are the victims, some feminists reject a view of the atonement that requires sacrifice, suffering and death. Life, not death and suffering, should be the motif.

I have not affirmed or glorified suffering per se; suffering, abuse and tor-

---

[27]Joanne Carlson Brown and Rebecca Parker, "For God So Loved the World?" in *Christianity, Patriarchy and Abuse: A Feminist Critique*, ed. Joanne Carlson Brown and Carole R. Bohn (Cleveland: Pilgrim Press, 1989), p. 2.

ture are neither good nor wished on another. Rather, my picture is that suffering and disease connect with sin, and both are to be eliminated. Healing and well-being (life) are elevated. The issue concerns how to eliminate sin and suffering. As we have seen, Christ's healing of us requires his suffering because what he takes on and removes is virulent and deadly.

Self-sacrifice and servanthood are goods. But as with many other good things, self-sacrifice and servanthood can be misused. That they can be turned into abuse and oppression does not mean that we must jettison the healing or restorative structure of the atonement, or deny that these features may play an important role in healing. Healers serve the ill, sometimes jeopardizing, even sacrificing, their own health and well-being for the good of the community. Indeed, self-sacrifice often is part of the very love that underlies relating to, caring for and helping others. God in love sends the great Physician to take on and remove our sin; otherwise we are left without a cure for our deep human predicament. The atonement and its accompanying suffering and sacrifice are part of God's love. As Lewis points out, both self-serving need-love and sacrificial gift-love are not to be abandoned but radically transformed by God.[28]

Holistic Shalom

One final issue must be addressed. While many are comfortable with atonement as spiritual healing or restoration, they are less sanguine with including the physical (body, mental and emotional) dimension in the model. The atonement, they argue, addresses sin, not sickness. Among others,[29] Wilkenson argues that since sin and disease belong to different categories, what applies to sin does not apply to disease. "Disease is not sin, but a consequence of sin. Disease carries no penalty which must be atoned for as sin does. Disease does not interfere with a man's fellowship with God like sin does. . . . Once we recognize that sin and disease belong to different categories we can readily see that the atonement will affect them in different ways."[30] Furthermore, if physical healing were part of the atonement, physical healing should be "available for all in this life in the atonement."[31] Again, forgiveness is a permanent state, whereas Scripture

---

[28]C. S. Lewis, *The Four Loves* (New York: Harcourt Brace Jovanovich, 1960).
[29]W. Kelly Bokovay, "The Relationship of Physical Healing to the Atonement," Διδασαλια 3, no. 1 (1991): 24-39.
[30]Wilkinson, "Physical Healing and the Atonement," p. 162.
[31]Ibid., p. 161.

and experience show that healing is not. Those forgiven remain forgiven, whereas those healed or restored to life at some point again become ill and eventually die. Since Isaiah's other five uses of *heal* are figurative, Isaiah 53 likewise must employ *heal* figuratively for the healing from sin (as in 1 Pet).[32]

That physical and spiritual healing differ in the ways just noted is true and important, but from these differences it does not follow that "it is not theologically valid to maintain that physical healing is available in the atonement or [by] request in this present life"[33] or that physical healing is eschatological only. Different modes of application of healing do not negate the physical dimension of the atonement. The diverse modes merely suggest that the multidimensional atonement works variously. If Brown is correct that *rāpā'* is properly understood in a broader sense of "restore," there is no reason to think that the restoration, even in Isaiah's other uses, is devoid of physical (or political or economic) content.

> It is incorrect to state that in the prophetic books, sickness and pain are merely figurative expressions representing sin and alienation, as if "healing" is equated there only with forgiveness and reconciliation. . . . It is probable that in the biblical mentality, societal life in general was viewed in more holistic terms than it is today, with religion, family life, political and economic stability, and general health and welfare seen as thoroughly intertwined. Thus, concepts such as *šālôm* were more wide-reaching in their importance, and the idea of Israel being 'sick' and in need of 'healing' might not have been perceived *strictly* as metaphorical by the ancient hearer.[34]

Claus Westermann helpfully notes that the denigration of physical healing reflects a presupposed separation of the soul from the body and the resultant valuing of the former over the latter.

> [Physical] healing and salvation are different in character. Each word points to a basically different way in which God acts. The event of salvation has a different structure from the event of [physical] healing, even though both have much in common. Christian theology has always tried to bring healing and salvation into a close relationship, and has done this by subordinating healing to salvation. Usually [physical] healing has been made a sign either that points to

---

[32]Richard L. Mayhue, "For What Did Christ Atone in Isa 53:4-5?" *Master's Seminary Journal* 6, no. 2 (1995): 128.

[33]Wilkinson, "Physical Healing and the Atonement," p. 163.

[34]Brown, pp. 185, 188.

salvation or that proves the authority of the salvation-bearer. . . . Once healing is defined *merely* as a sign it is straightway degraded. . . . Healing is the non-essential, salvation the essential.[35]

When we treat individuals as whole persons, we understand that physical healing is an essential part of our total well-being. Indeed, as Westermann continues, "The relation of salvation and healing in the Old Testament cannot be so defined that healing becomes secondary to salvation. Rather there are two basically different ways in which God deals with men: salvation and blessing."[36] If we treat both physical healing and spiritual healing (salvation) as restorations, we can locate both in Christ's atonement. In both we encounter God.[37]

Furthermore, a parallel exists between the two aspects in at least one important respect. The fact that our sins are forgiven does not mean that we cease to be sinners. As Luther noted, to be saved is *not* to be free from sin but to be a justified sinner. We are simultaneously righteous (without condemnation) and sinners (but not allowing sin to reign in our lives—Rom 6:11-14). Similarly, the fact that we are healed does *not* mean that we are free from future illness. We are simultaneously healed and subject to illness and ultimately death. But in both cases we are to implement God's healing with a healthy, Spirit-led life (Rom 8:9-13).

The integrity of the two aspects of healing is strengthened by the end of the Isaiah passage, where the Servant is described as making intercession for the transgressors. This fits into not only the spiritual dimension of sin but also the medical dimension that invokes prayer. I have already referred to James's recommendation that the church anoint and pray for the ill that they be healed. Isaiah's Servant intercedes for his people and their sins, and since sin is connected with illness, his intercession plays a role in effecting a cure.[38] The healing model of the atonement thus makes room not only for

---

[35]D. C. Westermann, "Salvation and Healing in the Community: The Old Testament Understanding," *International Review of Mission* 61 (1972): 9.

[36]Ibid., p. 18. "The Lord blesses his people with shalom" (Ps 29:11).

[37]Ibid., p. 13.

[38]The intercessory role might be modeled after that of Moses, who was seen in Jewish literature as the one who saved his people by intercession. The *Testament of Moses* portrays Moses as the eternal liberator, who through both his suffering and his death mediates on behalf of Israel for their sins (David P. Moessner, "Suffering, Intercession and Eschatological Atonement: An Uncommon/Common View in the Testament of Moses and in Luke-Acts," in *The Pseudepigrapha and Early Biblical Interpretation*, ed. James H. Charlesworth and Craig A. Evans (Sheffield, U.K.: Sheffield Academic Press, 1992), pp. 202-27.

bearing our diseases but also for healing intercession on our behalf.

Of course the critics are correct that whereas God does not deny salvation to anyone, intercession does not always bring the results we desire. God does not always remove the illness or suffering. Exploration of the reasons for this would move us into a discussion of the difficult doctrine of divine providence, which lies outside of our present scope. However, it is worth reflecting on the idea that if healing can bring a person into relationship with God, so can *not* being healed. Interviewed on "Speaking of Faith" in April 2005, the Holocaust survivor Elie Wiesel denied the interviewer's claim that because he accused God of abandoning his chosen people by failing to intervene on their behalf in the Holocaust and numerous pogroms, he was an atheist. Rather, Wiesel stated, the fact that he could accuse God stems from his deep faith in God. It reflects the Jewish tradition of contending with God, rooted in Abraham (Gen 18:23-33) and Job (Job 40:1-2). Since atheists do not believe that God exists, for them arguing with God has no meaning. In effect, they would have no one to argue with. To argue with God requires a deep faith that God exists; because God exists we can contend with him. Thus just as we can encounter God when we are healed, so we who are not healed can encounter God in the struggle to understand why healing did not come. "Healing can also be acknowledged as God's deed, in that the person to whom it is not given, by accusing God, holds fast to the healing of God."[39]

Implications for Today

Certain practical consequences follow from the doctrine of atonement as healing or restoration. First, we can have the assurance that our sins are forgiven and that we have a restored relationship with God. The result of this restoration is the tremendous freedom that we have in Christ: our lives need not be lived under the law (Gal 5:1), worrying about whether we keep or break the laws. This is not the freedom to sin but the freedom to live a life of righteousness (2 Cor 5:21) and of service to God and others (Rom 6:1; 12:1-2). This is shalom of the spirit.

Second, we can be assured that God desires well-being for us. In sickness and suffering, in calamity and hardship, God seeks our good. The oft-quoted passage from Jeremiah in the context of restoration is relevant: " 'For I know

---

[39]Westermann, "Salvation and Healing," p. 18.

the plans I have for you,' declares the LORD, 'plans to prosper you and not to harm you, plans to give you hope and a future' " (Jer 29:11). This is the shalom of our physical and social being. Intercession and praise for healing, and even arguing with God (Lk 11:5-8), are consistent with the atonement. James is not out of date (Jas 5:13-16).[40]

Conclusion

I have rooted my model of atonement as healing or restoration in Isaiah, who sees the atonement as healing our sin and its resultant sickness. We have seen this model developed in Matthew, Luke, Paul and Peter, where atonement is fulfilled in the life and death of Jesus Christ, through whom we encounter God in his fullness and love. Atonement, in its deepest rhythms, necessitates that the great Physician take on our sin and suffering as the only way to finally address the human predicament and to restore us to shalom with God, with ourselves and with our community. Until the Physician disposes of the sin and sickness, it is on him, its virulence leading to his death. But the good news is that death is not the end, for Christ or for us. So the elder begins his letter with a holistic greeting, "Dear friend [Gaius], I pray that you may enjoy good health and that all may go well with you, even as your soul is getting along well" (3 Jn 1).

---

[40]Some contemporary studies indicate that persons for whom intercessory prayer has been offered tend to do better medically than a control group for whom no prayer was offered. Randolph Byrd, in a 1994 study of four hundred patients admitted to a coronary care unit at San Francisco General Hospital, found that those "assigned to intercessory prayer groups suffered less with congestive heart failure during recovery, . . . had less frequent intubation, and experienced fewer cases of pneumonia and cardiopulmonary arrests" (Gary Thomas, "Doctors Who Pray," *Christianity Today*, January 6, 1997, p. 20). This and other studies suggest that intercession plays some role in the healing process.

Christus Victor Response

GREGORY A. BOYD

I appreciate the fact that Bruce Reichenbach (in contrast to Joel Green) attempts to organize and understand the rich diversity of metaphors for the atonement in the biblical narrative around a single, dominant theme. I agree with Reichenbach that certain biblical metaphors are conceptually more fundamental than others and can thereby provide the framework within which the other metaphors can be best understood. I further applaud Reichenbach's excellent work in demonstrating the importance of healing for our understanding of the atonement. I wholeheartedly agree that through Jesus' life, death and resurrection God brought healing to humans and to the cosmos on every level.

At the same time, I have to confess that Reichenbach failed to convince me that healing-related metaphors and teachings are conceptually the *most* foundational atonement metaphors and teachings in Scripture. He thus failed to convince me that the healing motif provides the broadest and most appropriate framework for understanding the ultimate significance of Jesus' life, death and resurrection. More fundamental than these, I submit, are metaphors and teachings related to cosmic conflict and spiritual warfare. While the healing dimension of the atonement can be understood as an aspect of God's victory over the devil, God's victory over the devil cannot be understood merely as an aspect of the healing dimension of the atonement.

To illustrate, suppose a scientist named Dr. Joe produced an airborne, self-replicating organism that would instantly annihilate every virus it came in contact with. Once released into the atmosphere, all viral diseases would eventually be eradicated from the earth. Now, those who had been suffering from viral diseases would be perfectly correct in proclaiming, "Dr. Joe healed us of our infirmities!" But this clearly would not be *the most fundamental thing* that could be said about what Dr. Joe accomplished. It would not provide a complete description or explanation of Dr. Joe's achievement. For the most fundamental and significant thing Dr. Joe accomplished was the annihilation of the viruses that were causing human and animal sickness in the first place. He didn't just heal people and animals: *he conquered viruses!* He routed viral sickness itself.

The annihilation of viruses explains the fact that people and animals are now healed of viral afflictions, but the fact that people and animals are now healed of viral afflictions does not in and of itself explain the fact that viruses have now been annihilated. After all, multitudes of people and animals had recovered from viral afflictions before Dr. Joe's creation without all viruses themselves being destroyed. What changed with Dr. Joe's achievement is that the vicious organisms that had for eons thrived in the earth's atmosphere and tormented humanity and the animal kingdom had finally been defeated. So, while we would of course celebrate the fact that people and animals are now healed, we would only be properly describing and explaining Dr. Joe's achievement if we construed these healings as a beneficial result of his victory over the viruses themselves.

I submit that this is precisely the relationship between Jesus' victory over "the powers," on the one hand, and the healing dimension of the atonement, on the other. Certainly Jesus' life, death and resurrection frees us (at least in principle) from our spiritual, psychological and physical infirmities. But this is not the most fundamental thing that can be said about what Jesus accomplished. The ultimate reason Jesus brings us healing is because he defeated "the one who has the power of death, that is, the devil" (Heb 2:14). All the "works of the devil" have in principle been brought to an end because the devil himself has been defeated (1 Jn 3:8). While it is, therefore, perfectly appropriate to celebrate the benefits we receive from this cosmic victory, including our healing, we must never forget that the benefits are fundamentally rooted in this cosmic victory. To return to my viral analogy, we are not only healed: the cosmic viruses themselves have been destroyed! Indeed, we are healed only *because* the cosmic viruses themselves have been destroyed.

The cosmic foundation of the good news of what Jesus accomplished permeates Scripture. To continue my analogy, the viral "rulers and authorities" have been conquered through the cross and therefore "disarmed" (Col 2:15). The cosmic "murderer" who has "from the beginning" been behind every spiritual, psychological and physical ailment humans have ever experienced has at long last been "driven out" (Jn 8:44; 12:31). The cosmic virus that is "the ruler of the power of the air," perpetually polluting the atmosphere of our planet, has been terminated (Eph 2:2). The "god of this world," who exercises an infectious power over the whole world, has been defeated (2 Cor 4:4; 1 Jn 5:19). The venomous "ruler of this world" who has for eons been the power behind all that is contrary to God's beautiful design for creation has at long last been vanquished (Jn 12:31; 14:30; 16:11). The deceiver who owns and corrupts all the kingdoms of the world has finally been dethroned (Lk 4:5-6; cf. Rev 18:3; 20:3, 8). The toxic "strong man" who oppresses all who had become "his property" has finally been overpowered (Lk 11:21-22). Yes, humanity, along with the entire cosmos, is healed in Christ. But this pervasive warfare motif in Scripture explains why.

Jesus did not just heal our blindness: according to Scripture, he confronted and overcame darkness itself (1 Jn 1:4-5). Jesus did not just set captives free: "he made captivity itself a captive" (Eph 4:8). Jesus did not simply free sinners: he destroyed the power of sin itself (e.g., Rom 7:11; 8:1-2). Jesus did not merely free us from condemnation: he silenced the accuser himself (Rev 12:10). And Jesus did not simply heal our infirmities: he destroyed the lord of death himself (Heb 2:14). We significantly weaken and distort the biblical depiction of Christ's accomplishment if we centralize the anthropological benefits instead of the cosmic foundation of these benefits.

The centrality of Jesus' engagement with and victory over hostile forces is evidenced in everything Jesus was about. It is particularly obvious in Jesus' healing ministry, a point I did not have space to adequately emphasize in my original essay. Peter provides us with a succinct summary of what Jesus was centrally about when he proclaims, "God anointed Jesus of Nazareth with the Holy Spirit and with power" so that "he went about doing good and healing *all who were oppressed by the devil*" (Acts 10:38, emphasis added). Though Bruce Reichenbach repeatedly insists that "God, directly or indirectly, brings calamities" (p. 121), Jesus and the Gospel authors uniformly attribute infirmities to Satan and demons.[1] For example, Acts 10:38

---

[1]John 5:14 and John 9:1-3 provide the only possible exceptions to this. Neither verse *requires* our concluding that God brought the infirmities on these individuals. Yet, even if we grant this, neither verse warrants overturning the otherwise uniform teaching that Satan, not God, is ultimately behind disease and infirmities. For a discussion of John 9, see my *God at War* (Downers Grove, Ill.: InterVarsity Press, 1997), pp. 231-34. I should at this point also mention

clearly presupposes that all the illnesses and infirmities Jesus confronted were ultimately (if not at times directly) ways in which people were oppressed by the devil. God's purposes are revealed not in the infirmities but in the healing of infirmities and, even more fundamentally, in the routing of demonic powers that bring them about. It is one aspect of Jesus' general warfare on behalf of the oppressed. The ultimate meaning of Jesus' healings, therefore, is found in their warfare significance.

This is what we find throughout the Gospels. When Jesus encounters a woman who "was quite unable to stand up straight," for example, Luke describes her as "a woman with a spirit that had crippled her for eighteen years." Jesus then asked, "ought not this woman, a daughter of Abraham whom Satan bound for eighteen long years, be set free from this bondage" (Lk 13:11, 16)? This was not a calamity *God* brought on this woman. It was an affliction *Satan* brought on her. What God brought was healing, and he did so by routing the spirit that afflicted her through Christ.

So the Gospel authors sometimes refer to infirmities with the word *mastix,* which literally means "flogging" (Mk 3:10; 5:29, 34; Lk 7:21). In keeping with Acts 10:38, this suggests that infirmities are one means by which Satan oppresses and torments us (Lk 11:21-22). Sometimes Jesus affirms that a specific demon is behind a specific illness (e.g., Lk 11:14). Other times a healing is treated as an exorcism, and an exorcism described as a healing (e.g., Mt 4:24; 12:22; Lk 7:21). This doesn't imply that healing and exorcisms are identical, for they are often listed and treated separately. But it does highlight the close connection between infirmities and demonic oppression, on the one hand, and healing and spiritual warfare, on the other.

Of course, everything I have just said would need to be significantly nuanced. For example, my virus analogy could be taken to imply that humans are *merely* victims in the cosmic war, which, of course, is not true. While "the powers" afflict us like a demonic virus, and while the central thing Jesus did was to destroy this virus and thereby set us free, it is also true that we would never have become vulnerable to these rebellious powers in the first place were it not for our own freely chosen rebellion. To claim, as I believe

---

that, while it is of course undeniable that God brought afflictions on people in the Old Testament—and once, even in the New Testament (Acts 5:1-11)—nowhere does Scripture suggest the conclusion that this is God's general *modus operandi* or that this is the general explanation for why sickness, disease or calamities occur in the world. For discussions of various passages that some think teach otherwise, see *God at War,* pp. 80-93; 144-54; and my *Satan and the Problem of Evil* (Downers Grove, Ill.: InterVarsity Press, 2001), pp. 394-416.

we must, that the oppressive powers are *ultimately* behind evil in the world does not in any way minimize the responsibility humans take in propagating evil. The lame claim that "the devil made me do it" has never been biblically or experientially justified.

Along similar lines, to proclaim that we have *in principle* been set free because the oppressive powers have been demolished does not mean that every individual is *in fact* set free. For, in the same way that we willingly choose to succumb to the powers, we must willingly choose to participate in Christ's victory over the powers. This further means that the "objective" accomplishment of Jesus' work would not be individually salvific were it not for the "subjective" work of the Holy Spirit, opening up our hearts to apply this work to our lives (see, e.g., Acts 16:14; 1 Cor 12:3). On top of this, to affirm that the powers have *in principle* been defeated by the incarnation, life, death and resurrection of the Son of God is not in any way to deny that we and the entire cosmos continue to be afflicted by the powers, as the New Testament and our own experience clearly teach. We live in the interval between D-day and V-day. The victory has been won, but it has not yet been fully manifested.

When Christ's victory *is* fully manifested, humans and the entire cosmos will be healed on every level. Yet it is always important to remember that, while this healing is a marvelous *aspect* of Christ's victory, it is not *the victory itself.*

Penal Substitution Response

THOMAS R. SCHREINER

Bruce Reichenbach helpfully reminds us of the therapeutic or healing dimension of Christ's atoning work. God's restorative work of bringing shalom into our lives and the cosmos is certainly one of the results of the work of Christ on the cross. Reichenbach also underscores some of the same themes that are central to the penal substitution view. Human beings are in a sorry state because "we are inveterate covenant breakers" (p. 119). We have sinned and fallen short of God's standards, and the consequences, as Reichenbach says, are both spiritual and physical. The blight of sin touches every part of our existence, and physical sickness is one consequence of sin, though, as Reichenbach indicates, it is not always due to personal sin. All sickness is due to the fact that we live in a sinful world, and yet it cannot invariably be attributed to personal sin, as if our sickness testifies to a judgment of God for particular sins.

Reichenbach spends some time on Isaiah 53 and maintains that the sacrifice was substitutionary, taking issue rightly with Hooker's view that Isaiah 53 was not formative in the New Testament understanding of Jesus' death until the writing of 1 Peter (p. 134). He proceeds to argue that the atonement described in Isaiah 53 involved the forgiveness of sins and healing of sicknesses. He rightly spies the healing dimension of the atonement in Matthew 8:17, so that forgiveness of sins and physical healing are not neatly separated from one another (p. 134). Reichenbach does not argue that all believers have a promise of physical healing in this life, or that those who remain sick have sinned in some way. We can rightly say that all sickness is ultimately (though not always personally) due to sin, and that in the cross we have forgiveness of sins and healing, but such healing will only be experienced fully at the day of resurrection when all sorrow, tears and illness pass away.

One of the interesting features in Reichenbach's essay is that he does not specifically argue for the centrality of the healing theme over against other interpretations of Christ's death. He presents well the theme of healing, but he does not attempt to argue that it is the fundamental theme in the Scriptures relative to the atonement. Hence, it appears that he does not fulfill one of the stated objectives of the book. In the remainder of my response, therefore, I will attempt to show why penal substitution is more central than a therapeutic theme.

The fundamental problem with the therapeutic view is that it centers on human beings instead of God himself. The God-centeredness of biblical revelation is shunted to the side and the consequences of the atonement for human beings comes to the forefront. I could raise the same criticisms with respect to Boyd and Green. In every case the holiness of God is virtually ignored, and the issue of his justice being satisfied is muted. Such are the consequences of anthropocentric views of the atonement that concentrate on the healing of human beings, the defeat of demonic powers or the nature of the human condition. The truth that the fundamental human sin is idolatry, the refusal to submit to God's lordship and to give him the praise and honor he deserves as Lord (Rom 1:18-25), falls into the background and is scarcely mentioned in such approaches. The awesome beauty of God's holiness becomes nearly invisible when the focus shifts to human beings and the benefits we accrue from the atonement. No view of the atonement can be central if it fails to put God at the center of what happens in the cross, and more particularly, if it fails to reckon with God's holiness and justice in the face of the affront and offense of sin.

Even though Bruce Reichenbach affirms substitution, he probably does not mean the same thing as I do in using the term. In any case, he avoids the term *penal substitution.* He argues that Jesus as our physician had to take our sin upon himself. Otherwise, there would be no cure for sin. But like Boyd he provides no explanation as to why God required the death of his Son to cure us of our sins. It seems quite conceivable that God in his sovereignty and love could cure us without his Son suffering the pain of death. We know that physicians can cure us without contracting the diseases we have, and thus it would help to understand why the disease of sin could be cured only through Christ's death. Reichenbach does not tackle this matter in any detail; therefore we are left only with his claim that the death of the Son was needed for the cure. Precisely at this point we need biblical exegesis to verify and support what is fundamental for Reichenbach's view of the atonement.

I refer readers to my chapter, where an attempt is made to demonstrate exegetically that the penal substitution view explains most satisfactorily the drama of the atonement. The penal substitution theory is paramount because it reckons with the God-centered character of the Scriptures, and it demonstrates both God's love and justice in salvation history. Nor is this an abstraction, as some claim, for we are talking about an event—the cross of Christ—that actually occurred in space-time history! The cross of Christ is not separated from the history of salvation or the story line of Scripture; it represents the apex of the biblical story line, and as each of the Gospels demonstrate, Jesus' death and resurrection are the climax of the story.

Penal substitution also takes seriously human sin. Sin is not merely a disease that deforms us, nor are we merely the victims of outside powers. As the twentieth century testified in more blatant ways, human beings are radically evil. We are in thrall to Satan and demons, but the very story line of Scripture (Gen 3) indicates that we are in bondage because of human sin. We are in bondage to sin (Rom 5—7), and yet we willingly and gladly sin. As sons and daughters of Adam we sin because we find it to be delightful (Eph 2:3), and we think it will bring us life. Sin at its heart is a deep-seated rebellion against God and his lordship. The gospel speaks powerfully to us because it does not gloss over the human condition, recognizing that we need to be delivered from the evil that dominates us.

God in his holiness cannot abide evil. As we often read in the Old Testament, his wrath righteously burns against human sin. So too in the New Testament, God's wrath is revealed from heaven against all sin and human disobedience, because we long to be independent from God and cast him away so that we can be the captains of our fate and the masters of our souls. The Scriptures teach that God's holiness must be satisfied and appeased so that our sin is forgiven. God sent his Son out of love, and the Son willingly came in love to appease his own wrath and win our salvation. God's holiness is satisfied in the cross, so God is both just and the justifier of the one who has faith in Jesus (Rom 3:21-26). Penal substitution fits Scripture so remarkably, not because it is abstract and impersonal but because it blazes white-hot with God's personal holiness that cannot tolerate any sin because of his righteousness. It shines the searchlight on human sin in all its depravity and corruption, and it shows that we are unutterably proud, profoundly selfish, and ardent haters of God. But in the cross we find the greatest mystery of all. God's merciful love and his awful wrath meet at the cross. I do not understand why people say this provides no basis of ethics or that it is separated from Christ's ministry on earth, or that it does not conform with the biblical story line. Justification by faith is the wellspring of all Christian living, for we live each day in the grace that has been given to us in the gospel.

Kaleidoscopic Response

JOEL B. GREEN

Bruce Reichenbach introduces and explores one of the most powerful portraits of Yahweh in the Scriptures of Israel: "I am the LORD, who heals you" (Ex 15:26). Yahweh's work of healing is the centerpiece of a constellation of images, such as care for and sovereignty over the cosmos, working justice on behalf of the oppressed, extension of love and mercy, renewal of the fatigued, forgiveness, and restoration. Healing is God's setting things right. Similarly, in the Synoptic Gospels, Jesus' ministry is distinguished by his typical behavior as a healer and his portrayal as one who exercised in a direct way the saving power of God. Jesus' healing was pivotal to the meaning of his ministry, declaring his identity as the authorized agent of Yahweh's beneficence, the presence of which signals in Jesus' ministry the currency of God's end-time dominion. What is more, both Old and New Testaments evidence the role of God's people, whether individually and collectively, in the healing work of God. Clearly then, from the standpoint of biblical theology, salvation understood in terms of healing is a welcome emphasis indeed.

Nevertheless, questions remain with regard to Reichenbach's presentation of the atonement as healing and, indeed, of the adequacy of healing as a metaphor for the atonement more generally.

First, in spite of his concern with holistic shalom, Reichenbach's discussion of healing too often allows for a dichotomy between the physical and the spiritual.

In the New Testament world, the most common usage of the Greek terms associated with "salvation"—*sōzō* ("to save"), *sōtēr* ("savior"), *sōtērion* ("saving"), and *sōtēria* ("salvation")—was medical. "To save" was "to heal," and physicians were sometimes designated "saviors." Miracles of healing in the Roman Mediterranean were claimed by and for "holy men," as well as attributed to kings, emperors and military leaders.[1] Deliverance from the enemy, cataloged as "salvation," "peace" or "healing," was as much a religious statement as a political one. Consider Philo's words concerning the Augustus's success as a military-political leader: "This is the Caesar who calmed the torrential storms on every side, who healed pestilences common to Greeks and barbarians, pestilences which descending from the south and east coursed to the west and north sowing seeds of calamity over the places and waters which lay between them."[2]

This perspective is very much at home in the Scriptures of Israel, where the language of "salvation" might refer to deliverance, healing, health and prosperity. Like water to the thirsty (Is 12:3), salvation addresses the threat of sin (Is 64:5) and sickness. Says Yahweh:

> For the hurt of my poor people I am hurt,
>   I mourn, and dismay has taken hold of me.
> Is there no balm in Gilead?
>   Is there no physician there?
> Why then has the health of my poor people
>   not been restored? (Jer 8:21-22)

Intercultural perspectives can help us here. If "sickness" is any unwanted condition, or substantial threat of unwanted conditions, of self,[3] then notions of health and sickness are not "givens," as though all people at all times and in all places represent themselves in the same way. Rather, ideas and experiences related to "health" and "sickness" are tied to how a people measures human well-being. It follows from this that representations of sickness and hopes for health might take on different forms, as one moves from culture to culture. People in the contemporary West tend to think in terms of diseased individuals (rather than communities), with "ailments" falling in the category of the physical or bodily; hence, cures are sought via biomedical intervention. Deeply committed to a biomedical model of health and healing, we focus our concerns and hopes on the life of one individual at a time. For people portrayed in the biblical materials, the source of sickness rested

---

[1] Cf. Wendy Cotter, *Miracles in Greco-Roman Antiquity* (London: Routledge, 1999), pp. 11- 53; more generally, Ceslas Spicq, *Theological Lexicon of the New Testament* (Peabody, Mass.: Hendrickson, 1994), 3:344-49.

[2] Philo *The Embassy to Gaius* 144-45, in *Philo* (Cambridge, Mass.: Harvard University Press 1962), 10:73-74.

[3] I have adapted this definition from Robert A. Hahn, *Sickness and Healing* (New Haven, Conn.: Yale University Press, 1995), p. 22.

not only in the bodies of the sick but also and sometimes especially in their social environments and in the larger cosmos. In this case, healing might entail restoring a person to community, some form of bodily intervention, the redress of cosmic imbalances—or, more typically, some combination of all of these.

I mention all of this because, in spite of Reichenbach's sensitivities to these matters, his presentation sometimes slips into either-or terms. For those of us weaned on medical practices and health care systems in the Western world, this is no surprise. We often misconstrue the nature of healing in Scripture by focusing too narrowly the reach of "healing." In this respect it is worth remembering that humanity was created in the image of God (Gen 1:26-27), entailing relationships of harmony within the human community as well as with God and the entire cosmos. Consequently, "healing" from a biblical perspective must entail restoration to health in the fullest sense. Healing, then, is human recovery.

In short, a more holistic approach to healing is demanded by the evidence. This is why "healing" serves so well as a way of articulating the biblical message of salvation.

Second, in what sense does Bruce Reichenbach account for the fact that the character of Jesus' life, his teaching and ministry practices, resulted in his crucifixion on a Roman cross? Sundered from engagement with the circumstances of Jesus' death, any model of the atonement, including this one, remains an abstraction. Reichenbach is clear, helpfully so, that the healing model of the atonement embraces not only Jesus' death but also his life. What is lacking, however, is a clear articulation of how his model accounts for the reality of Jesus' crucifixion as the consequence of a life in the service of God's purpose over against all sorts of opposing social, political and religious agenda. To put it more crassly, in order to achieve atonement as healing, why did Jesus have to die? To push further still, in order to achieve atonement as healing, why did Jesus have to die as a threat to Rome?[4]

Third, can Reichenbach provide evidence that healing as a model for the atonement is part of the church's theological tradition? One of the hallmarks of this model of the atonement is its central focus on the subjective side of

---

[4]That such a case might be made, see, e.g., Graham N. Stanton, "Jesus of Nazareth: A Magician and a False Prophet Who Deceived God's People?" in *Jesus of Nazareth: Lord and Christ,* ed. Joel B. Green and Max Turner (Grand Rapids: Eerdmans, 1995), pp. 164-80; August Strobel, *Die Stunde der Wahrheit,* Wissenschaftliche Untersuchungen zum Neuen Testament 21 (Tübingen: Mohr Siebeck, 1980).

the atonement, and this is clearly represented in the theological tradition. It would buttress Reichenbach's case, though, if he were able to show that the healing view has played an important role in the development of atonement theology.

Fourth, and most importantly, in what sense can we speak of "healing" as a way of making sense of the saving work of Jesus on the cross? A plethora of soteriological images congregate around images of salvation as healing and health, including reconciliation, new creation, forgiveness, justification, peace and sanctification.[5] But these are images of salvation, not of the atonement; that is, they fill out the meaning of salvation but do not identify the means of salvation. Without developing a hyperconcern with the mechanics of the atonement, the mechanism of how the cross of Christ saves, I am nonetheless curious how Christ's work on the cross, when understood as healing, effects salvation.

Reichenbach recognizes this problem and attempts to address it in two related ways. First, borrowing from Isaianic language concerning the Servant of Yahweh, he observes that Jesus, as Servant, takes on all our inequities and gives us forgiveness of sins. Still working within the thought world of the Isaianic Servant, Reichenbach goes on to urge that Jesus, as Servant, takes on the punishment for our sins. Reichenbach thus shows how the atonement, understood in substitutionary terms, effects healing, but he does not show how the atonement, understood in terms of healing, effects salvation. Second, Reichenbach offers the analogue of the shaman at work in traditional cultures. Even if we were to admit that Israel or its surrounding cultures promoted such practices (a possibility that Reichenbach does not press), the model he sketches is still substitution or exchange, with healing the consequence of the shaman's taking on the illness and suffering.

In short, it is far easier to argue that salvation itself must be understood as healing or that healing is really a consequence of salvation than to argue that healing is the means by which salvation through Christ's (life and) death is made available.

---

[5]Joel B. Green, *Salvation,* Understanding Biblical Themes (St. Louis, Mo.: Chalice, 2003), pp. 52-60.

FOUR

Kaleidoscopic View

JOEL B. GREEN

A close reading of the New Testament supports two indisputable and intimately linked claims about the crucifixion of Jesus of Nazareth. The first is that Jesus' demise at the hands of Roman justice, represented theologically in the motto "Christ crucified," is the means for comprehending the eternal purpose of God, as this is known in Israel's Scriptures. The second is that the significance of Jesus' death is woven so tightly into the fabric of God's purpose that we may never exhaust the many ways of articulating its meaning for our salvation. My task in this chapter is to unpack these dense claims to demonstrate both that the significance of Jesus' death can be grasped neither apart from its historical context in the Roman world nor apart from the expansive mural of God's purpose in creation and redemption, and that on its own no one model or metaphor will do when it comes to the task of articulating and proclaiming that significance in the world today.

The Death of Jesus, God's Messiah, in Context

What do we know about the manner of Jesus' execution? On this the evidence is far more ambiguous than is generally realized and popularly portrayed. Literary sensibilities in Roman antiquity did not promote graphic descriptions of the act of crucifixion.[1] As Cicero remarked in his defense of a Roman senator:

> But the executioner, the veiling of the head and the very word 'cross' should be far removed not only from the person of a Roman citizen but from his thoughts, his eyes and his ears. For it is not only the actual occurrence of these

---

[1]Martin Hengel, *Crucifixion: In the Ancient World and the Folly of the Message of the Cross* (Philadelphia: Fortress, 1977), pp. 38, 77-81. This is (over)emphasized in Werner H. Kelber, *The Oral and the Written Gospel* (Philadelphia: Fortress, 1983), pp. 193-94.

things or the endurance of them, but liability to them, the expectation, indeed the very mention of them, that is unworthy of a Roman citizen and a free man.[2]

Although remarkably full accounts, even the Gospels lack the sort of detail that apparently belonged to the shared cultural encyclopedia of the larger Roman world. In spite of the paucity and ambiguity of the evidence, Martin Hengel has suggested that crucifixion typically included a flogging beforehand, with victims generally made to carry their own crossbeams to the location of their execution, where they were bound or nailed to the cross with arms extended, raised up and, perhaps, seated on a small wooden peg (a *sedile*).[3]

Roman practices were guided by their interest in the deterrent value of crucifixion. Quintilian (c. A.D. 35[]90s) observed that, "whenever we crucify the guilty, the most crowded roads are chosen, where most people can see and be moved by this fear. For penalties relate not so much to retribution as to their exemplary effect" (*Declamationes* 274). Variation in the manner of how victims were affixed to the cross would have served not only as sadistic entertainment but also the need to leave the victim alive as long as possible for maximum deterrent effect. This interest is related to the fact that Rome did not embrace crucifixion as its method of choice for execution on account of the overwhelming physical pain it caused. This lack of interest in torturous pain is emphasized by contrasting accounts of crucifixion with the portrait of heinous suffering memorialized in the martyr tale of 2 Maccabees 6:18—7:42, in which seven brothers and their mother serially experienced scalping, dismemberment and their bodies thrown into heated pans for frying. The act of crucifixion resulted in little blood loss and death came slowly as the body succumbed to shock.[4] This form of capital punishment was savage and heinous, but for reasons other than bodily torture. In the honor-and-shame-based culture of Greco-Roman antiquity, bodily torture was not the worst sort of injury. Indeed, even in the martyr tale of 2 Maccabees 6—7, the emphasis falls on dying with nobility, with honor, rather than experiencing the shame of rejecting one's ancestral faith. More than pan-frying or dismem-

---

[2]Cicero *Rabirio Perduellionis* 16, in Hengel's *Crucifixion*, p. 42.
[3]Hengel, *Crucifixion*, pp. 22-32.
[4]The often-repeated view that crucifixion resulted in death by asphyxiation is no longer tenable, at least in cases where the executed was fixed to the cross with arms outspread—see F. T. Zugibe, "Death by Crucifixion," *Canadian Society of Forensic Science* 17 (1983): 1-13.

berment, then, crucifixion brought with it the pain of humiliation. In their depiction of the ordeal Jesus endured in the hours before crucifixion and during the time of his hanging on the cross, the Gospel records themselves make this clear—focusing as they do on the myriad attempts to dishonor Jesus: spitting on him (Mt 26:67; 27:30; Mk 14:65; 15:19), striking him in the face and head (Mt 26:67; Mk 14:65; Lk 22:63), ridiculing him (Mt 27:29, 31, 41; Mk 15:20, 31), insulting him (Mt 27:44; Mk 15:32; Lk 22:65), and derisively mocking him (Mk 15:16-20, 29-32; Lk 22:65; 23:11, 35-37); he even suffers the humiliation of having been abandoned by his closest friends. Executed publicly, situated at a major crossroads or on a well-trafficked artery, devoid of clothing, denied burial and left to be eaten by birds and beasts, victims of crucifixion were subject to optimal, unmitigated, vicious ridicule.

Rome did not expose its own citizens to such reprehensible punishment but reserved crucifixion above all for those who resisted imperial rule.[5] That this is true in the case of Jesus is evident from the announcement of Jesus' offense, the inscription on the cross: "The King of the Jews," which Gerhard Schneider takes as "the historically unimpeachable point of departure" in an examination of the charge brought against Jesus.[6] It is true that Jesus is not identified as a λῃστής *(lēstēs)*, an "insurrectionist" (cf. Mt 26:55; 27:38, 44), but the claim to kingship would be sufficient to serve as a threat to the emperor: "Anyone who makes himself king opposes Caesar" (Jn 19:12).[7]

That the Romans were involved in the legal proceedings concerning Jesus and were responsible for pronouncing the death sentence is undeniable, whatever one makes of the role of the Jerusalem Sanhedrin. Crucifixion was not a Jewish practice; so if Jesus had been sentenced to death by the Sanhedrin we might have expected, say, an account of stoning or beheading. More to the point, however, in the Roman provinces the power of capital punishment was held by the Romans; John's report of the words of the Sanhedrin to Pilate possesses historical verisimilitude on this point: "We

---

[5]This is now well documented in Hengel, *Crucifixion;* H.-W. Kuhn, "Die Kreuzesstrafe während der frühen Kaiserzeit: Ihre Wirklichkeit und Wertung in der Umwelt des Urchristentums," *Aufsteig und Niedergang der Römischen Welt* 2.25.1 (1982): 648-793 (706-18).

[6]Gerhard Schneider, "The Political Charge Against Jesus (Luke 23:2)," in *Jesus and the Politics of His Day,* ed. Ernst Bammel and C. F. D. Moule (Cambridge: Cambridge University Press, 1984), pp. 403-14 (404).

[7]Unless otherwise indicated, Scripture quotations are the author's translation.

are not allowed to execute anyone" (Jn 18:31).[8] How can we explain this level of Roman interest in Jesus?

Roman rulers were charged with taking whatever steps were necessary to maintain the "peace of Rome," so the most straightforward way to account for the problem Jesus posed Rome is by reflecting on the potential of Jesus' popularity with the crowds. Pilate's interest would surely have been piqued upon hearing these words concerning Jesus from the Jewish Council: "He stirs up the people by teaching throughout all Judea" (Lk 23:5). Add to this the teeming masses present in Jerusalem for Passover and the Feast of Unleavened Bread, the scene of the triumphal entry, and Jesus' prophetic action in the temple, and it is easy to see how Jesus might have been regarded as a threat to public order. It is worth noting, though, that Jesus was on a collision course with Roman interests long before his arrival in Jerusalem. Though relatively unknown in the Roman world, he propagated a worldview that ran counter to official Roman ideology, and he encouraged others to do the same. If the followers can be charged with "turning the world upside down," "acting contrary to the decrees of the emperor," and "saying that there is another king named Jesus" (Acts 17:6-7), how much more the leader? Indeed, the juxtaposition of the dominion of Caesar and that of Jesus comes into focus in two key texts:

- "We found this man perverting our nation, *forbidding us to pay taxes to the emperor,* and saying that he himself is the Messiah, *a king.*" (Lk 23:2)

- "Therefore, the chief priests and the Pharisees called a meeting of the Sanhedrin, and said, 'What are we to do? This man performs many signs. If we allow him to continue like this, everyone will believe in him, and the Romans will come and overrun both our [holy] place and our nation.'" (Jn 11:47-48)

These and related texts demonstrate that the problem of Jesus was also well-known to the Jewish leadership in Jerusalem.

From Jewish perspectives, the possible infractions associated with Jesus are several. The Temple Scroll designates those who betray Israel to a for-

---

[8]See Klaus W. Müller, "Möglichkeit und Vollzug jüdischer Kapitalgerichtsbarkeit im Proxess gegen Jesus von Nazaret," in *Der Prozess gegen Jesus,* ed. Karl Kertelge, Quaestiones disputatae 112 (Freiburg: Herder, 1988), pp. 41-83. It is true, though, that large numbers of Jews were crucified under the Jewish king and high priest Alexander Janneus (107□76 B.C.), who is remembered for his crucifixion of eight hundred Pharisees (Josephus *Antiquities of the Jews* 13.14.2 §380; *Jewish Wars* 1.4.6 §97; Nahum Pesher [4Q169] 3-4.1.7).

eign power as deserving of the penalty of "hanging on a tree" (11QTemple 64.6-13; see Deut 21:22-23), and blasphemy was long regarded as an infraction punishable by death. Regarding the first, we may recall that John reports Caiaphas's decision concerning the execution of Jesus: if Jesus were allowed to continue his public ministry, Rome would destroy the temple and the nation (Jn 11:47-53). Regarding the latter, both Mark and Matthew have it that Jesus was found guilty of blasphemy (Mt 26:59-68; Mk 14:55-65).[9] Additionally, Graham Stanton and August Strobel have shown that Jesus had to be eliminated as a religious deceiver, or magician, and false prophet.[10] This is suggested by the evaluation of Jesus as a deceiver in Matthew 27:63 and John 7:12 but even more so in the allegations brought against Jesus in Luke 23—namely, that he "perverts our nation"/"the people" (vv. 2, 14). Reference to "perverting" constitutes a formal allegation against Jesus as a false prophet, rooted in Deuteronomy 13 and 17. In a disputed report, Josephus ties the portrait of Jesus as miracle-worker together with his "leading the people astray,"[11] and this comports well with later rabbinic traditions describing Jesus as a magician who deceived and led Israel astray (*b. Sanhedrin* 43a; 107b; cf. *b. Shabbat* 104b). Writing in the mid-second century A.D., Justin Martyr observes similarly that though Jesus' miracles of healing should have elicited recognition of him as Messiah, some drew the opposite conclusion: "they said it was a display of magic art, for they even dared to say that he was a magician and a deceiver of the people" (*Dialogue* 69.7; cf. Deut 13:5). These diverse testimonies lead to the same conclusion, that Jesus was charged as a deceiver and false prophet.

The proximate basis for Jesus' arrest and trial, though, is more likely to

---

[9]See Darrell L. Bock, "The Son of Man Seated at God's Right Hand and the Debate over Jesus' 'Blasphemy,'" in *Jesus of Nazareth: Lord and Christ: Essays on the Historical Jesus and New Testament Christology*, ed. Joel B. Green and Max Turner (Grand Rapids: Eerdmans, 1995) pp. 181-91, and *Blasphemy and Exaltation in Judaism: The Charge against Jesus in Mark 14:53-65,* Wissenschaftliche Untersuchungen zum Neuen Testament 2/106 (Tübingen: Mohr Siebeck, 1998).

[10]Graham N. Stanton, "Jesus of Nazareth: A Magician and a False Prophet Who Deceived God's People?" in *Jesus of Nazareth: Lord and Christ,* ed. Joel B. Green and Max Turner (Grand Rapids: Eerdmans, 1995), pp. 164-80; August Strobel, *Die Stunde der Wahrheit: Untersuchungen zum Strafverfahren gegen Jesus,* Wissenschaftliche Untersuchungen zum Neuen Testament 21 (Tübingen: Mohr Siebeck, 1980).

[11]Josephus *Antiquities* 18.3.3 §§63-64; on the problem of the *Testimonium Flavianum,* see the survey and bibliography in Craig A. Evans, "Jesus in Non-Christian Sources," in *Studying the Historical Jesus: Evaluations of the State of Current Research,* ed. Bruce Chilton and Craig A. Evans, New Testament Tools and Studies 19 (Leiden: Brill, 1994), pp. 443-78 (466-74).

be rooted in the combination of triumphal entry and prophetic action in the temple. Jesus' relationship to the temple is of particular interest, since the temple charge—that Jesus claimed that he would destroy the temple and rebuild another not made with human hands—appears in the trial before the Sanhedrin as recounted by Matthew and Mark, and is otherwise well-established in the tradition.[12] "Rebuilding the temple" is a task allocated to the Messiah in one significant strand of eschatological expectation concerned with the restoration of Israel,[13] and this only underscores the political stakes of Jesus' action in the temple upon entering Jerusalem (Mt 21:12-13; Mk 11:15-17; Lk 19:45-46; Jn 2:13-16). Taken on its own, the temple act could have been overlooked, but when this act is comprehended within this eschatological framework and in tandem with the popular support evident in the triumphal entry and continuing throughout the time of Jesus' teaching in the Jerusalem temple, too much was at risk.

As the Gospel narratives have it, three stable elements characterize the period of Jesus' Jerusalem ministry: (1) Jesus' interaction with various representatives of the Jerusalem elite, (2) the omnipresence of "the people" who look favorably on Jesus' teaching, and (3) the persistent setting of the whole in relation to the temple. Because of the religious, political and economic centrality of the temple in Jewish ideology, this is crucial. This is the sacred space that embodies and propagates the order of the world, and provides the axial point around which socioreligious life is aligned. If in his prophetic action in the temple Jesus anticipates the demise of the temple system, if in a series of encounters with those groups associated with the temple Jesus finds himself in conflict on key issues related to scriptural interpretation and faithful praxis, if he claims divine sanction and authority for himself and his message, and if Jesus forecasts calamity and destruction as the old world order is overtaken by the new, has he not thus subverted the authority of the Jewish elite who have been divinely entrusted with the mediation of God's ways, who speak for God, who collect tithes and maintain the temple treasury, who handle holy things? In other words, Jesus ran afoul of the Jerusalem elite because he proclaimed by word and deed a vision of God's rule

---

[12]Mt 26:61; Mk 14:58; cf. Mk 15:29; Jn 2:19; Acts 6:14; *Gospel of Thomas* 71.

[13]Cf. 2 Sam 7:5-16; Zech 6:12-13; *Targum of the Prophets* Zech 6:12-13; *Targum of the Prophets* Is 53:5; *1 Enoch* 90:28-29; 4 Ezra 10:27; *Florilegium* (4Q174) 1.1-13; E. P. Sanders, *Jesus and Judaism* (London: SCM, 1985), pp. 77-90; Joel B. Green, *The Death of Jesus: Tradition and Interpretation in the Passion Narrative,* Wissenschaftliche Untersuchungen zum Neuen Testament 2/33 (Tübingen: Mohr Siebeck, 1988), pp. 277-81.

that ran counter to that of the Jewish leadership in Jerusalem, and it cost him his life.

In short, Roman and Jewish eyes and ears could see and hear quite different things in Jesus' deeds and words, and in the end these two streams of interpretation arrived at the confluence of one outcome: Jesus' capital sentencing. As Peter Stuhlmacher summarizes: "Jesus had to die because he made too many enemies who opposed his messianic ministry."[14]

Some may wonder what this rehearsal of historical reminiscence has to do with the theology of the atonement. What I have urged thus far is that the death of Jesus cannot be understood apart from the powerful social, political and religious currents he set himself against. The saving significance of Jesus' death cannot be understood apart from those same forces. Let me suggest how this is so.

The Gospels are unanimous in their testimony that Jesus anticipated his death; in the charged environment of Roman Palestine how could he not have done so? To admit this is to open the door to its corollary—namely, the probability that he reflected on its significance and did so in a way that intimately related it to his mission to redeem the people of God. By this I mean that Jesus was no masochist looking for an opportunity to suffer and die, but he saw that his absolute commitment to the purpose of God might lead, in the context of "this adulterous and wicked generation" (Mk 8:38), to his death. This, he discerned and embraced in prayer on the night of his arrest, was the cup given him by God (Mk 14:32-42; Lk 22:39-46).

His mission, as this is known to us in the Gospels, was directed toward revitalizing Israel as the people of God. Pursuing this aim compelled him to proclaim the intervention of God's rule and to embody the ethics of this kingdom, and this brought him into conflict with the conveyers of Roman and Jewish ideologies and practices. From this perspective nothing of significance in Jesus' practices is irrelevant to his execution; everything—his interpretation of Israel's Scriptures, his practices of prayer and worship, his astounding choice of table companions, his crossing of the boundaries of clean and unclean, his engagement with children, his miracles of healing and exorcism—leads to the cross. Calling twelve disciples as representative of restored Israel, weaving the hopes of a new exodus and the eschatological era into his ministries of word and deed, speaking of the fulfillment of

---

[14]Peter Stuhlmacher, *Jesus of Nazareth—Christ of Faith* (Peabody, Mass.: Hendrickson, 1993), p. 55.

God's promises to Israel, his prophetic action at the temple in anticipation of a temple not made by human hands—in all of these ways and more, Jesus countered the present world order and maintained that God was at work in his person and mission. This led him to a form of execution emblematic of a way of life that rejected the value of public opinion in the determination of status before God and inspired interpretations of his death that accorded privilege to the redemptive power of righteous suffering. The way was opened for Jesus' followers to accord positive value to his shameful death, and thus to learn to associate in meaningful ways what would otherwise have been only a clash of contradictory images: Jesus' heinous suffering and his messianic status.

This means that God's saving act is not God's response to Jesus' having become "obedient to the point of death—even death on a cross" (Phil 2:8). Rather, God sent his Son to save, and this is worked out in a kaleidoscope of purpose statements: to fulfill the law (Mt 5:17), to call sinners to repentance (Mt 9:13), to bring a sword (Mt 10:34), to give his life as a ransom for many (Mk 10:45), to proclaim the good news of the kingdom of God in the other cities (Lk 4:43), to seek and to save the lost (Lk 19:10), and so on. Even the ransom saying is exegeted by the parallel description of Jesus' mission: "The son of man came not to be served, but to serve" (Mk 10:45). God's saving act is the incarnation, which encompasses the whole of his life, including his death.

To admit all of this, however, is to press for interpretations of Jesus' death that bind together the life of Jesus and his death. It is not enough to affirm that the cross is the culmination of Jesus' life without taking the further step of articulating how this is so. Indeed, apart from this larger narrative, we have little on which to base any claim regarding the soteriological significance of Jesus' execution.[15] Within the Gospel tradition, it is precisely the collocation

---

[15]Someone might say, as Rudolf Bultmann certainly said, that for his part Paul seemed quite capable of interpreting Jesus' death (and resurrection) without any concern for the manner of Jesus' life, that Jesus' earthly life, apart from the "that" of his earthly life, was irrelevant to Paul: "Jesus' manner of life, his ministry, his personality, his character play no role at all; neither does Jesus' message" (*Theology of the New Testament* [New York: Charles Scribner's, 1951, 1955], 2:293-94). But this way of construing Paul's interests has been countered repeatedly—with reference both to evidence of Jesus-tradition in Paul's letters (e.g., David Wenham, *Paul and Jesus: The True Story* [Grand Rapids: Eerdmans, 2002]) and to the theological significance of the life of Jesus for Paul (e.g., Richard B. Hays, *The Faith of Jesus Christ,* Society of Biblical Literature Dissertation Series 56 [Chico, Calif.: Scholars Press, 1983]; Richard N. Longenecker, "The Foundational Conviction of New Testament Christology: The Obedience/Faithfulness/Sonship of Christ," in *Jesus of Nazareth: Lord and Christ,* ed. Joel B. Green and Max Turner [Grand Rapids: Eerdmans, 1994], pp. 473-88).

of Jesus' life and death that funds a robust soteriology. Thus Jesus was able to gather together Israel's history and hopes and from them shape a view of himself as the one through whose suffering Israel, and through Israel the nations, would experience redemption. In elucidating the significance of his looming death, Jesus pushed backward into Israel's history and embraced Israel's expectations for deliverance. At the table on his last night with his followers, at a meal copious with the imagery of Passover and exodus, he intimated that the new exodus, God's decisive act of deliverance, was coming to fruition in his death, the climax of his mission. Moreover, he developed the meaning of his death in language and images grounded in the constitution of Israel as the covenant people of God (Ex 24:8), the conclusion of the exile (see Zech 9:9-11) and the hope of a new covenant (Jer 31:31-33) so as to mark his death as the inaugural event of covenant renewal. How could Jesus contemplate such thoughts? Taken together with his prophetic action in the temple, the symbolic actions at the table of Jesus' last meal with his disciples signify the disestablishment of the old ordering of Israel's life and, by means of God's great act of deliverance in his sacrificial death, the establishment of a new basis of Israel's life before God.[16]

In other words, a model of the atonement with a solid claim to being biblical cannot represent the death of Jesus in terms that do not integrate seriously the reality of his crucifixion as the consequence of a life in the service of God's purpose and in opposition to all manner of competing social, political, and religious agenda. Atonement theology, understood in this light, cannot be reduced to the relationship of the individual to God, nor to an objective moment in the past when Jesus paid the price for our sins, nor, indeed, to a notion of salvation segregated from holiness of life in the world.

The Atonement: The Necessity of Multiple Views

At one level, my claim in this section is easily defended, given the diversity of voices in the Scriptures and in the Christian tradition with respect to ways of understanding the atonement. Perhaps more controversial is the related claim that the church's glossolalia with regard to the soteriological effect of the cross

---

[16]I mean thus to underscore the significance of the Last Supper as a point of entry into our understanding of Jesus' death, even if its importance has been variously assessed—e.g., Joachim Jeremias, *The Eucharistic Words of Jesus* (Philadelphia: Fortress, 1966); Rudolf Pesch, *Das Abendmahl und Jesu Todesverständnis*, Quaestiones disputatae 80 (Freiburg: Herder, 1978); I. Howard Marshall, *Last Supper and Lord's Supper* (Grand Rapids: Eerdmans, 1980); and Bruce Chilton, *Rabbi Jesus: An Intimate Biography* (New York: Doubleday, 2000).

is a function of the catechetical and missiological needs and impulses of the church. This is not an extraordinary hypothesis, however, since it simply places on exhibition the model proposed by the late J. Christiaan Beker with regard to how we make sense of unity and diversity in Paul's understanding of the gospel. My challenge, then, is to document briefly something of the plethora of images of the atonement in Scripture and the Christian tradition, and then to explain the derivation and necessity of this diversity.

The diversity within the Scriptures. In speaking of the atoning significance of the cross, Paul's letters employ two formulas, which themselves represent widespread and early Christian thought. The first presents the "giving up" of Jesus for the salvation of humankind, either as an act of God (e.g., Rom 8:32) or as an act of self-giving (e.g., Gal 1:4). The second formula takes the form of a slogan, "Christ died for our sins" or "Christ died for us" (e.g., 1 Cor 15:3; 1 Thess 5:10). These expressions point plainly to the saving significance of Jesus' death, but without tying down in what way the cross is salvific. Moving beyond these stereotypical expressions, Paul, and with him other New Testament writers, generated a wide array of models for communicating the saving importance of the cross.[17] Taken as a whole, these images tend to congregate around five spheres of public life in antiquity: the court of law (e.g., justification), the world of commerce (e.g., redemption), personal relationships (e.g., reconciliation), worship (e.g., sacrifice), and the battleground (e.g., triumph over evil).

An expansive terminology attests this variety. With regard to images of sacrifice, for example, Paul and John refer to Jesus as the "Passover lamb" (1 Cor 5:7) and "the lamb of God who takes away the sins of the world" (Jn 1:29; cf. Jn 1:36; Rev 5:6); language regarding the handing over of Jesus can hark back to the binding of Isaac (i.e., the *Akedah;* Rom 8:32; cf. Gen 22); 1 Peter observes how Jesus "bore our sins in his body on the tree" (1 Pet 2:24; cf. 1:19); and Jesus' death is portrayed as "blood of the covenant" (Mk 14:24; cf. Ex 24:8) and as "first fruits" (1 Cor 15:20, 23; cf. Lev 23; Deut 16). Another example: although the language of "reconciliation" is rare in the

---

[17]See, e.g., John Driver, *Understanding the Atonement for the Mission of the Church* (Scottdale, Penn.: Herald, 1986), pp. 71-209; Joel B. Green and Mark D. Baker, *Recovering the Scandal of the Cross* (Downers Grove, Ill.: InterVarsity Press, 2000), pp. 35-115; Morna D. Hooker, *Not Ashamed of the Gospel* (Grand Rapids: Eerdmans, 1994); Herman-Emiel Mertens, *Not the Cross, But the Crucified,* Louvain Theological and Pastoral Monographs 11 (Grand Rapids: Eerdmans, 1992), pp. 31-61; Vincent Taylor, *The Atonement in New Testament Teaching,* 2nd ed. (London: Epworth, 1940).

New Testament (καταλλασσ☐, e.g., Rom 5:10-11; 2 Cor 5:18-20; Eph 2:16; Col 1:20, 22), the concept inhabits other texts as well, including references to "peace" (e.g., Eph 2:14-18) and the many acts (e.g., Rom 16:16), pleas (Philemon), and testimonies (e.g., Acts 15:8-9; Gal 3:26-29) of reconciliation that occupy the pages of the New Testament. In these ways the New Testament writers draw on the life worlds of their audiences while at the same time working to induct them into the world of Israel's Scriptures and the ways of Israel's God.

We should not imagine that the variety of New Testament images of atonement is simply a function of the different writers of its books. Paul himself can write of substitution, representation, sacrifice, justification, forgiveness, reconciliation, triumph over the powers, redemption and more. John can speak of illumination as well as sacrifice. Although in Hebrews the notion of sacrifice is paramount, Jesus is presented as both the perfect high priest and the perfect sacrificial victim. First Peter speaks of Jesus' death as a ransom and sacrifice, while the book of Revelation presents Jesus' death in terms of military triumph and redemption. This variety might appropriately lead us to the conclusion that the significance of Jesus' death could not be represented without remainder by any one concept or theory or metaphor. This is due first to the universal profundity of Jesus' death as saving event, to the variety of contexts within which Jesus' death required explication and to the variety of ways in which the human situation can be understood.

Within this variety we can discern common threads. Thus each image of the atonement presumes a portrait of the human situation, of human need. We find in the New Testament an abundance of terms and phrases for conceiving the condition that characterizes human existence apart from God: slavery, hard-heartedness, lostness, friendship with the world, blindness, ungodliness, living according to the sinful nature, the reprobate mind, the darkened heart, enemies of God, dead in trespasses and more. How we articulate the saving significance of Jesus' death is tied to our conception of the human situation. People who are blind need illumination. Slaves need liberation. The lost need to be found.

Second, the message of atonement is all-encompassing. That is, it cannot be reduced to one group of people, to one individual or to some aspect of the human person. What happened on the cross had universal significance: for Jew and Gentile, for slave and free, for male and female. The work of Christ on the cross had as its object even the cosmos, giving rise to images of new creation (2 Cor 5:17) and all-encompassing reconciliation (Col 1:15-20). The atonement is not narrowly focused on the individual's relationship to God but involves persons in their relationships to others, both neighbor and enemy, and to the world. The cross is less about a transaction after which persons are no longer guilty, and more about salvation as a call to reflect in day-to-day life the quality of life oriented to the other and on exhibition in Jesus' death on behalf of others. Atonement is divine gift, but it summons and enables human response.

Finally, in the restoration of broken relationships, God's initiative is paramount, and this initiative portends no distinction between the will or action of God the Father and God the Son. For example, Romans 5:1-11 presents the death of Christ as the ultimate expression of the love of God: "But God demonstrates his love for us in that while we were still sinners Christ died for us" (v. 8). In this important text we are told that *God* demonstrates his love by means of what *Christ* did. We might have anticipated that God's love would be revealed in God's own deed, and this would certainly have been the case were Paul sketching an atonement theology oriented toward the role of the cross in the Son's assuaging God's wrath. Instead, Paul asserts the oneness of the purpose and activity of God and God's Son on the cross. As the apostle puts it elsewhere, "in Christ God was reconciling the world to himself" (2 Cor 5:19). In this passage where descriptive terms for the saving effects of Jesus' death congregate (2 Cor 5:14—6:12: substitution, representation, sacrifice, justification, forgiveness and new creation), Paul carefully shows how the work of God and of Christ are one. There is no hint of mutual reconciliation. The "world" is estranged from God and needs to be brought back into relationship with God, but we find no hint that God is estranged from the "world." Rather, Paul affirms that God's love always has the upper hand in divine-human relations and that the work of Christ had as its effect the bringing of the "world" back to God.

The diversity of the tradition. Across the centuries that followed, theologians developed numerous models for expressing the saving significance of Jesus' death.[18] Interestingly, the ecumenical councils that produced the great creeds of the Christian church, thus defining classical orthodoxy for us, never selected one interpretation of the saving significance of the cross as definitive. Instead, from earliest times we find multiple

---

[18]See, e.g., Gustaf Aulén, *Christus Victor* (London: SPCK, 1931); Mertens, *Not the Cross*, pp. 63-84.

models, including three "classical" theories of the atonement:

- *Christ the conqueror,* which framed reflection on the cross and resurrection in terms of cosmic conflict, within which Jesus' death spells victory over sin and the powers of evil, including the devil (e.g., Irenaeus, c. A.D. 130-c. 200)

- *Satisfaction,* which understands the cross as "satisfying" the debt owed to God by a sinful humanity (e.g., Anselm, A.D. 1033-1109)

- *Moral influence,* which views Jesus' life and death as a demonstration of God's love capable of moving humans to repentance and love of God and neighbor (e.g., Abelard, A.D. 1079-1142).

Theologians have worked with other models as well: redemption, reconciliation, liberation, mediation and more. As Clement of Alexandria (c. A.D. 155-c. 220) put it, "The Savior uses many tones of voice and many methods for the salvation of humanity" (*Exhortation to the Greeks* 1).

Theologians have also developed some of these models further. For example, the biblical understanding of salvation as "illumination" is clearly on a trajectory with Abelard's model of moral influence. Most notably, the satisfaction model has been transformed into the well-known model of penal substitutionary atonement. In fact, the model of penal substitutionary atonement is so pervasive in American Christianity that many Christians may wonder whether the saving significance of Jesus' death can be understood in any other way. This is because we have failed to drink deeply from the wells of our own tradition.

A kaleidoscope of images. What motivates this diversity of interpretation? A satisfying answer would move in at least two directions at once. First, given the wealth of images for divine-human interactions in the Scriptures of Israel, we might not be surprised that early Christians, returning again and again to search the Scriptures, brought forth treasures both old and new. Reading the death of Jesus in light of Israel's Scriptures, and reading those Scriptures in light of the death of Jesus, they found telling images everywhere: substitution, sacrifice, forgiveness, deliverance and more. Seeking to inscribe new followers of Jesus into Israel's Scriptures, they worked to make those ancient images familiar ones; as Paul would put it in a related context, "These things happened to them to serve as an example, and they were written down to instruct us, on whom the ends of the ages have come" (1 Cor 10:11). Similarly, in the wake of both the Old and New Testament writings, with their compounded array of images of the saving work of Christ, the church has worked faithfully to embrace the message of the atonement without presuming that one image subsumed or trumped the others. In other words, the biblical narrative, which we seek to inhabit and to put into play in our lives as communities of Jesus' followers, authorizes an expansive range of images and models for comprehending and articulating the atonement.

Second, as Herman-Emiel Martens has observed, interpretations of Jesus' death are tied to particular cultures and times, so that no interpretation can be regarded as the only authentic or definitive one.[19] The case of Anselm easily makes the point. In his attempt to address the question "Why did God become human?" *(Cur Deus Homo?)*, Anselm turns not to the Bible per se but to his own social context, a feudal world, in which the importance of honoring one's liege was integral to the maintenance of order and peace. For Anselm, then, sin was an insult to the honor of God, which could be restored only through the death of the sinless One, Jesus. With Anselm, then, we are not navigating the world of innocence and guilt but of honor and shame.

The same could be said of Pauline language for the atonement. In 2 Corinthians 5, for example, he employs the language of "reconciliation," sketching an argument in ways that are context specific. Paul needs to counter the triumphalistic boasting of his opponents at Corinth and resolve the disharmony between himself and his "children" at Corinth. Rooting the message of reconciliation fundamentally in the sacrificial death of Jesus and asserting that reconciliation entails living no longer for oneself but for Christ (and thus for others), he addresses his first aim. His impassioned appeal to the Corinthians to be reconciled to God (2 Cor 5:20; 6:1-2), followed by an affirmation of his own open-handedness to the Corinthians (2 Cor 6:11-13; 7:2), deals with the second.

Similarly, Galatians 3:10-14 expounds the salvific character of the cross of Christ in ways well-oriented to the context Paul is addressing. At this juncture in his argument with Galatian Christians enamored with legal observance, Paul needs to overcome the obvious problem of the essential partitioning of Jew and Gentile—a distinction centered on the status of the *law-abiding* Jew in contrast to the *lawless* Gentile. Gentiles lived under God's curse as persons outside the law; how then could they share in the blessings

---

[19]Martens, *Not the Cross,* p. 63.

of Abraham? Paul's first answer was that those who use the law to drive a wedge between Jews and Gentiles have abused the law and therefore fall under the same divine curse. How then can *anyone* participate in the blessings of Abraham? Second, borrowing the imagery of Deuteronomy 21:22-23, Paul writes that Jesus has in his crucifixion borne the curse of God—that is, he has been placed outside the community of God's covenant. More than this, he has done so "on our behalf." In his death he has exhausted the power of the law to segregate people from the covenant. It is not accidental that in constructing his argument Paul refers to "Christ" bearing the "curse," for this places in provocative juxtaposition two profoundly contradictory images: the one "anointed by God" is the one "cursed by God." If Jesus has identified with humanity in having been placed outside the covenant of God's people as one who bears the divine curse, his divine "anointing" signifies the acceptance of the "outsider," both Jew and Gentile. The death of Christ thus marks the new eon in which Gentiles may be embraced, in Christ, as children of Abraham.

What we have found illustrates the phenomenon to which J. Christiaan Beker referred when he wrote of contingency and coherence in the thought of Paul.[20] "Contingency" connotes the expression of the gospel's coherence (or central beliefs) in the particular situations to which Paul addresses himself in his letters. Accordingly, we may understand as central to the overarching plan of God the saving significance of Jesus' death, while allowing that the articulation of that significance is worked out in particular contexts. The hermeneutical task that occupied Paul and Peter and other New Testament writers, and Christian theologians and preachers subsequently, is located at the interface of this central affirmation of the atoning work of Christ and its contingent interpretation. This continues to be the hermeneutical task today, and this explains not only the presence of but also the mandate for multiple models of understanding and communicating the cross of Christ.

The Atonement: Two Models

In order to illustrate this diversity, I want in this final section to sketch two models of the atonement, both of which are already at home in Christian

---

[20]J. Christiaan Beker, *Paul the Apostle* (Edinburgh: T & T Clark, 1980). The fecundity of Beker's model beyond the particulars of his thesis regarding Paul has been picked up by others— e.g., I. Howard Marshall, *New Testament Theology* (Downers Grove, Ill.: InterVarsity Press, 2004), pp. 32-34.

Scripture, but presenting different degrees of currency for contemporary audiences in North America: (1) the atonement as sacrifice, and (2) the atonement as revelation. In outlining these two proposals I want to be sensitive to the importance of locating the saving significance of Jesus' death in relation to the narrative of his life, through which we understand his execution on a Roman cross in social, political and religious terms. I want also to follow the theological compass points I identified earlier in relation to the atonement and speak to the nature of the human situation, the nature of God's initiative, and the all-encompassing consequences of the cross. Finally, I want to explore how these models might address both the subjective (i.e., how the cross of Christ transforms humans) and objective (what the event of the cross itself signifies in the divine economy) sides of the death of Jesus.

The atonement as sacrifice. In their development of the saving significance of Jesus' death, early Christians were heavily influenced by the world of the sacrificial cult in Israel's Scriptures and by the practices of animal sacrifice in the Jerusalem temple, whether contemporary or in recent memory. The expression "Christ died for all," widespread in this and variant forms throughout the New Testament (e.g., Mk 14:24; Rom 5:6, 8; 15:3; Gal 2:21; 1 Pet 3:18), is thematic in this regard, as are references to the salvific effects of the blood of Christ (e.g., Acts 20:28; Rom 5:9; Col 1:20). Jesus' death is presented as a covenant sacrifice (e.g., Mk 14:24; 1 Cor 11:25; Heb 7:22; 8:6; 9:15), a Passover sacrifice (e.g., Jn 19:14; 1 Cor 5:7-8), the sin offering (Rom 8:3; 2 Cor 5:21), the offering of first fruits (1 Cor 15:20, 23), the sacrifice offered on the Day of Atonement (Heb 9—10), and an offering reminiscent of Abraham's presentation of Isaac (e.g., Rom 8:32). The writer of Ephesians summarizes well: "Christ loved us and gave himself up for us, a fragrant offering and sacrifice to God" (Eph 5:2). This last text reminds us that, for the New Testament writers, images of sacrifice were not deployed abstractly to clarify the atoning work of Jesus' death. As Christ loved us and gave himself up for us, we are told, so are we to "live in love" as "imitators of God, as beloved children" (Eph 5:1-2). That is, imagining the death of Jesus in sacrificial terms draws us into a life of sacrifice marked by worship of God and ethical comportment.[21]

---

[21]This correlation has been observed repeatedly—see, e.g., Driver, *Understanding the Atonement,* pp. 129-46; Roger T. Beckwith, "Sacrifice," in *New Dictionary of Biblical Theology,* ed. T. D. Alexander and B. S. Rosner (Downers Grove, Ill.: InterVarsity Press, 2000), pp. 754-62.

Given the importance of sacrifice to Old Testament notions of atonement, we should not be surprised at the magnetic draw of Israel's sacrificial cult on Jesus and his followers. There, the concept of atonement is the resolution of estrangement between two parties whose relationship has been interrupted or broken by sin or other infraction, and is generally tied to rites of sacrifice and mediation. In divine-human relations, God is the source of atonement, and it is God who arranges a sacrificial system through which he mediates atonement.

Among the sacrifices and sacrificial offerings developed in the Old Testament, the most important for our purposes is the purification offering (הַחַטָּאת, *ḥaṭṭāʾt*, e.g., Lev 4:1—6:7; 6:24—7:10; see Lev 16), the focus of which is on cleansing the effect of sin, cultic impurity. This way of explaining the atoning work of sacrifice has been argued persuasively by Jacob Milgrom, though his view is susceptible to a reduction of the purification offering to a concern only with contamination of the temple. Clearly, however, this rite cannot be segregated from forgiveness of sins (e.g., Lev 4:20, 26, 31; 16:16). Milgrom himself interprets atonement as redemption through the substitution of an animal for a human being (Lev 16) as well as purification of the sanctuary and, by extension, of the community of God's people (e.g., Lev 15:31; 16:19).[22] From early in the twentieth century, debate swirled around whether sacrifice emphasized "expiation" (sacrifice as the means by which God frees and cleanses people from the onus and blemish of sin) or on "propitiation" (sacrifice as a means of averting God's wrath). However, the linguistic evidence prioritizes the sense of "to wipe away" or "to cleanse," though not exclusively so,[23] and this is supported by the integrated reading of sacrifice offered by Milgrom.

The importance of forgiveness is highlighted in a text like Leviticus 19:22:

---

[22]Jacob Milgrom, *Leviticus,* 3 vols., Anchor Bible (New York: Doubleday, 1991-2001), and *Studies in Cultic Theology and Terminology,* Studies in Judaism in Late Antiquity 36 (Leiden: E. J. Brill, 1983). See further, B. Lang, "כפר," in *Theological Dictionary of the Old Testament,* ed. G. Johannes Botterweck (Grand Rapids: Eerdmans, 1995), 7:288-303; Gary A. Anderson, "Sacrifice and Sacrificial Offerings (Old Testament)," in *Anchor Bible Dictionary,* ed. David Noel Freedman (New York: Doubleday, 1992), 5:870-86.

[23]Against "propitiation" see, e.g., C. H. Dodd, "ἱλάσκομαι, Its Cognates, Derivatives, and Synonyms in the Septuagint," *Journal of Theological Studies* 32 (1931): 352-60. For an argument favoring the notion of "propitiation," see Leon Morris, *The Apostolic Preaching of the Cross,* 3rd ed. (Leicester, U.K.: Inter-Varsity Press, 1965). For a recent, thorough examination of the linguistic data, see Richard E. Averbeck, "כפר," in *New International Dictionary of Old Testament Theology and Exegesis,* ed. William A. VanGemeren (Grand Rapids: Zondervan, 1997), 2:689-710.

"And the priest shall make atonement for him with the ram of guilt offering before the LORD for his sin that he committed; and the sin he committed shall be forgiven him." Sin has resulted in an estranged relationship between the sinner and God, and it is this separation that must be addressed. Serving as mediator, the priest resolves the broken relationship through a sacrifice. How is this so? First, basic to this legislation is the opposition of life and death—with death a great evil to be avoided and with everything related to death (whether the corpse itself, bloody discharge or disease) rendering people unclean and unfit to enter into God's presence. (When we remember that severed relations with Yahweh constitute death in Israel's Scriptures, it is easy to see how the sinner is thus regarded as unclean.) Second, the choice of an unblemished animal serves as an analogy for the election of Israel, set apart for life in relationship to and service of God. Third, in the rite of sacrifice, the laying of hands on the beast's head signals the importance of "identification" or "representation"—with sinners identifying themselves with the beast and the beast now representing sinners in their sin. And so the shedding of blood—with blood understood as the substance of life, sacred to God—signifies the offering of the lives of those for whom the sacrifice is made.

What of the relationship of God's wrath to the sacrificial cult? Most generally, it is crucial that we not confuse the wrath of Yahweh with the retributive, begrudging and capricious dispositions of the Greek and Roman gods to whom sacrifices were offered in order both to placate the deities and to solicit their favor. In spite of popular views of the "Old Testament God," divine wrath in the Old Testament is not well-represented by views of this kind. In fact, Old Testament scholars today continue to debate in what sense it is appropriate to attribute anger to God.[24] What is clear is that the God of Israel is "slow to anger and abounding in steadfast love" (e.g., Ex 34:6; Num 14:18), and for the Old Testament anger is God's response to sinful acts, not descriptive of God's general disposition toward humanity.[25] More pointedly,

---

[24]See Jan Bergman and Elsie Johnson, "אַף," in *Theological Dictionary of the Old Testament*, ed. G. Johannes Botterweck (Grand Rapids: Eerdmans, 1977), 1:348-60; Gary A. Heron, "Wrath of God (OT)," in *Anchor Bible Dictionary*, ed. David Noel Freedman (New York: Doubleday, 1992), 6:989-96.

[25]"Wrath is not an attribute of God. His acts are not in general determined by it" (Wolfhart Pannenberg, *Systematic Theology* [Grand Rapids: Eerdmans, 1988], 1:439). See John Goldingay, *Old Testament Theology*, vol. 1: *Israel's Gospel* (Downers Grove, Ill.: InterVarsity Press, 2003), p. 140.

if God's anger can be understood in numerous passages in the Old Testament in relation to retributive punishment, then it is crucial to recall that the antidote to God's wrath is not therein developed in sacrificial terms. Although the animal sacrifice may *represent* the one(s) for whom the sacrifice is offered, we find no exposition of the ritual act as "satisfaction" or "penalty."[26] John Goldingay observes, "The problem of sin in Leviticus is not that sin involves infidelity or disloyalty which makes God angry but that sin pollutes, stains, and spoils, and thus makes people repulsive. . . . Sacrifice does not directly relate to anger."[27]

This foray into the background of sacrificial images in the Old Testament presses the question how Jesus' death, understood as a sacrifice, might be comprehended as resolving the estrangement in divine-human relations. If, as we have seen, "assuaging God's wrath" and "payment of the penalty of sin" are wide of the mark, then how are we to understand the sacrificial death of Jesus? Different texts point in different directions. Let me sketch three examples. First, Paul's reference to Jesus as τὸ πάσχα *(to pascha)*, "Passover lamb," in 1 Corinthians 5:7 is powerfully reminiscent of the Passover sacrifice so central to Israel's story. Celebrated annually, Passover both memorialized and reappropriated for generations of God's people God's election and great act of deliverance. Read in relation to Paul's directive regarding the presence of an immoral person within the church (1 Cor 5:1-13), his allusion to Passover marks the Corinthian believers as a community of persons set apart from the bondage of sin as the distinctive people of God.[28]

Hebrews devotes significant space to the sacrificial death of Jesus, which it develops along at least three lines. Most broadly, the death of Jesus signals the obedience of Jesus, even the pouring out of his life in a noble death, in which Jesus' obedience is representative of the obedience of all and is ac-

---

[26]See James D. G. Dunn, "Paul's Understanding of the Death of Jesus as Sacrifice," in *Sacrifice and Redemption,* ed. S. W. Sykes (Cambridge: Cambridge University Press, 1991), pp. 35-56 (44); more broadly, Robert J. Daly, *The Origins of the Christian Doctrine of Sacrifice* (Philadelphia: Fortress, 1978), pp. 11-35. Gordon Wenham imagines, however, that the "pleasing odor" from the sacrifice quiets "divine uneasiness" ("The Theology of Old Testament Sacrifice," in *Sacrifice in the Bible,* ed. Roger T. Beckwith and Martin J. Seman [Grand Rapids: Baker, 1995], pp. 75-87 [80]).

[27]John Goldingay, "Your Iniquities Have Made a Separation Between You and God," in *Atonement Today,* ed. John Goldingay (London: SPCK, 1995), pp. 39-53 (51); see further, John Goldingay, "Old Testament Sacrifice and the Death of Christ," in ibid., pp. 3-20.

[28]See the discussion in Richard B. Hays, *First Corinthians,* Interpretation (Louisville: John Knox, 1997), p. 83; Anthony C. Thiselton, *The First Epistle to the Corinthians,* New International Greek Testament Commentary (Grand Rapids: Eerdmans, 2000), pp. 405-6.

cepted by God as a perfect sacrifice—and so calls people to follow Jesus, leader and pioneer, in the journey of obedience to God.[29] In addition, Jesus' death ratifies the (new) covenant between God and his people, itself providing the measure of faithful behavior for God's covenant partners.[30] Then Hebrews develops the sacrificial death of Jesus in relation to the Day of Atonement, even if the author is selective in his choice of regulations related to the annual ceremony in Leviticus 16. Thus the Levitical material related to the scapegoat is bypassed in favor of the sacrificial goat—a decision that highlights the identification of Jesus as the sinless, sacrificial victim who cleanses the sin that is an affront to God in order to lead people into the holiest place—that is, into God's own presence.[31]

If, from the perspective of Israel's Scriptures, sin rendered people unclean and thus excluded them from God's presence, the institution of sacrifice was largely concerned with the removal of this impediment. As G. B. Caird put it, "A sense of pollution . . . implies an essential sanctity, and the imperative need of those whom sin has defiled is that which can cleanse the conscience from dead works (Heb. 9.14)."[32] What Hebrews describes, then, is the action of God to initiate covenant relations with humanity in Christ, to provide a forerunner who through his suffering and death not only enters the presence of God before us but wipes away all barriers so that we might enter with him, and so to work within the human being to transform the human condition.

As a third example, to return to Paul, the status of Jesus' death as a "sin offering" is clear in several texts, including references to the saving efficacy of Jesus' blood (Rom 3:25; 5:9; Eph 1:7; 2:13; Col 1:20), which must be understood symbolically in this way since the mode of Jesus' execution was not markedly bloody, and in Romans 8:3 (περὶ ἁμαρτίας, "concerning sin" or, more to the point, "as a sin offering"); 2 Corinthians 5:21 (ὑπὲρ ἡμῶν ἁρμαρτίαν ἐποίησεν, "[God] made [Christ] sin for us"). In these instances, Paul speaks to the efficacy of sacrifice in terms of exchange and represen-

---

[29]See John Dunnill, *Covenant and Sacrifice in the Letter to the Hebrews,* Society for New Testament Studies Monograph Series 75 (Cambridge: Cambridge University Press, 1992). On these motifs more broadly, see Sam K. Williams, *Jesus' Death as Saving Event,* Harvard Dissertations in Religion 2 (Missoula, Mont.: Scholars Press, 1975); David Seeley, *The Noble Death: Graeco-Roman Martyrology and Paul's Concept of Salvation,* Journal for the Study of the New Testament Supplement Series 28 (Sheffield, U.K.: Sheffield Academic Press, 1990).

[30]Compare Heb 9:19-21 with Ex 24:1-8.

[31]Cf. Barnabas Lindars, *The Theology of the Letter to the Hebrews,* New Testament Theology (Cambridge: Cambridge University Press, 1991), pp. 84-101.

[32]G. B. Caird, *The Language and Imagery of the Bible* (London: Duckworth, 1980), p. 17.

tation: sin and death transferred to the sacrificial victim, its purity and life to those who receive the benefits of the sacrifice. In this economy of sacrifice the death of Jesus wipes away sin and its effects. Substitution is clearly at the heart of sacrifice in these texts, but the metaphor is economic (exchange) rather than penal (satisfaction).

These examples evidence both subjective and objective aspects of the atonement, and demonstrate how God deals with the human predicament through the provision of the perfect sacrifice, Jesus Christ. Moreover, sacrifice draws attention to a life lived and given in obedience to God, a life and death marked as ignominious by the standards of the larger world but recognized as noble among those whose systems of valuation have been reset by God. Sacrifice ratifies the covenant between God and his people and casts Jesus' perfect obedience unto death as a call to and exemplar for the people of the covenant.

The atonement as revelation. At one level the smells and images of sacrifice are far removed from life in the twenty-first-century West. For many, this form of ritualized butchery seems as barbaric as the logic of sacrifice seems alien. Nevertheless, it remains just as true today, perhaps even more so than when Frances Young observed it three decades ago, that we find in contemporary literature serious engagement with ideas of sacrifice.[33] Colin Gunton has urged that the notion of sacrifice is in fact deeply embedded in human nature.[34] The journey of God's Son as this is spelled out in Philippians 2:6-11, with its central emphases on self-emptying and obedience even unto death, underscores the centrality of sacrifice for creatures made in God's image. This, I am sure, is why the message of Jesus' sacrifice is so immediately and naturally morphed into calls for other-oriented life as the hallmark of faithful discipleship.[35] Although some will undoubtedly work to

---

[33]Frances Young, *Sacrifice and the Death of Christ* (London: SCM, 1975).

[34]See Colin Gunton, "The Sacrifice and the Sacrifices: From Metaphor to Transcendental?" in *Trinity, Incarnation, and Atonement,* ed. Ronald J. Feenstra and Cornelius Plantinga Jr., Library of Religious Philosophy 1 (Notre Dame, Indiana: University of Notre Dame Press, 1989), pp. 210-29; Colin Gunton, *The Actuality of the Atonement* (Grand Rapids: Eerdmans, 1989), pp. 115-41.

[35]See Martin J. Selman, "Sacrifice for Christians Today," in *Sacrifice in the Bible,* ed. Roger T. Beckwith and Martin J. Selman (Grand Rapids: Baker, 1995), pp. 157-69. Cynthia L. Rigby argues for a way of construing substitution that does not valorize the feminine sins of self-deprecation and passivity to exercise power as agents ("Taking Our Place: Substitution, Human Agency, and Feminine Sin," *International Journal for the Study of the Christian Church* 4 [2004]: 220-34.) The ease with which Jesus' crucifixion is understood as an expression of his passivity or powerlessness (rather than a potent if ironic expression of power) is a reminder of our desperate need to locate atonement theology within the Roman and narrative contexts of the Gospels.

find modern analogs to stimulate our contemporaries to contemplate Jesus' sacrificial death, it may be that a more fruitful strategy is to induct Christians fully into the narrative world of Scripture that they will be so transformed by their encounter with this "full, perfect, and sufficient sacrifice for the sins of the whole world"[36] that they will embody his life as their own.

This, however, is already to move into the arena of the second model of the atonement to which I want to draw attention, the atonement as revelation. Rather than begin with the central importance of this model in Scripture, I want first to sketch five interrelated observations from the neurosciences about the nature of human formation and knowing that serendipitously prepare for a consideration of the revelatory significance of Jesus' death.

1. Too little input. In an intriguing discussion of "the machinery of the cerebral cortex," Christof Koch observes the general deficit of incoming sensory data necessary for an unambiguous interpretation of the object of our perception. This is true from the seemingly more mundane activity of our visual systems to larger-scale hermeneutical concerns, our reflection on and the practices of human understanding. Our limitations notwithstanding, our "cortical networks *fill in*. They make their best guess, given the incomplete information. . . . This general principle, expressed colloquially as 'jumping to conclusions,' guides much of human behavior."[37] Various terms name the structures by which we "fill in"—*imagination* ("a basic image-schematic capacity for ordering our experience" or "the power of taking something as something by means of meaningful forms, which are rooted in our history and have the power to disclose truths about life in the world"),[38] for example, or *conceptual schemes* (which are at once *conceptual* [a way of seeing things], *conative* [a set of beliefs and values to which a group and its members are deeply attached], and *action-guiding* [we seek to live according to its terms]).[39] To put it differently, life events do not come with self-contained and immediately obvious interpretations; we have to conceptualize them,

[36]From the "Prayer of Consecration," "A Brief Form of the Order for the Administration of the Sacrament of the Lord's Supper or Holy Communion," in *The Methodist Hymnal* (Nashville: Methodist Publishing, 1964), p. 832.

[37]Christof Koch, *The Quest for Consciousness* (Englewood, Colo.: Roberts, 2004), p. 23.

[38]Mark Johnson, *The Body in the Mind* (Chicago: University of Chicago, 1987), p. xx; and David J. Bryant, *Faith and the Play of Imagination,* Studies in American Biblical Hermeneutics 5 (Macon, Ga.: Mercer University Press, 1989), p. 5, respectively.

[39]Owen Flanagan, *The Problem of the Soul* (New York: Basic Books, 2002), pp. 27-55.

and in the main we do so in terms of imaginative structures or conceptual schemes that we implicitly take to be true, normal and good.[40]

2. The narrative shape of our interpretive schemes. "*Story* is a basic principle of mind. Most of our experience, our knowledge, and our thinking is organized as stories." So summarizes the cognitive scientist Mark Turner, who adds that "narrative imagining is our fundamental form of predicting" and our "fundamental cognitive instrument for explanation."[41] That is, it is increasingly clear from neurobiology that meaning-making is central to our day-to-day experience, that we will go to great lengths to impose structure on the data we receive from our sensory organs on the basis of what we take to be possible or normal, and that this "structure" comes in the form of narratives.[42]

3. Neuroplasticity, nature and nurture. "People don't come preassembled, but are glued together by life."[43] So writes Joseph LeDoux, calling attention to the essential neurobiological reality that human beings are always in the process of formation. At a basic level, formative influences are encoded at the neuronal level, in the synapses of the central nervous system. The organization of the brain is hard-wired genetically, of course, but genes shape only the broad outline of our mental and behavioral functions; the rest is sculpted through our experiences. In other words, although our genes bias the way we think and behave, from birth we are in the process of becoming, and this "becoming" is encoded in our brains by means of synaptic activity. Our hermeneutical equipment, then, is formed at the synaptic level, is capable of reformation and is even now providing the conceptual schemes or imaginative structures by which we make sense of the world around us.

4. Believing is seeing. My "perception" of the world is based in a network of ever-forming assumptions about my environment and in a series of well-tested assumptions, shared by others with whom I associate, about "the way

---

[40]Cf. Mark Johnson, *Moral Imagination* (Chicago: University of Chicago Press, 1993), chap. 8.

[41]Mark Turner, *The Literary Mind* (New York: Oxford University Press, 1996), pp. v, 20.

[42]On the role of narrative in forming and reporting beliefs, see the studies of Todd E. Feinberg, *Altered Egos* (Oxford: Oxford University Press, 2001); and William Hirstein, *Brain Fiction* (Cambridge, Mass.: MIT Press, 2005); they demonstrate the incredible lengths to which we will go to make storied sense of what we take to be true.

[43]Joseph LeDoux, *Synaptic Self* (New York: Viking Penguin, 2002), p. 3; cf. Susana Cohen-Cory, "The Developing Synapse: Construction and Modulation of Synaptic Structures and Circuits," *Science* 298 (2002): 770-76; Peter R. Huttenlocher, *Neural Plasticity,* Perspectives in Cognitive Neuroscience (Cambridge, Mass.: Harvard University Press, 2002).

the world works." Ambiguous data may present different hypotheses, but my mind disambiguates that data according to what I have learned to expect. Patients who have experienced selected lesions to the brain demonstrate the inability to see what they cannot believe to be true,[44] just as those of us with unaffected brains operate normally with a strong hermeneutical bias on the basis of prior beliefs, so that we actually perceive stimuli when none are physically presented.[45] The narratives we tell and embody regulate how we construe the world.

5. *Which stories?* It is therefore crucial to inquire: What story is shaping the worlds we indwell? What story are we embodying? Alternatives abound: "The little engine that could"—if only it worked hard enough and kept pushing and kept pushing, it could conquer that mountain; the promise of "unrelenting progress"; "I did it my way"; "Might makes right"; and so on. If we perceive the world and shape our identities in relation to the narratives we construct and inhabit,[46] then this is a pressing question indeed.

Setting out these observations in this way is useful for three reasons. First, it underscores the importance of the narrative structure of Scripture itself, including the narrative structure of the gospel. In this sense Scripture itself promotes a narrative structure by which to comprehend the world. Second, it draws attention to the importance of the story of Jesus, whether in Matthew or Paul or the whole of the biblical canon, for making sense of the purpose of God. Third, it corroborates what social-scientific investigation has already identified regarding conversion—namely, that conversion includes a reordering of life in terms of the grand narrative shared with and recounted by the community of the converted.[47]

Within the narrative of Luke, for example, the disciples lack understanding, and can make no sense of Jesus' statements regarding his im-

---

[44]E.g., V. S. Ramachandran, *A Brief Tour of Human Consciousness* (New York: Pi, 2004), chap. 2.
[45]See Aaron R. Seitz et al., "Seeing What Is Not There Shows the Costs of Perceptual Learning," *Proceedings of the National Academy of Sciences* 102, no. 25 (2005): 9080-85. The importance of "belief" has only begun to be studied empirically—cf.. e.g., Daniel L. Schacter and Elaine Scarry, eds., *Memory, Brain, and Belief* (Cambridge, Mass.: Harvard University Press, 2000).
[46]Cf., e.g., Jerome Bruner, *Making Stories* (New York: Farrar, Strauss & Giroux, 2002).
[47]See David A. Snow and R. Machalek, "The Convert as a Social Type," in *Sociological Theory 1983,* ed. R. Collins (San Francisco: Jossey Bass, 1983), pp. 259-89; Wayne A. Meeks, *The Origins of Christian Morality* (New Haven, Conn.: Yale University Press, 1993), pp. 18-36; Nicholas H. Taylor, "The Social Nature of Conversion in the Early Christian World," in *Modelling Early Christianity,* ed. Philip F. Esler (New York: Routledge, 1995), pp. 128-36.

pending suffering (Lk 9:44-45; 18:31-34). Their failure continues until the concluding moments of Luke's narrative, when Luke reports that Jesus "opened their minds to understand the scriptures" (Lk 24:45).[48] Prior to this, what is lacking are the categories of thought, an interpretive schema adequate to correlate what Jesus holds together in his passion predictions, Jesus' exalted status and his impending dishonor. Their horizons of perception are too narrowly circumscribed, patterned as they are according to a conceptual scheme more conventional in Roman Palestine. Jesus "opened the Scriptures" for them by claiming that it was "necessary that the Messiah should suffer these things and then enter into his glory"; then, "beginning with Moses and all the prophets, he interpreted to them the things about himself in all the scriptures" (Lk 24:25-27). Here is Jesus' hermeneutical lesson. By correlating the persecution of the prophets with messiahship, he is able to assert that the Scriptures provide a script for the eschatological king who would suffer before entering into glory.[49] Thus in God's economy the high status of God's anointed One is not contradicted by humiliation; rather, in his passion and exaltation, Jesus embodied the status-reversal comprising salvation. His death was the focal point of the divine-human struggle over how life is to be lived, whether in humility or in self-elevation. God's purpose embraces both rejection by humans and divine exaltation, and recognition of this *fabula,* this story behind the story—fully embodied by Jesus—serves as the theological pattern by which to order the scriptural witness. As the book of Acts demonstrates on almost every page, this narrative pattern orders not only the biblical witness but indeed the very lives of Jesus' followers, their mission and community. They interpret the world in terms of this narrative, which they incarnate in their lives of mission, *koinonia* and persecution. All of this is the result of a hermeneutical conversion centered in the death and resurrection of Jesus Christ.

If Luke's narrative emphasizes illumination, this is because the primary obstacle that must be overcome as God restores his people is "ignorance" (e.g., Acts 3:17; 17:30). This was observed by J.-W. Taeger, who argued that the human situation in Lukan thought was one characterized by ignorance

---

[48]I have developed this more fully in Joel B. Green, "Learning Theological Interpretation from Luke," in *Reading Luke,* ed. Craig Bartholomew, Joel B. Green and Anthony Thiselton, Scripture and Hermeneutics Project (Grand Rapids: Zondervan, 2005), pp. 55-78.

[49]See Mark L. Strauss, *The Davidic Messiah in Luke-Acts,* Journal for the Study of the New Testament Supplement Series 110 (Sheffield, U.K.: Sheffield Academic Press, 1995), p. 257.

needing correcting rather than sin needing forgiveness.[50] Aside from the enigma Taeger thus introduces into Lukan studies concerning the heightened interest found in Luke-Acts specifically on forgiveness of sins,[51] Taeger's view suffers from an anemic understanding of "knowledge" and "ignorance," as though the human deficit could be measured in terms of "lacking information." For Luke, ignorance is actually misunderstanding—an abysmal failure to grasp adequately the purpose of God. Even when obeying God, people within the Lukan narrative obey him as they have come to perceive him, and the extent of their misperception is so grand that their attempts at obedience actually run counter to the divine will. What is needed is a theological transformation: a deep-seated conversion in their conception of God and thus in their commitments, attitudes, and everyday practices. Consequently, the resolution of "ignorance" is not simply "more and better data," but "repentance" and divine forgiveness.[52] Luke's work is thus a narrative of enlightenment, so that prior understandings might be razed and the now-reconstructed understanding of the purpose and promises of God—an understanding that arises from the story of the Scriptures grasped in light of the advent, death and resurrection of Jesus—might be welcomed.

We can find a similar focus on shaping a people's interpretive schema in 1 Peter. Clearly, the axis of Peter's "narrative" is Jesus Christ. His readers are to find their home "in Christ" (1 Pet 3:16; 5:10, 14). The warrant for his directives concerning faithful living is Jesus' own suffering, death, resurrection and triumph. And Jesus is the interpretive matrix for understanding the pattern of God's story, the lens through which to read our story within the story of God. Elements of the story of Jesus that Peter highlights include Jesus' preexistence (1 Pet 1:11; cf. 1:20), his life of faithfulness (1 Pet 1:2), his suffering and death (1 Pet 1:2, 11, 19; 2:4, 7, 21-25; 3:18-19; 4:1; 5:1), his ascension (1 Pet 3:22), and his pending, final revelation (1 Pet 1:7, 11, 13; 5:1). Among these, of special importance is Jesus' suffering and death, and espe-

---

[50]J.-W. Taeger, *Der Mensch und sein Heil: Studien zum Bild des Menschen und zur Sicht der Bekehrung bei Lukas,* SNT 14 (Gütersloh: Gerd Mohn, 1982): *"Der Mensch ist kein salvandus, sondern ein corrigendus"* (p. 37).

[51]Lk 1:77; 3:3; 5:20-21, 23-24; 7:47-49; 11:4; 12:10; 17:3-4; 23:34; 24:47; Acts 2:38; 3:19; 5:31; 10:43; 13:38; 15:9; 22:16; 26:18; cf. Joel B. Green, " 'Salvation to the End of the Earth' (Acts 13:47): God as Saviour in the Acts of the Apostles," in *Witness to the Gospel: Theology of Acts,* ed. I. Howard Marshall and David Peterson (Grand Rapids: Eerdmans, 1998), pp. 83-106.

[52]Cf. Peter Pokorný, *Theologie der lukanischen Schriften,* Forschungen zur Religion und Literatur des Alten und Neuen Testaments 174 (Göttingen: Vandenhoeck & Ruprecht, 1998), pp. 62-63, 66-67.

cially its relationship to the eternal purpose of God—which Peter documents repeatedly.[53] Jesus' suffering is *exemplary,* providing a model for his followers of innocent suffering (1 Pet 2:19-20; 3:16-17; 4:1-2, 13-16); *redemptive,* providing a model for his followers of effective suffering (1 Pet 2:12, 15; 3:1-2); and *anticipatory,* providing a model for his followers of how God will vindicate the righteous who suffer (1 Pet 2:20; 4:13-14; 5:1, 10). This means that although it is true that Peter draws heavily on Israel's Scriptures, it is equally true that the biblical story is now fundamentally branded by the crucifixion of Jesus. Jesus' execution functions for Peter as the conceptual scheme by which life is lived and the world is made to make sense. The cross of Christ provides a way of comprehending life, orients a community around its identifying beliefs and values, and guides the actions of those whose lives carry its brand.

Avid readers of C .S. Lewis's The Chronicles of Narnia series will recognize the importance of this "insider perspective." In *The Last Battle,* having passed from this world into the next through a stable door, the dwarves are served a lavish feast of "pies and tongues and pigeons and trifles and ices, and each Dwarf had a goblet of fine wine in his right hand. But it wasn't much use. They began eating and drinking only the sort of things you might find in a Stable"—hay or an old turnip, raw cabbage or dirty water. "You see," said Aslan. "They will not let us help them. They have chosen cunning instead of belief. Their prison is only in their own minds, yet they are in that prison."[54] Similarly, from a point of view illumined by conventional wisdom, Peter's readers are humiliated, rejected, ostracized and exiled, but from a perspective radiated by the passion of Jesus, they are God's elect, precious, honored.

When the human predicament is imagined in terms of "blindness" or "unfaith" or "lack of perception," it is natural to find soteriological images of illumination and revelation. Dotting the horizons of the Gospel of Mark are questions regarding Jesus' identity, but it is only "when the centurion, who stood facing him, saw that in this way he breathed his last" that someone shares God's perspective regarding Jesus; then, the centurion said, "Truly this man was God's Son!" (Mk 15:39; cf. Mk 1:1, 9-11; 9:2-8). For John, the theme of revelation is thematic, as he indicates in the opening of his Gospel,

---

[53]See 1 Pet 1:11, 19 (Is 52:13—53:12); 2:4-10 (Ps 118:22; Is 8:14); 2:21-25 (Is 52:13—53:12); 4:1-2, 17.
[54]C. S. Lewis, *The Last Battle* (New York: Collier, 1956), pp. 147-48.

"The true light, which enlightens everyone, was coming into the world" (Jn 1:9). John 9 presents what is for the Fourth Evangelist a characteristically layered approach to the problem of epistemology, trading on literal and ironic notions of blindness and sight in order to demonstrate that authentic sight is symptomatic of a faith that perceives what God has revealed. The narrative crescendoes toward the coming of the "hour" when Jesus will be "lifted up," a glorification that finds its acme in the cross when the full glory of God is revealed (Jn 17:1). Paul too writes of a hermeneutical conversion centered on the cross. In a pericope abundant with images of the saving significance of Jesus' death, he confesses, "From now on, therefore, we regard no one from a human point of view. . . . So if anyone is in Christ, there is a new creation: everything old has passed away; see, everything has become new!" (2 Cor 5:16-17). This is the work of the cross.

The death of Jesus on the cross is surely one of the most profound visual representations of the character of God. In large part, this is due to the historical-narrative realities that color this portrait—highlighting the topsy-turvy nature of the cross when viewed against the backdrop of Roman sensibilities, while accentuating how the life of Jesus finds its keenest expression in a Roman crucifixion. This objective moment of revelation is thus capable of impressing itself on the hearts and minds of people throughout history, promoting a real change in how people construe the whole of God's creation and make their homes in it. "See, everything has become new!"

These are two of many ways of construing the soteriological import of Jesus' execution by the Romans. Such interpretations abound in the New Testament. None captures the fullness of Jesus' passion, but each adds to our appreciation of the mystery of the saving work of Jesus on the cross.

Conclusion

From a perspective shaped by the biblical narrative, there is no Christianity apart from the cross of Christ. However inconvenient or humiliating it might have seemed, the cross became the chief icon by which to rally a robust Christian identity and to ground a Christian ethic. This event, Jesus' crucifixion, exhibited the character of God's saving mercy so that Jesus' suffering and death was "for us."

In order to project this profundity, the cross can never be sundered from these two anchor points: (1) the ancient Mediterranean world within which Jesus was sentenced to death on a Roman cross, and (2) the eternal purpose of God. Between these two nonnegotiable points, much can be said about *how* this event could accomplish and signal the salvation of God's people. At the interface of the particular moment of Jesus' crucifixion and the eternal mission of God, we can find not one but many models of the atonement. So limited is the ground on which we walk and so infinite the mystery of God's saving work that we need many interpretive images, many tones, many voices.

Undoubtedly, some models will be more attractive than others. Some will communicate better to this people at this time, others in another time and to a different people. Some that attract champions may fail to represent faithfully the apostolic witness to the gospel, lacking in their coherence with the biblical narrative in terms of their grasp of the human situation or their portrait of God, or problematic in their efforts to narrow too much the consequences of God's saving work. Those that counter the narrative of Scripture as this is understood within the classical faith (see the ecumenical creeds of the early church and their precursors in the "rule of faith") should be left aside. But this cautionary word should not cause us to overlook that the biblical narrative, which we seek to inhabit and to put into play in our lives as communities of Jesus' followers, authorizes an expansive range of images and models for comprehending and articulating the atonement.

Christus Victor Response

GREGORY A. BOYD

I applaud almost every aspect of Joel Green's excellent essay. Among other things, Green did a marvelous job elucidating the rich variety of atonement metaphors used throughout the New Testament. He rightfully notes that the biblical narrative "authorizes an expansive range of images and models" (p. 170) for comprehending and articulating the atonement and he effectively shows that, given this rich variety, "the significance of Jesus' death [can]not be represented without remainder by any one concept or theory or metaphor" (p. 167). In other words, we need the multiplicity of metaphors we find in the New Testament. I firmly believe he is right.

I further appreciate Green's insistence that the meaning of Jesus' life and death can't be divorced from the first-century sociopolitical context Jesus lived in. I also enthusiastically support Green's insistence that the meaning of Jesus' death can never be properly understood if it is separated from every other aspect of Jesus' life. Over and against much evangelical thinking on the atonement, which tends to isolate it to the work of the cross (as I argue against Schreiner's perspective), Green rightly emphasizes that Jesus' incarnation, countercultural lifestyle, teaching ministry, healing ministry, deliverance ministry, death and resurrection are all connected. (Though, as will become clear, Green and I differ on what can be said about this connection.)

Finally, I must add that I am also in essential agreement with Green's analysis of the sacrificial metaphors used throughout the New Testament. Over and against the penal substitution view of the atonement, Green argues that while the New Testament depicts the world as needing to be reconciled to God, it never depicts *God* as needing to be reconciled *to the world*. So, too, while the New Testament depicts humans as needing a sacrifice to be restored to God, the New Testament never depicts *God* as need-

ing a sacrifice to love and forgive humans. Jesus expresses the Father's un-
fathomable love for the world: he does not divert the Father's wrath away
from the world, toward himself.

Clearly, I take little issue with anything Joel Green affirms. My difficulty
with Green's essay is rather in what he seems to deny. In a word, Green
seems to deny there is any intrinsic logic to the variety of New Testament
atonement metaphors. More specifically, Green denies that any metaphor or
set of metaphors can be taken as intrinsically more fundamental than others.
There is, then, no normative, transcultural, overall framework within which
all the variety of New Testament metaphors are to be arranged and properly
understood. Rather, in Green's view, different individuals and groups will at
different times find some metaphors of the atonement to be more significant
and paradigmatic than others, depending on what issues they are confronting in their particular historical circumstances. This, Green suggests, is as it
should be.

For all that I admire in Green's essay, I find this aspect of his kaleidoscopic view of the atonement troubling. There are six considerations I wish
to raise in response.

First, and perhaps most fundamentally, Green's analysis strikes me as potentially relativistic. Now, I must immediately acknowledge that Green, to
his credit, offered several reflections that protect him against wholesale rel-
ativism. For one thing, Green affirms "the eternal purpose of God" as a transcultural reality that is revealed in Christ (p. 157). He also insists that the significance of Jesus' life and death must be anchored in first-century historical
realities. And, finally, regardless of the metaphors an individual or group
take to be most significant and paradigmatic, Green believes there is a biblical "mandate" for the church to continually embrace the rich variety of New
Testament atonement metaphors (p. 171). If heeded, this mandate would
provide a continual check against any individual or group becoming too my-
opic in their understanding of the significance of Jesus' life and death.

This certainly helps, but it does not fully assuage my concern. The meaning an individual or group finds in any *particular* metaphor (or set of metaphors) within the New Testament's variety is inevitably affected by the
meaning the individual or group finds in the rich variety considered *as a
whole*. And the meaning an individual or group assigns to the rich variety as
a whole is affected, if not determined, by the metaphor (or set of metaphors)
an individual or group takes to be paradigmatic (in the sense of being foun-

dational for interpreting the other metaphors). Thus, if this last element is left to the vicissitudes of historical circumstance, the overall significance of Jesus' incarnation, life, death and resurrection is, at least to a large degree, left to the vicissitudes of historical circumstance. This leaves me unsettled.

Yes, Green rightfully insists on a transcultural "eternal purpose of God" that is in various ways revealed through each aspect of the rich variety of metaphors in the New Testament. But if "the eternal purpose of God" is not also revealed in the way that this variety is arranged—if this is rather left to the vicissitudes of historical circumstances—then to a large extent the actual content of "the eternal purpose of God" is relativized. For, again, the meaning of each aspect of the variety is affected by the meaning of the variety considered as a whole, and the meaning of the variety as a whole is largely determined by the historically contingent decision of what metaphor (or set of metaphors) will (and will not) be considered foundational to the understanding of the others.

Second, Green's analysis makes it nearly impossible to provide an objective critique of competing atonement theories, his three objective referents notwithstanding. The primary disagreement between competing theories has not been that some completely ignore aspects of the variety of metaphors found in the New Testament. All views (at least within the orthodox Christian tradition) at least try to adhere to Green's "mandate." Rather, the primary disagreement between competing theories has been the differing ways competing views arrange the variety of metaphors that comprise the biblical data, that is, the logical relationship each view believes exists amidst this data, which metaphors they consider foundational for an understanding of others, and so forth. But this is the very thing Green seems to think is not revealed in the New Testament.

Hence, it seems that in Green's analysis all the competing theories of the atonement are at one and the same time equally right *and* equally wrong. They are equally right insofar as their views are rooted in biblical metaphors (and do not violate any of the three objective referents Green specifies). But they are equally wrong insofar as they think their unique way of arranging the biblical data—and thus their unique interpretation of "the eternal purpose of God" revealed in Christ—arises out of the biblical data itself. Among other problems with this implication is that it seems to lead to a logical contradiction. At least at points, certain views of the atonement do not simply differ from certain other views of the atonement on points of emphasis: they contradict one another. It is therefore logically impossible for them to be equally right on these points. Both may be wrong, but both cannot be right. And this means we are logically forced to debate the merits of competing ways of arranging the biblical material on the basis of the biblical material itself.

Third, as I mentioned in my own essay, if we believe that Jesus reveals reality, I do not see how we can or why we should abandon attempts to integrate the variety of metaphors and teachings found in the New Testament into a single, transcultural, coherent framework. In all other intellectual disciplines, we have advanced our understanding of reality by sticking to our conviction that *reality is one* while striving to arrive at a conceptual scheme that reflects this oneness (i.e., a conceptual scheme that organizes a variety of data into a broader whole). Why should we assume things are altogether different in theology? To suppose otherwise, I fear, is to significantly acquiesce to the increasingly prevalent postmodern conviction that there is no (at least knowable) ontological referent to our theological language.

Fourth, while Green does a marvelous job elucidating the variety of New Testament metaphors for the atonement, he actually offers no evidence or argument in support of the most foundational aspect of his kaleidoscopic view, namely, his conviction that this variety has no intrinsic logic or inherent order. We can grant Green's argument that no single atonement metaphor exhausts the significance of Jesus' life and death while nevertheless insisting that a single metaphor (or set of metaphors) is foundational to the others and as such provides a conceptual framework within which the variety of metaphors is best understood. We can grant that the New Testament "authorizes" the use of many different metaphors in expressing Jesus' significance without thereby granting that personal or cultural circumstances alone should determine which "authorized" metaphor is considered most fundamental or significant. It seems to me that Green mistakenly assumes that in demonstrating the one he has argued for the other, but in fact this is simply not the case.

Fifth, I believe that something of the intelligibility and transforming power of certain New Testament metaphors is compromised when they are not construed in a particular overall framework, namely, the one provided by the Christus Victor understanding of the atonement. For example, I contend that the court-of-law metaphors (e.g., justification) take on increased intelligibility and power when they are understood against the backdrop of a cosmic conflict in which Satan holds us in bondage as our "accuser" (Rev 12:10). The commerce metaphors (e.g., redemption) take on more intelligibility and power when understood against the backdrop of our enslavement to "the powers." The personal relationship metaphors (e.g., reconciliation) take on added intelligibility and meaning when construed in the context of our bondage to one who blinds our minds and imprisons our hearts. And the worship metaphors (e.g., sacrifice) take on increased intelligibility and meaning when they are understood as aspects of cosmic war. Loving sacrifice is the central means by which evil is defeated in the world.

In short, the intelligibility and power of the gospel to a significant degree hangs in the balance of how one arranges the rich variety of metaphors in the Bible. And the most intelligible and powerful way to arrange these is within the context of God's ongoing battle against "the powers" that are hostile to God, the creation and humanity.

Finally, I submit that Joel Green's proposal is potentially dangerous on a practical level. As I indicated in my chapter, we must not ever separate theory from praxis in our thinking about the atonement (or on any other theological issue). How we conceptualize the relationship between New Testament metaphors—which is to say, how we construe the overall significance of Jesus' incarnation, life, death and resurrection—has significant practical consequences.

For example, when the atoning work of the cross is even theoretically separated from Jesus' teachings and life, Christians can (and do) sometimes end up with a cheap, merely legal, understanding of grace. This is why, especially in America, we have so many *believers* and so few genuine *disciples*. This disastrous failure in praxis is, I submit, most fundamentally rooted in a misunderstanding of the atonement. To leave the arranging of the variety of New Testament metaphors to the vicissitudes of personal or cultural circumstances is thus to leave major aspects of the Christian life up to the vicissitudes of personal or cultural circumstances. And this, I believe, is unwise, to say the least.

What makes this consideration particularly important is that both Scripture and history teach us that the human heart is "deceitful above all things" (Jer 17:9 TNIV) and idolatrous. As church history makes painfully obvious, the easiest thing in the world for us fallen creatures to do is to convince ourselves we are following Christ while we are in fact following Caesar, our nation, our culture or some such thing, and to unconsciously (or consciously) revise our understanding of Christ to conveniently accommodate this idolatry. For this reason, if for no other, I believe we desperately need a strong presentation of not only the rich variety of the New Testament metaphors but also the warfare framework, which, I believe, expresses the intrinsic logic and proper relationship of this rich variety. We can only wonder how much violence "in Jesus' name"—throughout history and yet today—would have been avoided had Christians been perpetually confronted with the New Testament teaching that everything Jesus was about centered on living in outrageous, sacrificial love as an act of resistance to "the powers" that rule all societies, all governments and all nations.

Penal Substitution Response

THOMAS R. SCHREINER

In some ways Joel Green's thesis is the easiest to defend, for he is surely right that the significance of the atonement is multifaceted, and including only one theme cannot do justice to the richness of what God has accomplished in Christ. Green's essay reminds us of the dangers of reductionism, and I hope I, for one, take it to heart. Furthermore, his sketch of the narrative and social world of Jesus' ministry grounds Jesus' death in the historical and cultural context of his day, so that Jesus' death is not abstracted from his ministry and everyday life in Palestinian Judaism. In addition, the Old Testament context of Jesus' death is explored, so that we see the fulfillment accomplished in Christ in terms of a new exodus and a new covenant.

Even though Green rightly reminds us of the diverse themes relative to the atonement, he is not as persuasive in contending that all the themes are equally important. Green maintains that since we have a diversity of themes relative to the atonement in Scripture, all the themes are of equal importance, or at least no one theme is fundamental. Green does not present a cogent and tightly argued case for his position. His argument seems to be as follows: (1) A number of different metaphors are used to depict the atonement. (2) Therefore, no one theme can claim pride of place. The conclusion might be true, but it needs to be defended with arguments and evidence in support of the particular thesis, and Green does not prosecute his case in detail. It seems to me that a more stringent defense of this thesis would have been more valuable than the long section on the two models of the atonement. We know that Green thinks a number of different models are important, but the mere presence of a diversity of themes does not logically or scripturally lead to the conclusion that no theme is foundational.

Perhaps Green's most substantive argument supporting his view is the situational nature of the biblical writings. That is, biblical writers present different dimensions of the atonement insofar as they speak to the circumstances and social location of their readers. Such variety suggests that no single metaphor for the atonement is fundamental or brings coherence to the other themes. Each theme has its own independent value and contribution in the kaleidoscope. Such a view is quite interesting, and I think it would have been helpful if Green had pursued this line of argument in more detail. I would maintain (space forbids detailed argument) that the root problem in the human condition is human sin, and penal substitution grounds our redemption, illumination, freedom, forgiveness, victory over demonic powers, moral life, and so forth. In other words, the kaleidoscope has an anchoring color (penal substitution) that brings coherence to all the dimensions of the atonement.

Another factor in Green's thesis is his conception of the situations addressed, which seems to focus on contingency more than coherence. Green remarks that the human predicament emphasized in the Scriptures reflects the historical context, whether the issue is reconciliation in 2 Corinthians or "legal observance" in Galatians. Virtually all scholars agree that the circumstances addressed in New Testament documents affect the theme emphasized by the writers. Green's illustration from Anselm, however, suggests that he thinks themes relative to the atonement are reducible to the human context, especially since he says what obtains in Anselm's case also applies to the "Pauline language for the atonement" (he introduces the matter by saying, "The same could be said . . ." [p. 170]). In reply, we must remember the biblical truth that God is the Lord of history, so that the situations addressed in the Scriptures truly reflect the genuine predicament of human beings before God. That is, we truly are guilty before God, enslaved to sin and in desperate need of reconciliation. No wedge should be introduced in the Scriptures between the situation addressed and the transcendent Word of God. Postmodernism has reminded us that we do not have a God's-eye view of all of reality, but we must avoid the reductive conclusion that the New Testament documents merely represent a human perspective of the human dilemma. We may not understand exhaustively, but we certainly understand truly, for God is able to break through our dullness and reveal himself to us (1 Cor 2:6-16).

I also differ with Joel Green's construal at a number of different points. For instance, he argues that there is "no hint of mutual reconciliation" in the biblical text, but such a judgment fails to read the biblical text in terms of the larger storyline of Pauline theology, since it is clear that God's wrath is revealed against the ungodly (Rom 1:18; 2:5; cf. Rom 3:25-26). The message of reconciliation (see Rom 5:10-11; 2 Cor 5:18-21; Eph 2:14-18) must not be read in isolation but in a context in which people are separated from God (Eph 2:12), are children of wrath (Eph 2:3) and face final judgment (2 Cor 5:10).

Green falls prey to a false disjunction in saying that "the cross is less about a transaction after which persons are no longer guilty, and more about salvation as a call to reflect" in everyday life our new relationship with Jesus (p. 168). Note how he uses the cold and mechanistic word *transaction* to describe the forgiveness of sins. When I sin against my wife and she forgives me, her forgiveness is precious, personal and living. Hence, forgiveness must not be lessened with a cold word like *transaction*. Why not say instead that the cross is about experiencing the glory and beauty of God's forgiveness, *and* a new life lived in joy and self-giving in light of our salvation?

I was pleased that Green believes that the biblical terms for atonement convey the notion of both expiation and propitiation, though, contrary to the position I would defend, he sees expiation as primary. But it should be pointed out that Green does not really support his preference for expiation but simply claims that Jacob Milgrom verifies his assertion (p. 173). Naturally we cannot defend everything in the articles we write, but I see no reason to change my view that propitiation is fundamental in biblical thought since Green does not sustain his case by doing exegesis but simply directs readers to secondary sources.

In speaking of the unblemished animals offered in sacrifice Green sees "an analogy for the election of Israel" (p. 174) but he says nothing about Christ as an unblemished sacrifice (1 Pet 1:19; cf. 2 Cor 5:21; Heb 7:26-28; 9:14; 1 Pet 2:21-25). Further, he says that putting one's hands on the head of the animal sacrificed signifies "identification" and "representation." But in what sense does the animal represent the sinner? It seems clear that the animals functioned as a substitute, for they suffer the punishment (death) sinners deserve. Indeed, the notion of substitution seems to be acknowledged by Green, though he does not use the term since he says the blood "signifies the offering of the lives of those for whom the sacrifice is made" (p. 174).

Green rightly says that God's wrath is not arbitrary and cannot be likened to that of pagan gods, but I think he underestimates remarkably the pervasiveness of God's wrath in the biblical story. I direct readers here to my chapter, and simply observe that many other examples could be given where God's wrath burns because of human sin. It seems to be nothing short of extraordinary that Green asserts that sacrifices are not related to God's anger. Notice that he operates at the level of assertion here and not argument. He simply asserts his position and then cites John Goldingay in his defense. He says that "we have seen" in his chapter that satisfying God's wrath and sacrifices as a "payment of the penalty of sin" are not biblical (p. 175), but he actually does not argue for his case exegetically. In my judgment Green's view of sacrifices is abstracted from the Old Testament narrative. When we are told that blood makes atonement (Lev 17:11), such atonement cannot be segregated from God's anger that burns against his people when they sin. Hence, when Israel sins at the golden calf, the Lord's anger is provoked (Ex 32:10), and Moses offers to make atonement to mollify that anger (Ex 32:30). So too we are often told that sacrifices are a pleasing aroma to the Lord, presumably because they pacify his anger. We must beware of distortions of the view of God's wrath, as Green insists, but at the same time those who downplay God's wrath betray a modern rather than a biblical worldview.

Green also claims that Paul articulates Jesus' death in terms of representation and exchange in economic rather than penal terms. Green's discussion is quite brief here, so I may misunderstand him, but the disjunction posited between exchange and penal substitution seems quite improbable. If we think of Jesus' death as an exchange, then it follows that payment has to be made, and the payment is Jesus' death instead of ours. But why is the exchange made in the first place? Why can't we just be saved by the inherent power of Jesus' life? Second Corinthians 5:21 teaches that Jesus was made sin on our behalf, and we become God's righteousness in him. We know that the wages of sin is death (Rom 6:23), and hence it follows that Jesus took the punishment of death we deserved, that he absorbed the penalty that belonged to us. The language of representation and exchange in the biblical account cannot be segregated from penal substitution, for Jesus represented us *by* taking the punishment from God that we deserve.

Joel Green is a very fine scholar, and his essay contains much that is interesting and valuable, but he does not defend adequately the view that all dimensions of the atonement are of equal significance. Nor does he ground his criticisms of penal substitution and his notions of the wrath of God in exegesis, and hence I remain convinced that penal substitution is the anchor of the atonement.

Healing Response

BRUCE R. REICHENBACH

Although Christians locate the atonement within ontology in that the atonement is a real event in the life, death and resurrection of Jesus of Nazareth, the interpretation of the atonement (how it functions and what meaning it has) requires a connection with understandings of the nature of God, of human nature, and of the cultures in which it occurred and is interpreted. Joel Green's thesis is that the only way to understand the atonement is through diverse models or images that emerge from the spheres of life that both writers/speakers and readers/listeners share. Green identifies five dimensions of public life—law, commerce, personal relationships, religion and warfare—that supply fecund contexts for the models or motifs that writers use to understand atonement: respectively, justification, redemption, reconciliation, sacrifice and triumph over evil. To this list I would add the sphere of medicine, from which develops the healing motif or paradigm. He notes that not only does the diversity of models or images emerge from the diversity of these spheres, but a diversity of models also can be found in a single writer, depending on the point he wants to make in a given context. Likewise, Green argues, atonement images connect with diverse views of the human predicament (i.e., we are condemned due to sin, held in slavery, alienated from God, polluted by sin, under the control of Satan or suffering as a consequence of sin).

Although Green's thesis is well worth noting, one might legitimately wonder whether he is a relativist when it comes to employing metaphors to explicate the atonement. In *Recovering the Scandal of the Cross* he asks, "Who controls the metaphors that shape our lives?" Paul, he writes, serves "as midwife to a conversion of worldview," "deconstructing the old and reconstructing the new."[1] If Paul can use "several dozen metaphors . . . to lay bare the

---

[1]Joel B. Green and Mark D. Baker, *Recovering the Scandal of the Cross* (Downers Grove, Ill.: InterVarsity Press, 2000), p. 66.

benefits of Christ's death," why stop with these?[2] Will any culturally relevant motif be acceptable?

Green, however, is not a relativist; he does not say that any and all cultural dimensions or motifs provide adequate bases for explication. Rather, he suggests that just as the ontology of the atonement cannot be isolated from its historical, social, political and religious context, so the interpretation of that event is grounded both in the spheres operative in the time of Jesus and in the spheres operative for subsequent interpreters to make sense in their day. While he praises certain models for using contemporary cultural forms, for not "privileging certain persons or groups over others" or for "easily lending [themselves] to reflection on the ethical implications of Jesus' saving activity," he also critiques the standard views on the grounds that they find no support in the New Testament, "give a less-than-biblical view," give culture too great an influence, or do "not allow God's relation with Israel and the character of God as revealed in Jesus Christ fundamentally to shape [their] concept of God."[3] As such, he treads a delicate balance between the normative role of the New Testament and its cultural forms, and the comprehending role of the interpreter's cultural context. As a result, the accusation he raises against defenders of the penal substitution view—that they have "turned to the world around [them] at those points where [they] should have relied on the Bible and [have] gone to the Bible when [they should have] engaged [their] own cultural context"—warrants some significant discussion of how these diverse criteria function in selecting appropriate models or metaphors.[4]

Green himself presents two models, not to be taken as overarching but rather as illustrative, of the diversity that we find in Scripture and that also may have varying appeals to twenty-first-century minds. The first, atonement as sacrifice, connects us with the sacrificial system that the New Testament world inherited from the Old Testament. But even here, he notes, atonement as sacrifice is treated differently by the same and by different biblical authors in diverse contexts. In 1 Corinthians 5 Paul connects Christ's sacrificial death with the Passover, which sets the Israelite celebrants apart from the Egyptians as they readied for their exodus from slavery; Christ's atonement too "marks the Corinthian believers as a community of persons set apart from the bondage of sin as the distinctive people of God" (p. 175). In Hebrews

---

[2]Ibid, p. 58.
[3]Ibid, pp. 124, 131-33.
[4]Ibid, pp. 149-50.

the writer connects Christ's sacrifice with the Levitical sacrifices that cleansed and purified those contaminated by sin. And elsewhere in Paul, "substitution is clearly at the heart of sacrifice, . . . [where] the metaphor is economic (exchange) rather than penal (satisfaction)" (p. 177). Green's marshaling of the diverse understandings of sacrifice further strengthens his position that the same image may be used in different contexts with differing emphases.

At the same time, we have to wonder whether Green treats the penal dimension of atonement fairly when he suggests that " 'assuaging God's wrath' and 'payment of the penalty of sin' are wide of the mark" (p. 175).[5] Green rejects a God who has anger or wrath on the grounds that (1) God is gracious, and this is foundational to his character, (2) God takes the initiative in salvation, (3) anger ascribed to God is at best metaphorical, (4) it "is not a divine property or essential attribute of God," and (5) it is to be rightly understood as God "letting us go our own way."[6]

I will address each of Joel Green's points. First, God's graciousness is not inconsistent with divine anger. God is angry at Israel for building the golden calf, yet at the bequest of Moses he relents from imposing the disaster he had threatened (Ex 32:9-14; see Deut 9:19-20).[7] Indeed, in the very passage from which Green quotes (Ex 34:6), God's slowness to anger is paired with his abounding in love and faithfulness and his forgiveness of wickedness. The latter do not negate the anger, but temper it. Second, God's graciousness thus connects with anger; it does not prevent it from being a divine property.[8] God's anger and love are paired, just as are justice and mercy. Consequently, anger does not prevent divine initiative, but provides a context in which God takes action to reveal his love for the sinner. Third, Green allows that God has positive emotions (e.g., love) and divine intercourse with humans (e.g., gives perfect gifts, is faithful, is generous, pronounces judgment). So why draw the line at anger? The reasoning Green gives in his *Recovering the Scandal of the Cross*—that "given our limited vantage point

---

[5] "Whatever meaning atonement might have, it would be a grave error to imagine that it focused on assuaging God's anger or winning God's merciful attention" (ibid, p. 51).

[6] Ibid, pp. 51-57.

[7] Although Moses does not sacrifice here to assuage God's anger, he makes a strong request to God not to carry out what he has revealed, which at least in part counters Green's contention that "the Scriptures as a whole provide no ground for a portrait of an angry God needing to be appeased in atoning sacrifice." Repentance and turning from evil ways are what often bring about God's relenting (Jer 18:8; 26:3).

[8] See Richard Gaffin, "The Scandal of the Cross," in *The Glory of the Atonement*, ed. Charles E. Hill and Frank A. James III (Downers Grove, Ill.: InterVarsity Press, 2004), pp. 150-53.

as human beings (and so the human perspectives from which the books of the Old Testament were written), perhaps we attribute 'anger' to God only because we have no language other than human language with which to comprehend God"—would equally militate against all the "positive" predicates he ascribes to God throughout the book.[9] To remove the property of anger harkens back to the Platonists who removed all emotion from God because a perfect God has to be unchanging. But God cannot be properly understood apart from his emotions of love, care and, yes, even anger. Totally "de-anthropomorphizing" God makes him totally transcendent to the affairs in which he has a part. Fourth, it is therefore difficult not to see wrath as a divine property. He is angry with persons and angry at their sin, the two being connected (Ex 4:14; Num 11:1; 12:9; 16:22; 22:22; 32:13; Jn 3:36; Rom 1:18; 2:5; 3:5; Rev 11:18; 14:10). Fifth, "letting us go our own way" is not wrath itself but flows from God's anger at our sin and his treatment of humans. Romans 1—2 conveys God's disgust at our sinful behavior, yet for a time he allows it to play itself out in our lives because he has given us freedom and provides no opportunity for us to have an excuse. God's punishment is delayed (Rom 3:25). In short, to rightly reject the idea of a capriciously vengeful God still leaves open the fact that according to both the Old and New Testaments sin brings about God's wrath.

Green and Schreiner debate whether Romans 3:21-26 provides grounds for seeing a penal role in Christ's sacrifice. Green takes the passage as emphasizing an economic model (pp. 176-77) where God is only the subject of the sacrifice.[10] But for Paul God is both the subject who presents the sacrifice of expiation and the one who receives it both to avert God's wrath (Rom 3:5) and to address concerns of justice highlighted by God's delaying the deserved punishment for sin.[11] The latter interpretation lends credence to the contention that Paul entertained a penal understanding of the atonement, which despite Green's rather strong critique is consistent with his emphasis on a pluralism of atonement models.[12]

In his second model Green treats the atonement as revelation. Here we get

---

[9]Green and Baker, *Recovering the Scandal of the Cross*, p. 54.

[10]Ibid., p. 96.

[11]James D. G. Dunn, *Romans 1-8,* Word Biblical Commentary 38 (Waco, Tex.: Word, 1988), p. 173; Leon Morris, *The Epistle to the Romans* (Grand Rapids: Eerdmans, 1988), p. 181.

[12]For a careful defense of this, see D. A. Carson, "God Presented Him as a Propitiation," in *The Glory of the Atonement,* ed. Charles E. Hill and Frank A. James III (Downers Grove, Ill.: InterVarsity Press, 2004), pp. 119-39.

a feeling for elements of the postmodern role of perspective and interpretation in shaping a thesis. In addressing this motif in the narrative of Luke, Green takes as a central thesis the disciples' inability to comprehend or, better, their misunderstanding of the events they witnessed because they lacked "the categories of thought, an interpretive scheme adequate to correlate what Jesus holds together in his passion predictions, Jesus' exalted status and his impending dishonor" (p. 181). Thus Luke ends his Gospel narrative with Jesus enlightening two disciples by explaining to them the Old Testament prophecies that showed that the Messiah had to suffer such things before being glorified. Illumination or revelation thus becomes the interpretive theme of Luke and also of Acts. The disciples "interpret the world in terms of this narrative, which they incarnate in their lives of mission, *koinonia* and persecution. All of this is the result of a hermeneutical conversion centered in the death and resurrection of Jesus Christ" (p. 181). Thus Green sees Luke's Gospel as a "narrative of enlightenment," in which the death and resurrection of Christ provide the interpretive key to transform the disciples' "conception of God and thus . . . their commitments, attitudes and everyday practices" (p. 182).

His similar treatment of 1 Peter reemphasizes this point about a shaping image. The focus here is Jesus Christ: "Jesus is the interpretative matrix for understanding the pattern of God's story, the lens through which to read our story within the story of God" (p. 182). Christ's life and death offer a new conceptual scheme that not only gives a new perspective but also becomes the motif around which the Christian story and our own story can be developed and lived out.

I raise here the question whether revelation or illumination is the *meaning* of the atonement, or whether, rather, Green is describing the *function* of the atonement narratives, namely, forming a foundational conceptual piece in terms of which we structure our theological and daily narratives. I agree with Green's treatment of motifs as forming the basis of conceptual schemes and conative structures, and providing guidance for action, that is, as functioning as organizing hermeneutical principles. In this regard his treatment of the use of the atonement is very enlightening. But to note this as the function of the atonement motif is not to state, develop or clarify its meaning. Though the doctrine of atonement might be revelatory in that it provides diverse ways to understand the significance of Christ's life, death and resurrection for our perspective, beliefs and actions, it does not thereby provide the meaning of atonement (in the same way, e.g., as does Green's treatment of atonement as sacrifice). Thus Green's treatment of atonement as revelation differs significantly in character from and should not be paralleled with his treatment of atonement as sacrifice.

Green might reply that in my criticism I have fallen into the very trap that Wittgenstein warns us against, namely, bifurcating meaning and use. For the later Wittgenstein the meaning is not something distinct from its use but is its use, especially insofar as it is connected with a language game.[13] Further, language games are diverse, at best overlapping in different spheres. So Green might connect his view of atonement as revelation with the language game that theologians play when attempting to understand and put into practice doctrine about Christ's atonement. I say this is a direction Green *might* go, not where he does go. To take this route Green would have to defend this view against the criticism that meaning and use or function are different, as indeed this discussion of the atonement reinforces, and that even the notion of language games presupposes some structure of what it is to be a game.

My criticism does not denigrate what Green has to say about the role of hermeneutics in understanding the atonement. He highlights the centrality of core beliefs as forming the interpretive base of worldviews. Though these core beliefs may be of diverse characters—scientific, historical, psychological, theological and so forth—they have similar functions in that they shape our understanding of the world and impact our commitments.[14] He reminds us of this core function of the doctrine of atonement, both in Scripture and in twenty-first-century theological thought and life. When this is truly grasped, conversion of one's perspective becomes radically possible.

Much can be gleaned from the insights in Joel Green's contribution, not the least that the doctrine of atonement must be rooted in a diversity of elements: Scripture, the historical and cultural context in which it was written about, the intention and concerns of the respective writers in their diverse contexts, and the context in which it is preached and shared today. The doctrine also is rooted in an understanding of God, humans, the human predicament and the action of God to address that predicament. And hermeneutically, Green has called us to recognize the importance of the doctrine as a central motif or paradigm in understanding diverse dimensions of Christian belief and praxis.

---

[13]Ludwig Wittgenstein, *Philosophical Investigations* (Malden, Mass.: Blackwells, 2001), §§7-27, 43, 108.

[14]Nicholas Wolterstorff, *Reason Within the Bounds of Religion* (Grand Rapids: Eerdmans, 1976), chaps. 12-13.

Contributors

James K. Beilby (Ph.D., Marquette University) is associate professor of systematic and philosophical theology at Bethel University. He has published or edited numerous books, including *For Faith and Clarity* (Baker, 2006), *Epistemology as Theology* (Ashgate, 2005), *Naturalism Defeated?* (Cornell University Press, 2002), and *Divine Foreknowledge: Four Views* (InterVarsity Press, 2001).

Gregory A. Boyd (Ph.D., Princeton Theological Seminary) is senior pastor at Woodland Hills Church in Maplewood, Minnesota. He has authored numerous books, including *The Myth of a Christian Nation* (Zondervan, 2006), *Seeing Is Believing* (Baker, 2004), *Repenting of Religion* (Baker, 2004), *Is God to Blame?* (InterVarsity Press, 2003), *Satan and the Problem of Evil* (InterVarsity Press, 2001), and *God at War* (InterVarsity Press, 1997).

Paul Rhodes Eddy (Ph.D., Marquette University) is professor of biblical and theological studies at Bethel University. He has published or edited numerous books, including *John Hick's Pluralist Philosophy of World Religions* (Ashgate, 2002), *Across the Spectrum* (Baker, 2002), and *Divine Foreknowledge: Four Views* (InterVarsity Press, 2001).

Joel B. Green (Ph.D., University of Aberdeen) is professor of New Testament interpretation at Asbury Theological Seminary. He has authored or edited more than twenty books, including *Recovering the Scandal of the Cross* (with Mark D. Baker; InterVarsity Press, 2000), *Gospel of Luke* (Eerdmans, 1997), *Salvation* (Chalice, 2004), *The Theology of the Gospel of Luke* (Cambridge University Press, 1995), and *Dictionary of Jesus and the Gospels* (with Scot McKnight; InterVarsity Press, 1992).

Bruce R. Reichenbach (Ph.D., Northwestern University) is a professor of philosophy at Augsburg College. He has also been a visiting professor at Juniata College, Daystar University in Kenya and Morija Theological Seminary

in Lesotho. He has published in the areas of philosophy of religion *(Reason and Religious Belief,* coauthor; *Evil and a Good God, The Law of Karma* and *Is Man the Phoenix?),* philosophy of biology *(On Behalf of God: A Christian Ethic for Biology,* coauthor), and critical thinking *(An Introduction to Critical Thinking).*

Thomas R. Schreiner (Ph.D., Fuller Theological Seminary) has been a professor of New Testament at Southern Seminary since 1997, and (since 1983) has also taught New Testament at Azusa Pacific University and Bethel Theological Seminary. He is the author of a number of books, including *Paul, Apostle of God's Glory in Christ* (InterVarsity Press, 2001) and commentaries on Romans, 1-2 Peter and Jude. Currently, he is working on a theology of the New Testament. He also serves as the preaching pastor of Clifton Baptist Church in Louisville, Kentucky.